UNCLOTHED

UNCLOTHED

Memoir of a Naked Soul

Casandra M. Austin

Cover Design by: Angelique Giron

ISBN-13: 978-1540881076
ISBN-10: 1540881075

Dedicated to my beloved son, Amari;

I am because you are.

This book is also dedicated to those

who have experienced adversities of all sorts.

Keep your faith and be strong.

Disclaimer

This is a work of creative nonfiction. The events are portrayed to the best of Casandra Austin's memory. While all the stories in this book are true, some names and identifying details have been changed to protect the privacy of the people involved. The reader should not consider this book anything other than a work of literature.

Contents

Preface

- Nearly 1 in 4 adults, and youth aged 13-18 in the U.S. experience mental illness in a given year.
- Suicide is the 10th leading cause of death in the U.S.
- Suicide is the 3rd leading cause of death for people aged 10-24.
- Suicide is the 2nd leading cause of death for people aged 15-24.
- Millions of Americans suffer from mental illness.
- Every 9 seconds in the U.S. a woman is assaulted or beaten.
- Over 315,000 children are victims of abuse.
- 1 in 5 girls and 1 in 20 boys is a victim of sexual abuse.
- Children are most vulnerable to criminal sexual abuse between the ages of 7 and 13.

Everyone has a story. I decided to share my own. *Unclothed: Memoir of a Naked Soul,* is my way of bearing all. This is me telling my truth; the part of me that has been unknown and hidden to many for a long time. My hope is through my transparency, others can remember what it's like to be human, experience adversities, and to be broken. But, also to remember the importance and rewards of forgiveness, healing and loving ourselves as well as others.

Society has become so consumed with external factors, that it seems what really matters has been lost – people. The lack of compassion in the world is truly disheartening. Empathy is missing. A lot have forgotten about the old golden rule, "to treat others how you would like to be treated."

Many have become disconnected and desensitized. People are either acting or treating others like robots. We have forgotten about the power of the human spirit. We have lost touch with ourselves and the fact that we have experienced, felt and known pain at some time or another in our own lives. Judgment is passed onto others without truly knowing one's internal struggles, pain or day to day worries. The perpetual cycle of hurt people hurting other people is normal. I aim to create a new normal.

By working in the criminal justice system for nearly a decade, I realized I experienced a lot of, if not the same adversities, as the juvenile and adult offenders. There were many times I wanted to say, "I know, I went through that too!" Or, "You can forgive. You don't have to hate them forever. Take your power back!" I wanted to share that I knew what it felt like to face trial and tribulations, to get knocked down and feel like the world is standing on top of you.

I experienced the aches and pains of broken hearts, one right after the other. I experienced the misery of suffering silently from depression and recurrent suicidal thoughts. I had disappointments and was betrayed by those closest to me. I knew all about the struggles of being a single mother. I had felt judgment from others, when no one dared to attempt to understand me. I also used to turn to alcohol and partying to suppress the pain, or have sex to feel loved and wanted. I felt if I could personally share my empathy toward them and their pain, then maybe they would be more susceptible to change and actually believe they too could change. Seeing them in the state they were in, motivated me to continue moving forward with my journey in forgiveness, healing, self-love and being whole. I wanted to be an example for them, that they too could experience the freedom I was experiencing.

Domestic violence, child abuse, sexual assault, race relations, mental health issues and other societal concerns needs to be more openly and candidly discussed to raise awareness regarding these prevalent issues. We must remove the stigmas, biases, fears and barriers surrounding these issues.

The staggering statistics mentioned in the bullet points are just a few examples of just how prevalent these issues are. My story reflects these numbers; hence why I have courageously decided to share it. If I can open the eyes of just one person, or raise awareness to a judgmental counterpart, or even inspire healing in another soul's life, my mission has been accomplished.

I implore anyone who graciously reads *Unclothed*, to take some time to self-reflect and then do some internal work. You may find it is long overdue. I am on a lifelong journey. I did not write this to show the means to an end, rather to show how the winding and twisting roads in life can change directions and form a new path, if one allows it.

If you, or anyone you know is having suicidal thoughts, please call the **National Suicide Prevention Lifeline at:**

1-800-273-TALK (8255).

"There is no greater agony than bearing an untold story inside of you..."
~ Maya Angelou

INTRODUCTION

Darkness, loneliness, and feelings of helplessness consumed me as I contemplated ending my life. Inadequacy, fear, and thinking I simply had no purpose on this earth dominated my mind; leaving no room for rational and positive self-talk to enter. I felt that the endless cycle of hurt and pain were constant variables in my life. The only way to escape it was to kill the soul residing in my shell. I could not see the light at the end of the tunnel. As darkness consumed my thoughts, feelings and vision I grabbed the bottle of Celexa which had been prescribed to me for depression. My thoughts continued to spiral downhill to a place darker then the depths of the bottom of a well.

Suicide was a periodic thought I battled with for years. It was the day after Valentine's Day. I felt overwhelmed. Insecurity, hopelessness, doubts, fears, failures, feeling unloved... the list went on and on. My mind and heart, both, were cluttered with random emotions, sensitivity and the impression that everyone was "out to get me." It was a thought pattern I developed early in life; the sentiment of feeling sorry for myself - that no one loved me - all because I was still bound and restricted by the afflictions of my past. I, however, never anticipated these barriers would be the cause of a nervous breakdown.

As I opened my eyes, the bright, white lights shined - it was near blinding. I was lying down in an unfamiliar place. There was a tube in my nostrils. I was scared. *"Where am I?"* I thought. For a moment, I had forgotten what led me to this place. As my vision became clearer from the blurriness and confusion, I heard a voice call my name. "Casandra. Cas...."

CHAPTER ONE

Humble Beginnings

Being named after others, and in the way I was, gave my name meaning. Mom said I was named after my God-mom, Casandra. They were both pregnant at the same time. Unfortunately, my God-mom lost her baby due to a miscarriage. Therefore, Mom promised her she would name me after her. My grandmother's (Mom's mom,) name was Casandra as well. I was named after my God-mother and grandmother. A name which may have been common to others meant something to Mom because of the people in her life.

I was conceived and born out of wedlock. Mom and Dad did not get married until after I was born. They were pronounced husband and wife at the courthouse. I never saw any pictures or really heard much else about the day their union was official under God and man, other than their anniversary was in June. Mom hyphenated her last name to include both her's and Dad's.

I thought it was admirable to not give up her entire identity when she got married. It was as if it was her own way of holding onto herself, as a reminder of her individuality in this world and who she really was deep down.

Mom is a red headed, Caucasian (with fair skin and freckles), educated woman who was born and raised on a farm in Iowa. Her family moved to the central Illinois area when she was in high school. Dad is an African American who was born in Mississippi, but raised on the eastside of Springfield, Illinois. His parents moved up north; I suspect to escape the Jim Crowism that still existed down south. Dad was the first African American Mom dated. Dad's older sister did not approve of their relationship. She felt white people were the enemy and Dad was a "traitor." Mom's family did not seem to favor her choice in a significant other either; though they kept their opinions to themselves.

Mom's family was more conservative. They were financially better off and seemed to be in an overall better place. Some owned their own homes. They were educated and had decent jobs or had careers. They also had vehicles of their own and traveled often. Even the food they ate was different. They appeared to be overall, happier people.

Dad's family, however, seemed to be completely the opposite. Poverty, violence, abuse, alcoholism, drugs and instability were common factors that existed. A single-parent home was common. Sometimes only one or two people had a vehicle and gave everyone else in the family rides. Some of them moved from place to place, not owning their own home nor remaining in a stable environment. The neighborhoods they lived in were different as well, which were more destitute and susceptible to crime. Although the food was more flavorful, there were times when resources were extremely scarce and meals were created from whatever was available, which may not have been much. Apparently, Mom and Dad were from two different worlds.

By the time I came along, Mom's family was dispersed across different states in the country. Traveling had to occur for us to see one another. Dad's core nuclear family and some extended relatives lived in Springfield, where we lived as well. Their thoughts, views, opinions and religious beliefs would be what I was raised around and taught for most my childhood life. I hardly saw the two families interact with one another.

There were pictures of myself lying in a dresser drawer as a newborn baby growing up. Cribs were costly and the dresser drawer was more cost efficient. My existence was obviously unplanned. Mom and Dad may not have been in a place in their lives where they were ready to have a child; although Dad already had a son from a previous relationship, Kendall, my older half-brother. I, however, was Mom's first child and Dad's first daughter.

I did not remain the only child between Mom and Dad for long, a whole twenty-one months to be exact. When April was born, Mom said I was so upset and mad there was going to be another child. She shared that I had expressed, "I don't need no more dollies," and pinched April on her arm. She began to cry as I just stood there, dumbfounded. At such a young age, I certainly did not have a problem expressing myself.

I was approximately two years old and April was still a baby, lying down, wrapped up in a bundle with a diaper on. Mom was in the kitchen getting something for April. I was in the living room with a lit candle and a piece of paper, mesmerized by the flame and its glow. With curiosity plaguing my mind, I took the piece of paper, put it in the fire, and watched it beam before me. Instantly, I felt fear consume me. As the flame on the burning piece of paper grew closer toward my fingertips, I threw it on the couch and hid behind it.

Mom immediately ran into the living room, searching and calling for me. She found me petrified, hiding behind a couch engulfed with flame in a room full of smoke. She snatched me by the arm, pulled me from behind the couch, and gave what I remember, as the first "whoopen" of my life! Mom opened the front door wide to air out the living room as she yelled at me, "if you play with fire, you'll get burned!" This was my first lesson in life. Obviously, today, I can laugh about it.

The house we lived in was on 13th street, the eastside of Springfield. This was and still is, known as the "ghetto," or the "hood." Before April was born, Mom said we lived in Evergreen, which was and still is considered "the projects." These areas are still poverty stricken neighborhoods where crime, violence, and drugs remain. Mom and Dad kept a "tight leash" on us, as protection, to shield us of a world they did not want us to discover. Inevitably, we would all be exposed to what they attempted to keep unknown. After my youngest sister, Crystal was born, we moved to a slightly better neighborhood.

I reacted differently to Crystal's birth. Since I was older, I became more aware that I would be "a helper." I was excited about Crystal and wanted to be "mommy's little helper." So thrilled, I attempted to make a bottle for Crystal and spilled all sorts of ingredients on the kitchen floor. Even though I was excited about baby Crystal, I still felt there was going to be too many of us. I felt I would be ignored and all the attention would be pivoted toward the new baby. I also believe I had a prophetic epiphany of what was yet to come. Either way, I was disturbed as the disapproval covered my face and was obvious through my actions.

It was in the early hours of the morning, before dawn, and Mom had to go to the hospital where baby Crystal would enter the world. Reality settled in. I had to accept there would be three of us. April and I sat at Madea and Paw-Paw's house until Dad came back with Mom and the baby. Madea and Paw-Paw were the only ones at that time they allowed to watch us, because they were Dad's parents. When Mom and Dad returned to pick us up and take us home with baby Crystal, I immediately pinched Crystal just as I had pinched April. Madea pinched me back, "you don't go around pinchin' no babies." Although my arm felt as if a bee had just stung me, I did not mutter a single word, or contest her reprimand. I did as I was told and kept quiet.

Crystal wasn't even a year old yet when we moved to another house. This house Mom and Dad still reside in currently. I was about four years old, and eventually was going to start kindergarten. The house we moved out of had hardwood floors and was smaller. Our last night there, April and I had to make a pallet on the floor and slept in the clothes we were to wear the next day. Crystal was still sleeping in the crib, which they disassembled the following morning.

The new house was on 7th and Laurel, the southeast side of town. It had an upstairs and a downstairs, two bedrooms, a living room and dining room - which was turned into a sitting room - and 1 ½ bathrooms. The kitchen was big enough for a table and had a deep freezer in it. Although the three of us girls had to share a room; we eventually each had our own beds and dresser drawers. There was also an attic and a traditional unfinished basement. Of course, it was going to be more of a funhouse for us! We played hide and go seek, had scavenger hunts, made tents, slid down the stairs with sheets, along with other fun ideas we created to do.

At the onset of spring, Mom pulled the weeds out of the ground, and prepared the soil for planting seeds. She had us girls help her and gave us a short lecture on how long the bulbs lasted, how important it was to keep the ground moisturized with plenty of water, and so on and so forth. We shoveled the dirt around, pulled out unwanted weeds, and learned about different bugs in the ground. "There are 2 different kinds of bugs," Mom said, "the ones that help your plants, and the ones that eat your plants!"

We planted a few rose bushes, a variety of pretty spring flowers, sunflowers, several veggies and some fruit. It was fun planting them and watching the bulbs or seeds grow and blossom into what they were created to be; something like life. There was always something about this process which fascinated me. I observed this to be an incredible theory. A theory I would eventually try to live by: We all, everything created under the sun and the moon, start off as a seed. The seed then grows and blossoms into what God created it to be.

When the weather permitted, we walked down the alley which led to Iles Park, and played until we couldn't play anymore. On the way to and fro, we passed mulberry bushes. Mom helped us pick the ripe ones to eat. She always found an opportunity to teach us something about nature when outside, and helped us to differentiate between what was edible or not. Mom was good at picking the sweet berries, even though they stained our hands and often times our clothes. We did not care because of how yummy they were! The berries were mildly sweet and juicy. Sometimes we picked enough to make mulberry shakes when we got home.

We also walked to Lincoln Library to read and check out books to take home. We spent a few hours there and soaked up as much air conditioning as we could before we had to truck it back home. Most of the time, we did not have a vehicle. So, our legs, taxi cabs, the city bus or rides from friends and family were our only means for transportation. Stopping for breaks so our little legs could get a few minutes of rest was ideal. However, most of the time Mom wanted us to get there as quickly as possible. Because we did not have central air conditioning, going to the Library on a hot summer day was our chance to cool off. What a treat! The cool air drying the sweat off of my pasty skin, felt like the sudden cold air that initially escapes a freezer and greets you directly in the face upon opening its door. That refreshing feeling alone was motivation enough to go to the Library.

Summers were the best time of year for me, and my favorite. As long as we came home by the time the street lights were on; we were able to enjoy the weather and play outside with the neighborhood kids. We played outside all day when school was out. Popsicles were my favorite! When the ice cream van came around the block, ringing the bell, all of the kids ran to the van to pick out their favorite treats. I never had any money to buy anything, but it was still fun listening for him to come around the corner. Summertime also meant less time in the house. Later, I would try to do whatever it took to get out of the house for as long as I could.

We often went to Madea's and Paw-Paws during the summertime so all of us kids could play with each other. Dad was the master on the barbeque grill, and of course, I was the master at eating it as quick as it came off of the grill! The smell of the meat cooking was an aroma that was like heaven to my nostrils. Dad grilled the meat, while Madea was in the kitchen preparing all of the side dishes and cakes. She made the best cakes! Madea also had a garden in her backyard. She picked collard greens and had us wash them off so she could cook them for our barbeque feast. Those were the good times.

While the adults cooked and conversed with one another; we sat around this large sized pothole that was in the middle of the yard and played 'duck, duck, goose.' We also played red light, green light; Simon Says and other traditional childhood games. Sometimes we went half a block down to the Boys and Girls Club too.

Firecrackers were a treat as well during the summertime. My male cousins usually had them, but shared them with us all. I did not care for the firecrackers that resembled snakes. They started off as a small black pellet and when lit with fire, they grew and looked similar to a snake! Usually it was only us girls who screeched and screamed as we ran away from the artificial snakes growing on the sidewalk.

The winter months were brutal at times. Boiling water to take a bath and opening the oven for heat was something we adapted to quickly. Usually the bill got too high to afford. Because Dad did not work and stayed home with us girls, Mom did what she could to make sure we at least had a roof over our heads and food at the table.

When the electricity was temporarily shut off, lighting candles at night to have some sort of lighting in the house was also something we were used to. At times, it got so cold outside, the three of us girls made pallets on the living room floor, snuggled up together, and laid as close to the heater as we could. Back then, I never knew if our way of living was a normal routine for everyone else or just us. I had gotten so used to it, I thought it was a way of life when the winter months came rolling along.

Hard times came often for us. Mom was the only one who worked consistently. The jobs weren't great in pay either. Simply keeping a roof over our head was the focus. There were times when peanut butter and jelly crackers or sugar toast was all I could find to eat. I even put water in my cereal rather than use the disgusting powdered milk we sometimes had. It smelled just as bad as it tasted. I tried to make due with whatever we had.

Creatively so, Dad found ways for us to get by when going to the doctor or purchasing over the counter medications was not an option. He was pro natural remedies. Any time we were either ill or simply ran out of some sort of hygiene product, Dad had a back-up plan. No toothpaste? Use baking soda. Sore throat? Gargle warm salt water. Have a general head cold? Drink a concoction of some sort which usually consisted of tea and honey. Got a rash? Take an oatmeal bath.

We did not have an operable washer or dryer in the house either. When we did, it seemed to not last long before it broke down and there were no means to get it repaired or replaced. Going to the laundromat in a taxi cab was what we did to get the clothes cleaned. I hated going to the laundromat. It felt like we spent an entire day there, washing, drying and folding clothes. It was loud. The washers and dryers ran consecutively. Other folk's kids ran around, playing and chasing one another. I simply did not like going there.

Dad never came with us to the laundromat. I suppose it was his time to get a break from being around us girls all of the time. Mom made us help fold laundry. Dad's clothes were so heavy when pulling them out of the washer and putting them into the dryer. His jeans alone felt like a ton of bricks!

The laundry mat was not our only source for washing clothes. Our feet were the laundry machines. We used the bathtub at times as well. Mom or Dad filled the tub up with laundry soap and water, and in we went with no socks on and our pants rolled up. We stomped and swooshed the clothes around while they soaked in the soapy water. We repeated this same process when it was time to rinse the clothes out.

Mom then taught us how to wring the soaking wet clothes out. We had to be sure to squeeze as much excess water out as we could, to expedite the drying process. Mom had a folding laundry drying rack she hung most of the damp clothes on to dry. She also put clothes on hangers and hung them in the living room on the hooks that were attached to the mantle. We did not have much, but made do with what we had.

There was an Aldi grocery store several blocks away from our house. We walked there often to go grocery shopping with Mom. "Don't ask for anything," she told us on the way there. We were quite the quiet and well behaved little girls when in public with Mom. Mom often received praises on how well-mannered we were. When we were done grocery shopping, depending upon how much groceries we had, Mom pushed the grocery cart home to unload the groceries and then pushed the grocery cart back to the store.

I was extremely embarrassed when Mom did this. I dreaded anyone I knew seeing this. I would walk adjacent to one of my sisters or Mom, in an attempt to hide so no one could see me. Mortified, my skin turned red any time embarrassment took over my countenance.

At one point, Mom's dad gave us their old car. It was old, big and green and was loud when running. We didn't have the car for long. For the duration we did have it, Dad gave his sisters rides when they needed it, and in turn, they offered him gas money. There were times I was also embarrassed to ride around and be seen in the "big green machine," as I would call it. I often ducked down, hoping no one saw my fiery red hair and recognized me. I was too young to appreciate we had transportation for the moment, something we did not have very often. However, I began to notice not everyone lived in the manner in which we did. I became embarrassed that we were poor.

Other than the fun and hard times we experienced; I also experienced and witnessed horrible events that a child my age, or anyone for that matter, should never have to observe or endure. Waking up to screaming, yelling, cussing, fighting and crying seemed to be an everyday occurrence. Or, what I knew of it as - a ritual.

Since I was the oldest, I was sent to be the one to go downstairs and *investigate* what all of the commotion was about. I liked to consider myself as an *Inspector Gadget*. Mom and Dad argued and fought often like cats and dogs. More likely, it was Dad beating on Mom, as she screamed for him to "Stop!" or "Get off of her!" Either way, what I detected was two people fighting and arguing; over what, I did not know. But what I did know, and always knew, it was not right and it did not exemplify "love" in my eyes.

Hostility and animosity consumed the atmosphere to a point where it was suffocating. It was hard to breath; hard to see, and hard to navigate with all of the negative energy roaming about from room to room. It was as if I was standing outside on a hot summer day, with no breeze passing through and the humidity was smothering to the point of suffocation. Not knowing if one day would be a good day or a bad day, or if there would be smiles or tears. The suspense was not a thrill I sought out, rather, I wished for more stability and a knowing of what was yet to come.

I had some stability - I knew who my parents were, living under the same roof for a given amount of years, and Mom's ability to hold a job. I knew we would have clothes on our back, regardless if they were used, old, stained or tattered, and that I would have something to eat. Our basic needs were met. Yet, not knowing if I was going to either be waking up to or walking into a war zone was mentally and emotionally exhausting. It was draining and had a deep impact for many years to follow.

Unfortunately, the only time it seemed Mom and Dad did get along was when we were awakened out of our sleep. We were forced to hear the disgusting sounds most kids dread; their parents *making love*. Our bedrooms were only a few feet apart, so any sound made easily penetrated the walls. I even threw a ball or some other object at the wall and yelled, "shut up!" as I got older, in an attempt to get them to be quiet so I could sleep. I never quite understood the relationship between Mom and Dad. It was vulgar, confusing, hateful, unstable and consequently; the only example of *love* I had which molded me.

CHAPTER TWO
Booze, Beatings & Bruises

Blackened eyes, bruises, screaming and streams of tears were the memories I had of Mom. I never understood why she put up with Dad. He was an abusive alcoholic. One day, early in the morning, I watched Mom apply foundation on her face as she was getting ready for work. She was covering the black eyes Dad gave her. Mom was quiet as she stared in the mirror, carefully applying the foundation around her eyes. She knew I was standing in the doorway watching her, yet neither of us uttered a single word. It was a nonverbal moment for us. I knew what happened, why Mom was covering it up, and she knew I was aware of all of it.

I was no older than 5 or 6 years of age at the time. I wondered then, at such an early age, why did she put up with this behavior from him? Did Mom not love herself more than that to just leave him? Or did Mom depend on Dad so much with staying home with us girls that she did not believe she could bear the struggle of being a single-mother? I often wondered, what was the true reason as to why she continued to live this way?

Witnessing a man of Dad's size and stature hit and beat on a woman looked awful. Mom was set up to lose by default. Dad was about 6'4" and at least 200lbs. His hands were large. Dad looked so serious, as if he were mad at the world. Mom on the other hand, was about 5'4" and an average sized woman.

Regardless of her size, I knew it was wrong for Dad to beat on her. I instinctively felt the wrongness of a man beating on a woman. However, it appeared worse because of the differences in their overall builds. It was like watching Goliath beat up on itty-bitty, small David.

At the time, I had never heard about domestic violence or that it was "wrong" for a man to hit a woman. We were never taught any of this. Nevertheless, my soul knew it was wrong. I heard my mother cry, beg and plead for Dad to get off of her. I wished he would stop pounding on her. It pained me and my sisters so deeply we cried and confided in one another in our shared bedroom. Fearful of what happened… how bad he hit her… was at the forefront of my mind each moment I heard calamity.

Over the years to come, Mom worked a variety of jobs; from Sangamon State University, to the State Journal Register, Temporary Services, and various managerial positions at different fast food restaurants. Dad, however, never really worked, unless picking up a beer or a joint and throwing his fist at someone every time he was drunk or angry counts as work. He did work a couple of part time jobs here and there, but they were short lived. I suppose the real work was Dad having to stay at home with three growing girls while his wife worked all day.

Mom had hectic work schedules. If we weren't at school, at work with Mom or involved in an activity, we were home with Dad. There were many assumptions I made as to why he was so mad. Maybe it was because he was stuck with the three of us at home more times than not? Or perhaps he felt disappointed he didn't do much with himself? Whatever his reasoning, it was not sufficient enough to justify why I was the one who faced his wrath.

Mom worked so much and so hard; I started to believe she was a workaholic. I didn't blame her, considering the circumstances. She was a victim of abuse and was clearly not going to leave. Mom was away from home more often than not. When Mom was home, she was fighting with Dad or getting beat by him, sleeping, reading a book, or cooking. A part of me knew or assumed she felt some type of alleviation by working. Work was an outlet that allowed her to escape the imprisoned life she chose to live. This instigated Mom into working more than one job at a time. She was not only trying to keep up with the bills, but I strongly felt she wanted nothing more than to stay away from Dad. It must have weighed heavy on Mom's heart to be away from her girls. So heavy, she probably wanted to leave, but stayed for the sake of her children.

Mom, however, will always be remembered for "having her nose in a book," as Dad called it. Our house had books everywhere: on the two book shelves, which were in the front room, boxes in her room, and boxes in the basement. Mom particularly loved to read sci-fi books. It seemed as if she wasn't mentally present whenever she was reading a novel. Mom read while walking, riding the city bus, riding in the cab and cooking. In order to get her attention, we had to call for her more than once because she was so engaged with reading the book in her hands. She also seemed to have an answer for everything and was extremely intelligent.

Mom was not only intelligent, she was creative and talented as well. I loved looking through Mom's old things. She had the best clothes and heels from her day, paintings she painted herself, and outfits she sewed as well. It seemed she was once extremely gifted. I often wondered why she didn't dress the same or do the same things she did back then.

Mom had so many neat things to look through; old jewelry boxes full of old broaches and necklaces; different and stylish clothing from back in her younger days. I became infatuated with her things. It was like digging through a treasure chest! As long as she was asleep or at work, and Dad was either gone or downstairs, the world was mine in her closet!

I admired Mom so. There were old pictures of her in sporadic places throughout the house. Her red hair was thick, long and gorgeous. Her make-up was flawless. She looked like a completely different person from the woman I was seeing day in and day out. I wondered what happened? When did she change? Why? How? Well, maybe I knew the why and some of the how. Seeing how Dad treated her and the environment she lived in, it was impossible for her *not* to change. I saw lost hopes, dreams, goals and visions in her eyes. She gave up on herself. She was only existing and surviving, not living and thriving.

Dad on the other hand, typically had an opened can of beer next to him. The smell of booze on his breath was a familiar scent. So much so, I began to predict what mood he was in based off of if I could smell the alcohol or not. Being at home was like walking on eggshells - trying to maneuver my way around Dad to see if he was happy or angry.

Sometimes Dad was a happy drunk. He played his favorite music so loudly that the three of us girls came running downstairs, just to see him in a good mood. We also enjoyed the music and danced to it. Prince became one of my favorite artists. Dad had his Purple Rain record. It was as if time had stopped when the music was playing. The three of us girls twirled around in small circles and watched our nighties twirl as Dad tapped his foot on the ground to the beat of the music. Dad seemed to have entered into a different world himself, allowing the music to take him to a place where he was not reminded of his reality.

However, there were times Dad was also an angry drunk. I feared this man with every fiber in my being. Knowing what was yet to come, the very hairs on my arms would stand up. My heart would beat so hard I thought it would jump right out of my chest and onto the floor where others could see it.

I wondered what Dad was like before he turned into the angry alcoholic. I had heard stories about him being in the Navy, playing in live bands with friends, and traveling a lot. I also heard about Dad being a "ladies man" and having a large afro. In older pictures I found around the house, Dad was smiling and appeared to be in a good mood, but Dad never really talked about himself a whole lot growing up. We heard more stories from Mom, because she was more transparent with us. Dad, however, was often quiet. He spoke seldom, but when he did you heard him. His words, actions and simply his demeanor scared the living daylights out of me.

"You should've kept your legs closed!" Dad belted out at Mom one night. She was crying about how hard it was having us kids, and having to work long hours. Dad was being unsympathetic and complaining about having to stay home with us. Occasionally, Dad refused to watch us and Mom was forced to bring all three of us girls with her to work. Since I was the oldest, I blamed my own birth for the start of it all. My birth caused their lives to turn into hell and they took it out on us. I was nothing but a mistake.

I heard about Dad being in a tragic car accident when he was younger. He suffered a terrible and chronic back injury in result. Having a bad back prevented Dad from doing certain physical activities. His back was so bad, he often had us girls walk on it while he laid on the floor. Sometimes his back would go out for days at a time and he was restricted to lying on the couch. Sadly, I looked forward to these days. I figured Dad was in too much pain to holler at or beat on anyone.

I attempted to use the knowledge of Dad having a bad back to my advantage. When I was small enough, I hid under my parent's bed in their bedroom. With Dad being so tall, it was extremely difficult for him to get down underneath the bed and reach for me from such a low spot. As I hid under the bed, my hands trembled. I was terrified and consumed with fear of what may happen to me when I crawled from underneath the bed. I knew I could not hide under there forever. There were a few occasions when Dad was able to grab a hold of my ankle or leg. He then dragged me from underneath the bed until I was completely out in the open. That's when the beatings began. Whatever he had available to him he used; extension cords, telephone cords, belts, switches, you name it.

The combination of getting hit and me being pissed off and frightened all at the same time - were the perfect ingredients to send me into a frenzy. Sometimes I panicked to the point of hyperventilation. If Dad punched me in the stomach, I felt as if the wind was knocked out of me and I could not breathe. I had to get a paper bag just to catch my breath and regain control of my breathing.

His fists were what I feared the most. Don't get me wrong, getting beat with whatever object Dad had on hand was very painful. With his strength, he used great force. Yet, it was something about his large-sized closed fists and the power and force he used when hitting me, that felt like something more than a traditional whooping. It was personal. It not only hurt physically, but emotionally.

Getting hit with a closed fist by my Dad, as a little girl, made me feel as if something was wrong with me. I thought little girls were supposed to be "Daddy's princesses." Instead, I felt as if I were one of Dad's enemies. He despised me - waging war against me on a consistent basis. I did not feel protected *by* my dad. Rather, felt I needed protection *from* my dad.

I didn't know if it was because I was the oldest, or if there was really something wrong with *ME* as to why Dad was so mean and hateful. He made me feel as if I had done something wrong by merely existing- that my presence in the world was a curse to him and he was determined to do whatever necessary to break me down. Not feeling loved by a dad that is raising you was the worst feeling to have to endure.

"You're a punk!" Dad often told me if I cried during or after a beating. He taught me that expressing myself was a form of weakness and to hold everything inside; fear, hurt and pain included. I took the worst beatings from him, stared him directly in his eyes, and did everything within my willpower to not let a single tear fall. I mastered how to hold in all of my hurt, fear and pain.

Once, I was in the corner trying to hide from Dad. I was between the couch and his old-school record player. He wrapped the leather part of the belt around his hand so that the buckle was loose. He then beat me with the buckle part of the belt, as I stared at him in anger.

"So you think you're funny!" he yelled, as I glared at him.

Even though the belt buckle hurt like hell, I wanted to show him that the pain he inflicted upon me did not affect me, or at least that's what I wanted him to believe. This angered him more and caused the beatings to worsen.

"Go outside and get me a switch," Dad told April as he beat me.

"Make sure it's thin and leave the stems on it."

Dad stopped sending me to get my own switch some time ago, because I often ran away and sometimes did not return that day. It didn't take long before Dad began sending April to get it. She was "Daddy's little helper." The switch alone was not bad. It was what he *did* with the switch that hurt the most. I also knew that a switch beating was not going to be the only beating I received. Sometimes he dampened the switch with water and beat me. The excruciating pain felt worse than a typical sting and left red welts all over my skin.

After listening to Mom and Dad fight and argue, watch Mom run out of the door after Dad was physically violent toward her or receiving beatings of my own, I began going outside to clear my mind. I paced around, trying to push the unwanted memories so far back into my subconscious they would never resurface to remind me of the hell I was forced to live in. I picked dandelions after they had flowered and blew the white seeds into the air as I wished for a different and harmonious life. As the white seeds floated away from me, I believed that they each carried my wishes. Someday my wishes would return to me.

I became more fed up with the adversity I was forced to live in. I needed an escape. I had become clever and tactful in how I defended myself against Dad. I was about 11 years old when Crystal and I decided to push our dresser in front of our bedroom door. We both sat on it so Dad could not get in…

He had been drinking, and was mumbling something under his breath. There was a vent in our room, which was connected to the living room downstairs. Dad sat downstairs, in the same spot, in front of the television. Before one of us went downstairs, we put our head down on the ground so our ears were exposed to the holes in the vent. We listened to see if we could hear Mom and Dad fussing at each other, Dad yelling, snoring if he were asleep or him mumbling under his breath. We did this even if we wanted to get a drink of water - frightened if he was in a bad mood or not. Usually when Dad mumbled under his breath, he had been drinking and no one was around.

On this particular day, Mom was at work and we were at home with Dad. Crystal and I got on the floor and put our ears next to the vent. I heard him mumbling. The three of us girls fought over who would go downstairs to ask for something to eat or drink. Usually, it was me making one of them go, out of fear of what I might run into. Since I was the oldest, I felt I had authority to dictate who did what between us girls. Whenever Mom was gone, I was the target, Dad's punching bag. I wanted to have some sort of power and control for myself.

"You should've been watching them! You're the oldest!" Dad often told me before he beat me. If April or Crystal did something out of line, I was to blame for it. I got tired of being held responsible for their shortcomings. If I could help it, I made sure to boss them around and tell them what to do.

Every now and then Dad heard us listening at the vent. He yelled from his seat in the living room at us, "What are y'all up there doing?" Fearful to say anything at all, we chose not to respond. We quietly got into our beds and pretended to be napping.

"I said, what are y'all up there doing dammit?" By his tone and the elevation in his voice, we knew he was angry.

"Nothing, we're just in our room lying down." I was too scared to ask for anything, so I decided to wait until later - after either Mom got home or Dad was calmer.

All of the sudden, we heard Dad get up from his seat. The sound of Dad's heavy footsteps got louder as he approached the staircase. Crystal and I decided to push the dresser in front of our bedroom door in a desperate attempt to block Dad from releasing his frustration and anger upon us. When Crystal was a little older, she began to either help me or stand up for me at times. April feared Dad so much that she usually hid, in an attempt to stay out of his sight.

Unfortunately, Dad still barged his way in. However, this fight wasn't going to be an easy one. Crystal jumped on his back as I ran around him, down the stairs and right out the front door. This was the very first time I experienced running in this manner - with no designated distance or known destination. Running was a habit I developed early in life. I felt free, happy, liberated and had a clearer mind. Not only was it a means for me to escape the abusive environment I lived in, it was a form of *therapy* for me, a newfound world I had never experienced.

Verbal put downs, abuse, and neglect were my strongest childhood memories. In attempts to not allow the negative words to have an adverse impact on me, I tried to cancel them out by speaking positive affirmations. I marched around the house, chanting my mantras while convincing myself that one day things would change for the better. I proclaimed that I would be "somebody" and "live a good life;" whatever that may be or meant. Something inside of me wanted more in life. I wanted to feel happy inside, to be loved and feel wanted.

"I'm going to be somebody!"

"I'm going to be a lawyer or work for the FBI! "

"I am not going to stay here for the rest of my life!"

"I'm going to leave and make something of myself!"

Those were familiar words to my younger sisters, as I often said them out of anger or hurt after getting a beating or being berated. Dad frequently recited insults when he was angry and/or drunk.

"You ain't shit and you ain't going to be nothing!"

"You're so damn stupid!"

"You're a failure who has no friends!"

"Shut the fuck up!"

I tried to let these hateful words go in one ear and right back out of the other. I desperately wanted to combat his hatred with avoidance. I thought I could block him out, or ignore him. Yet, the words still found a way to penetrate through my tough skin, enter into my clogged ears, and get inside of my thick skull. They crept inside of me, every single part of me. Although I did not want to believe or accept these words, they still managed to saturate my being and each letter became infused into my identity.

When Mom came home from work, she looked so exhausted I wouldn't dare bother her with my daily troubles. I don't even know if she knew what happened when she was at work, I just assumed she already knew.

"Why don't you just leave him?!" I often pleaded with Mom. To both of my parents, I was being a mouthy kid. "You need to stay in a kid's place," Dad told me when he overheard me begging Mom to leave him. I didn't understand their situation. I did know that everything that continued to go on in that house was not right, did not feel like love, and made me angry. In result, I continued to boldly express my opinions and how I felt about all of the abuse, regardless of the consequences.

I wanted to see Mom fight for herself. Fight for what she thought was right and stand up for that; because I surely was not given enough examples of it. I felt women were strong and powerful creatures, who could overcome anything and be whomever they chose to be. I saw more in Mom than an abused and battered woman. I saw a woman with a strong work ethic, who believed in earning her pay the right way, regardless of how hard she had to work for less. I saw a talented and gifted baker and a brilliant person who had the answers for any and everything. I saw more in Mom and I wanted her to see more in herself.

There was only one time I witnessed Mom truly defend herself and retaliate against Dad after a beating. I was in the living room and Mom and Dad were in the kitchen arguing. I don't know what Dad did, but I remember Mom threw a pot of chili on Dad. He yelled as Mom came dashing through the living room. I laughed hysterically! I even tried to slip my foot out in front of Dad, in an attempt to trip him as he chased after her. Unfortunately, my foot failed to catch his leg. Yet, I was so proud and shocked at Mom for actually defending herself for once! It was simply hilarious to watch Dad as he tried to get the chili off of him!

Maybe Mom defended herself other times as well and I just didn't witness it. Either way, I was glad to see that she was capable of defending herself in some shape, form or fashion. When Dad beat on her, she appeared to be so helpless and defenseless.

"STOP Otis!!"

The three of us woke up. They were fighting once again. Crying and screaming was all I heard.

"Go see what's going on," April and Crystal whispered.

I walked downstairs to the living room and witnessed Mom lying back down on the floor as Dad was straddled on top of her and choking her. I thought he was going to kill her! I was both terrified and furious. I didn't have much time, or the strength to get him off of her. I had to do something!

I tiptoed around the two of them, went into the kitchen and dialed 911. I left the kitchen phone unhooked. I then went back into the living room to unhook the phone in there. I figured if two phones were unhooked, whoever was on the other end could hear what Dad was doing to Mom. Dad caught me in the act, hung up the phone in the living room and told me to "take your ass back upstairs!" I stayed. I sat on the stairs in the front room, listening to make sure Mom was still shouting or attempting to do so at least. If I could hear her, she was still alive.

Eventually, the tragic episode ended and Mom left. I went back upstairs assuming it was all over. Soon, I heard a knock on the door, "Springfield Police." I slowly walked down a few stairs and sat quietly, so I could hear what was going on. Dad answered the door and let the two officers in.

"We received a phone call that there was a disturbance in the area," one of the officers told Dad.

"That must have been the neighbors," he replied.

I sat on the stairs angered and full of rage. *"That liar!"* I thought to myself. The officers apologized for the inconvenience and were about to leave.

My heart began to beat faster as blood was racing through my veins. My palms were sweaty and shaky. *"If I don't do or say something, we're going to be stuck here forever!"* I thought to myself. In desperation for an escape, I dashed down the stairs.

"He's lying, he's lying!" I shouted.

Dad looked at me in shock, speechless for once.

"He was just beating up my mom and he beats on me too!" I told the officers.

They then looked at each other with curiousness and confusion. One officer stayed in the front room with Dad, the other asked me to go into the living room with him. I was so amazed that my little trick worked! I told the officer how I was the one who called them and left the phones unhooked. I was proud of myself for outsmarting Dad. I felt relief. Finally, my voice would be heard.

"You're a smart little girl," the officer told me. I then told him what all happened in the house in great detail.

"Is there anywhere you can go? Like a family member's house?" He asked.

"Yes," I replied. "But I have two little sisters, they're upstairs." One of the officers told the other to go upstairs and check.

"Please don't go up there," Dad pleaded with him. I knew Dad didn't want them to go upstairs because it was a mess. Clothes were spread all over the floor and it appeared as if a tornado had run through the house. If we did not clean the house, it simply did not get done. Mom seemed to be too tired to clean once she got home. Dad seemed to feel as if he adhered to his responsibilities by staying home with us girls.

I felt like a slave each time I had to get on my hands and knees to wash the baseboards of the house, or iron Dad's gigantic clothes. Doing the dishes was the worst. They seemed to never end. Each time a dish was cleaned another one seemed to appear. "You never know who's going to stop by, so you need to keep the house clean." Dad recited this phrase often. I bet he did not imagine that this unexpected visit would be the police knocking on the door.

The officer stepped over the clothes, asked my sisters to put some shoes on and come with them. "Please don't take my kids!," Dad begged of them. The officers continued to have us get our coats and shoes on. They ignored Dad's pleas. I was immersed in joy as I watched Dad for once, *not* be in control.

The officers had the three of us get in the back of their squad car, told us "everything would be fine," and took us to Aunt Carol's house, Dad's youngest sister. "The operator told us they heard yelling and screaming in the background. So, we knew something was going on," the officer told me on the way to Aunt Carol's house. Madea answered the door when the officer knocked. They explained to her what was going on and asked was it okay if we came over. She let us in and we sat. The entire time I wondered where they took Dad and if he was in jail. Madea didn't ask us any questions.

"Finally!" I whispered to myself. The madness was finally over. I had taken control of my future. I was the catalyst for our freedom. My new life was going to start at this moment. I wondered what was next...

A few hours later there was a knock at the door, it was Mom! She told us to get our shoes on and we were going back home. To say I was "disappointed" is an understatement. My heart was crushed. I watched all of my hopes and dreams for some sort of normalcy go out of the door when it was opened for Mom. I began to develop a grudge against Mom. It was obvious she was not going to leave Dad. I was full of hatred and anger. Not only was Mom always at work and never came to my rescue when Dad beat on me; she also stayed with him!

Now I was not feeling loved by my Dad or my mother...

Mom had walked to get us, so of course, we were forced to walk back home. Mom read a book, as the three of us walked along with her. I shuffled my feet and kicked the rocks on the sidewalk, dreading returning to that treacherous house. Mom "had her nose in a book" again, with no regard that she was dragging her children back to the hell hole she chose to live in. I got upset.

"Is Dad home?" I asked.

"Yes," Mom replied.

"WHY!!?" I was so angry! I couldn't believe her.

"Why did you come get us then, why didn't you just leave us?"

Mom continued to walk and read in silence. I felt the police failed us by not taking Dad to jail and making it so easy for me to return to the hell I was forced to live in. I couldn't believe she was taking us back home! She was going back to this monster that just choked her nearly to death! By this point, I lost all faith in Mom. My vision of her changed. I saw weakness. I wanted her to be strong, at least for us. Here she had the perfect opportunity to begin a new life, and she blew it!

When we walked in the door, Dad was mumbling to himself. He was pissed off at me, but couldn't look me in the eyes. I didn't care what he was saying. I was infuriated that he was still home and the police didn't take him to jail.

"I thought you were supposed to go to jail." I told Dad. By this time, the fear in me was slowly leaving as boldness and anger took over. If Dad tried to put his hands on me, I would just call the police again; even though they didn't do much when I called the first time. This incident did move in my favor though. Dad didn't beat me for a while, and the fighting between him and Mom seemed to slow down. This phase only lasted briefly...

Bruises, red welts, scratches, and many other physical afflictions had become a common form of misinterpreted love I endured. The verbal and emotional abuse afflicted my mental and emotional state. I was never really sure of what exactly *LOVE* was. I had heard of the word and was told of its definition. Yet, those definitions did not match the examples I had at home. I was not taught how to love myself or others. In fact, I was shown quite the opposite.

I grew up to be full of hatred, resentment, and rage. I slowly turned into a callous being who did not know love. I had a temper that could boil a pot of water. I was a ticking time bomb. As I got older, I became physically aggressive. I had physical confrontations when someone would just say something I did not like. I felt the need to defend myself physically, rather than with words, or just ignoring. I learned that from Dad. He taught me that when you're angry, upset or mad, to pound your problems and feelings onto someone else.

Most of my physical altercations were between other family members; such as cousins and my sisters. One summer day, while playing with my cousins at Madea and Paw-Paw's house, I decided to help out and sweep their living room floor. My cousin Sharika came out of nowhere and snatched the broom out of my hand. Enraged she interrupted my peaceful moment, I snatched the broom right back from her and began punching her, like Dad had done to me.

I didn't see anything wrong with what I had done. Aunt Brenda, Dad's older sister, Sharika's mom, was furious! She could not believe I beat my younger cousin up and was unapologetic about it. I did not see the need to be remorseful. Dad never apologized to anyone when he beat on them-why should I?

As the years passed by, I began to believe April was Mom and Dad's "golden child." I never witnessed her get a beating, or receive much of a punishment, for that matter. I began to deeply resent April. I was always treated inferior to everyone else and wanted to know what was so "wrong" with me. Even though we were sisters, I felt as if I was the problem. It angered me to see April get treated better than I was. I was jealous.

As my anger grew, I eventually began to retaliate against April. There were times when I used to lock April in the closet in our room and call her "white girl," due to her extremely fair complexion. I even called her "Chuckie," after the doll on the horror film. I wanted her to feel how I felt – unwanted, unloved, and that her existence was unimportant. Deep down I knew that was not possible.

Incidentally, I now realize how cruel that was of me. Then, I felt I was just giving her what she deserved. She was a tattle tale at best, and did whatever possible to stay on Dad's good side. Now that I think of it, she was probably using her own personal survival skills and tactics she had developed to avoid Dad's temper. Nevertheless, our relationship was strained.

Crystal and I were closer, even though she was the youngest and I was the oldest. She helped me and came to my rescue when she got older when Dad beat me. She spoke of how unfair it was I got treated so poorly and sympathized with my pain. I felt she understood me and was not afraid to stand up against Dad on my behalf. I loved her for that.

CHAPTER THREE

More Secrets

Many times, I felt I was either being misunderstood or ignored. As a child, I did not have much of a say so in any matters. It was more of a "don't speak unless spoken to." Granted, I spoke out against what Dad was doing to Mom. However, other than the time I called the police on Dad, I never shared with anyone outside of our house the events which occurred until I got older. I learned how to keep things that happened only between those who were involved. I kept secrets inside of me, both mine and Mom's.

As Crystal grew out of her toddler phase, we spent more time at Madea and Paw-Paw's house. We did not go there often though. When we did go, it was mainly during the summertime or to visit on some holidays. It was more frequent when there were three of us. There were twelve of us that were usually there at the same time - cousins, siblings and all. I had both older male and female cousins. I landed somewhere in the middle in the age range between all of us.

Dad's sisters, Aunt Brenda (the oldest) and Aunt Carol (the youngest) pawned their kids off onto Madea and Paw-Paw, as Dad would put it. Dad despised them for doing this. He usually followed with cynical remarks about how his kids wouldn't spend days and hours at their house because we were his responsibility. Nonetheless, there were still times Dad dropped us off with the rest of them.

We usually spent most of our time together outside. Twelve kids were a lot to have playing inside of a modest house. Unfortunately, when I had to use the bathroom, going inside was not a simple task. Madea and Paw-Paw sat in front of the door on the front porch, to watch all of us kids as we played in the yard. We had to walk past the two of them to go inside and use the bathroom. They did not like a lot of traffic in and out of the house. By them sitting in front of the door, they could monitor all of us for the most part, while also minimizing the amount of times us kids went inside of the house.

Madea used snuff. She stuffed the tobacco in her lower lip and it just sat there. The house reeked of her tobacco breath. The bathroom smelled of soiled urine. The boys were careless in their aim, as the evidence covered the floor around the stool. The toilet was not clean either. It was covered with urine and feces residue. The lighting was dim. That bathroom was creepy. I wished I could just hold it, but I never could.

I still remember those bright, yellow shorts and the long tube socks I had on. I was squatting over the unkempt toilet urinating, while grabbing some toilet paper so I could wipe. I heard a knock at the door. "Someone's in here," I assertively mentioned, while trying to finish my business. Obviously, whoever was at the door was either deaf or had other intentions in mind.

It was Brian. He was my older cousin, Aunt Carol's oldest son. He slowly opened the door as I was wiping. I thought maybe he had to use the bathroom too, and was just being impatient. I tried to pull up my little yellow shorts as fast as I could, but unfortunately it wasn't fast enough.

Brian entered the bathroom. He closed the door behind him and stood in front of it. I was confused. *"What is he doing?"* I thought to myself. He had a smirk on his face. I felt doomed. Brian was five years older than me, standing taller and bigger than me in stature.

I was around nine years old when he grabbed me by the waist for the first time. I placed my hand on his stomach, trying to quietly push him away. With a firm grip around my waist, he used his available hand to unbuckle his pants. He ignored my opposition. He then lowered his pants just enough to expose himself. Perplexing thoughts raced about in my mind.

"What is he going to do?" I wanted to leave, but I was scared.

"Maybe he'll beat me up if I try to leave?" I wanted to escape, but did not know how.

"Will someone even hear me if I scream?" I remained quiet.

I complied with his aggressiveness and just stood there as he began to grind on my 'private part.' *"This doesn't feel right! He shouldn't be doing this!"* I desperately screamed inside, but not a single word left my lips. It probably lasted a few minutes, but felt like eternity. I wanted him to stop. *"Why is he doing this? Why ME?!"*

He didn't say a word as he stole my innocence - at least not until he was finished. He told me "don't say anything," as he buckled his belt. He walked out of the bathroom first as if nothing happened. He didn't even have to use the bathroom. I pulled up my shorts.

Soon, I felt a tingling, pulsating sensation down there. I was beyond confused. My body felt something different – a sensitivity I had never experienced before. Yet I felt shame and guilt welling up on the inside too. *"Why does this feel like this? Wasn't what he did wrong?"* I did not understand why my body responded differently on the outside. I was used to getting abused in a manner which hurt both externally and internally. This was different though. Inside, I felt disgusting and used. However, the outside did not hurt.

I was too distraught to consider telling anyone. Confusion and guilt grew within me. I did not want anyone to know what had happened. I did not want to have to explain the incident that occurred, or how it made me feel. I was having conflicting feelings and emotions. I could not even explain to myself what happened! How could I dare explain it to anyone else? A part of me felt it was "wrong," that my cousin intruded on me in the bathroom and proceeded to molest me. The shame was overbearing. I decided to walk outside and pretend as if nothing happened.

I walked over to the vacant fenced-in yard, which was connected to the house. I wanted to be alone. I walked around pulling dandelions out of the ground, trying to forget what had just taken place in the bathroom. Once again, I was blowing the white seeds into the air as I wished for my life to get better one day.

That was not the only episode. Each time it happened, it was in that same bathroom, while no one else was around. The second time he knocked on the door, I didn't even ask who was there. I *felt* him standing at the door. "Wait!" My plea landed upon deaf ears *again!* It was Déjà vu all over again. He did not miss a step. He entered the bathroom, closed the door and blocked me from having an exit. He aggressively grabbed my waist like he did the first time and proceeded to replay each grotesque step.

I spaced out. I concluded if this was going to continue to happen, I needed to mentally remove myself from that moment. I imagined my white seeds floating into the sky, and my wishes floating back down toward me. Then he was finished. I went back outside, just as I did the first time. Not uttering a single word, I picked my beloved dandelions out of the ground. They were always there for me, ready for me to pick them and dream. The white seeds gave me hope. I loved watching them float into the sky as I blew my secrets and wishes away.

I don't know how many times Brian took advantage of me. It all became a blur. In an attempt to avoid him, I began to go in the alley which was near their house to pee. I was only lucky enough to go in the alley when no one was near; which was rare. I also made sure to starting using the bathroom when we were at the Boys and Girls Club. I didn't know how long we would be at Madea and Paw-Paw's house. If I used the bathroom elsewhere, whenever I had the opportunity to do so, that was one more time I could avoid Brian.

I never thought to say anything to anyone, or tell for that matter on my older cousin. *"What if they ask me did it hurt?"* I did not want to answer any questions. I was torn between conflicting feelings and emotions. I was too confused and too ashamed to say anything. This wasn't like what I was experiencing at home.

I *thought* what my cousin did was "wrong", because he told me not to say anything. It reminded me of Dad drilling into me "what happens in this house stays in this house." When I heard familiar words such as these, I knew someone wanted me to keep a secret. These types of secrets were bad though.

"Am I supposed to tell?" I wondered.

I had not built up the courage, nor mustered up the strength, to be as vocal as I was at home. If only I had said something the first time it happened, that may have been the only time. Regardless, I kept those bathroom occurrences inside of me. I was too mortified to share my secret with another soul.

Ebony was the older cousin I looked up to. She was smart, pretty, popular and talented. She seemed to be everyone's favorite, including Dad's. I used to feel like I wanted to be just like her; even though we played our *game*. Ebony was Brian's younger sister, but older than me by two years.

Once again, while at Madea and Papa's house, something wrong was happening to me, and I didn't say anything. This time, however, it was not in the bathroom. It was in one of the bedrooms; in the same room that we all used to play Nintendo.

We had to blow into the Nintendo game to make it play. We often fought over who was next to play Mario Bro's. We all squeezed into the small bedroom, while watching whoever had the controller in their hands at the time. We did not have a video game system at home, so this was the first time we saw one. The three of us girls were usually the last ones to get a turn to play. My cousins treated us differently, compared to our other cousins. It was as if we were an outcast of Dad's side of his family.

Ebony and I were the only two people in that room when she wanted to "play a game." We both had on dresses. She told me to pull my dress up and she would do the same. She had me lay down on the bed as she laid on top of me. This was what I remembered as my first kiss. My oldest female cousin kissed me with her tongue inside of my mouth. She rubbed her hands all over my 'private part' and slowly grinded on me like her older brother had done to me before.

My body responded in the same manner it did when Brian caught me in the bathroom. I did not understand the external sensations I was having. It confused me. But I did not think what Ebony did was "wrong." She always looked after me. She painted my nails, took me places with her and her friends, did my hair and even let me wear her clothes sometimes. She was kind and gentle. I looked up to her like a big sister. She often gave me advice and asked her mom, my Aunt Carol, could I spend the night with them. I felt because of them, I could escape my life at home. I had to choose the lesser of two evils, so I chose to go with them.

I was never touched or hurt by either of them at Aunt Carol's house though. Whenever I spent the night at Aunt Carol's house, we never played our game. Brian was usually out running the streets and getting into trouble, providing me with no reasons to worry about not being able to pee in peace. It was only when we were at Madea and Paw-Paw's house that those concerns arose. I loved to be around my Aunt Carol. She went to fun places, and was nice to me.

I preferred to go over and spend the night at Aunt Carol's house. I did not want to gamble on what kind of mood Dad may have been in. With Dad, I never knew the level of severity the beatings would be, what I would witness in terms of him beating on Mom, or how bad his words would hurt my feelings. Yet with Ebony, she was so nice to me, always taking care of me and when she touched me it did not hurt, nor was she aggressive.

I thought by doing what she wanted that Ebony would like me more, maybe even as a little sister. I did not have much in the way of friends at the time, and April and Crystal were younger than I. I wanted someone I could look up to as well.

Thankfully, the last time Ebony made me play her game, Hank, her younger brother, walked in the room and caught her. "You're so nasty Ebony, you're nasty!" He yelled out in disgust. Ebony was startled, which indicated to me something was not right. Although I was more willing to be compliant to Ebony's demands, I was still relieved someone caught her and it would stop. By the look of embarrassment on Ebony's face, I knew those days of playing her games were over.

This was the last time Ebony ever put her hands on me. Like the countless times her older brother caught me in the bathroom, I could not count the amount of times she made me play her game in that room.

By the time I was the age of nine, I was used to Brian catching me in the bathroom, Ebony playing her game with me, and Dad beating and verbally tearing me down at home. I assumed anything that was physical toward me was normal. I spent years being abused physically, sexually, emotionally and mentally without saying a word to anyone about it. Again, another secret I had to compound on top of others.

Although I rationalized in my mind, "*this isn't as bad as the others.*" I knew it was wrong and chose not to repeat what occurred in that bedroom. I had two houses I had to keep secrets in, and only one vessel in which held them all - my mind, heart and soul. After Brian stopped catching me in the bathroom, and Ebony stopped playing her game with me, I decided it was safe for me to push those memories far back in my mind. I could pretend they never happened. I learned to hold all of my emotions and fears inside of my shell.

CHAPTER FOUR
School Days

The closet leading into the living room was full of shoes. There were several pairs of untied shoes out. Dad was making me learn how to tie my shoes and I couldn't get up until I figured it out. Kindergarten was right around the corner and they were going to be sure I was prepared. Shoes were scattered everywhere, in my lap and on the floor surrounding me. It felt like eternity as I learned how to tie the laces into two bunny ears.

The first day of kindergarten was an emotional experience. Mom walked me to my first day of school. I wore a blue and white polka dot dress, which would later be a hand-me-down dress for April and Crystal. The weather was beautiful. It was a sunny day with the perfect temperature. I kicked cicadas off the sidewalk while Mom read a book.

When Mom left me in the classroom alone, I cried. I did not know any of these people or if they would be nice to me or not. Mom and Dad kept us sheltered. The only time we went anywhere without their presence, was to a local family member's house. This whole school thing and being in a room full of strangers was new to me, as it is to most kindergartners.

I was too young to really understand the benefits of school and how it got me out of the house. However, I eventually saw that when Mom left me in the classroom by myself with a room full of strangers, I could become whoever I wanted to be. I chose to be the quiet little girl who kept to herself for the earlier part of my school years.

"She's such a joy," were one of the many praises I received from various teachers. They expressed to Mom I was "never a problem and was always quiet." I worked hard in school, even though I may not have been the smartest in the class. I was determined to show I could do the tasks that were set before me. I also enjoyed the warm feeling I got inside when I received a good grade or was commended on my work by a teacher. The feeling was foreign. Yet, the better I did in school and the more the teachers acknowledged it, the more frequently that warm feeling visited me.

Nonetheless, Mom reminded me that this was *not* my behavior at home. She spoke of how my sisters and I argued often. Mom did not understand though. It was different at school. The teachers were nice to me. I was not afraid at school or felt like I had to defend myself, even when I was teased for my appearance. I just tried to ignore any negativity that surrounded me and focused on what was most important to me and required of me.

As I sat at the table, I shook my leg impatiently. I was working on a worksheet and had noticed someone was already using the in-class restroom. I continued to work on the worksheet until I noticed the restroom was vacant. Consequently, I soon felt a warm sensation run down my legs as I lost all control of my bladder and its contents. I had become so used to being fearful of saying anything, that I kept my mouth shut and urinated on myself instead.

Mrs. Gilbert, my kindergarten teacher, asked me what happened. "It flew in through the window," I replied nervously, referring to the urine that covered my seat and the floor beneath me. Obviously, the teacher knew that was not the truth. However, my brain was already programmed to respond in fear, and that was the first thing that came out of my mouth. Instead of condemning me for the accident, she gave me a gray pair of school sweat pants, and sent me home in them with my original outfit in a plastic grocery bag.

Although I told a lie to my teacher, what I feared most was the punishment I would receive at home. I never repeated at school what happened at home - "What happens in this house stays in this house." The fear Dad instilled in me was plenty to keep me quiet. I was constantly under the impression, no matter what, do not tell anyone about anything that occurred at home.

I feared nothing more than to go home and get an awful beating from Dad while having to smell booze on his breath and hear him tell me I was "nothing." I even feared that he might take it out on Mom. Not being able to discuss my home life enabled my imagination to grow. I often created stories in my mind to fantasize about a life I wish I had.

"My parents don't smoke or drink!" I was in the second or third grade at the time and we were discussing a health-related topic. The teacher was pointing out the disadvantages of smoking cigarettes and the adverse effects it has on the lungs, as well as the adverse effects alcohol has on the liver. I was very aware of those facts and that I had told a fib. Both of my parents heavily smoked cigarettes and Dad was an alcoholic who enjoyed an occasional joint.

"What's that smell?" I asked Mom one evening as she cooked dinner. "You know what it is," she snapped back in an aggressive tone. Dad was smoking a joint, and I was becoming a very nosy little girl. I recognized that the fragrance was different compared to when they smoked cigarettes. It did not smell as bad and Dad acted differently after he was finished with his joint.

One day when Mom was at work, there were sections of the newspaper spread across the coffee table with a couple of heavy glass ash trays holding the papers down. It must have been summer break or we did not have school for whatever reason, because we were home all day with Dad. I asked Dad what he was doing, which was completely surprising due to the fear that was engrained within me to even speak to him. I figured if he had this stuff out, he was probably in a better mood, as I had never really witnessed Dad become angered or enraged when he smoked a joint.

He really did not give me much of a response. Instead, he instructed me to "sort the seeds away from the green stuff." I did just that. The smell was a fragrance I had never experienced, something calming, yet natural. April and Crystal were upstairs playing with one another. "Days of Our Lives," "Young and the Restless," and "Wheel of Fortune," were the television shows being broadcast in the background while Dad and I sorted through the seeds and green stuff.

I was too young and unaware at the time of what I was doing. I was simply happy Dad and I had an interaction which did not involve yelling, cussing, beating and crying. It was a calm, quiet and a pleasant experience. I dreaded the day school was not in session. I knew that meant I had to be home all day with Dad. This day wasn't so bad though. Dad was nice to me while I helped him sort his weed.

As I saw how much time per day I spent away from home at school, I began to enjoy going more often and put forth effort to be a good student. I was quiet, but observant and attentive. I heard the whispers and what other kids talked about when they thought no one was listening. I also heard them talk about me, sometimes to themselves and other times directly toward me.

Growing up as a light skinned, bi-racial, red headed girl was not easy. As these were just physical characteristics everyone else seemed to enjoy making a mockery out of. "Red head" "Kool-Aid" "white girl" "Oreo" "jungle fever," and "stuck up girl" were among the many names I was called during my childhood. These harsh, but typical name calling remarks was the start of my identity crisis and the start of me experiencing bullying amongst my peers at school.

I also experienced teasing and bullying at the Boys and Girls Club during the summers. I got picked on for having caramel colored skin, freckles and red, thick hair. I ignored them the best I could, fearing I'd be outnumbered if I stood up for myself. Around there, anyone was prone to getting jumped, and I had had enough of that at home. For the most part, I kept to myself and I only conversed with my family.

Although I did my best to ignore their antagonizing, I eventually let those negative words get to me. My self-esteem and the way I felt about myself was drastically affected. I already had a difficult time trying to avoid and ignore the abuse I endured by Dad.

Daily put-downs, being called every name in the book, and being treated as inferior were the ways of life I had come to know and hate. No matter how hard I tried to fight the cruel words which scorned me for years to come, I felt defeated each time I thought less of myself. It began to get to such a point, where I felt it did not matter where I went, I was always going to be a target. I was a target at home. I was a target at Madea and Paw-paw's house. I was a target at the Boys and Girls Club. Now, I was a target at school. I began to think something was truly *wrong* with me.

When having to take a standardized test in school, there were different options to mark one's ethnicity. During that time, there wasn't a "biracial" option, which perpetuated the confusion I had on what to mark down. I knew Mom was white and Dad was black. However, I was uncertain as to what that made me.

"Mom, what do I put down on the test at school? They asked us to mark our color. What color am I?" An innocent, yet bold question I asked of Mom. "Black, just mark black." Mom responded. From that point on, I knew I was biracial, but called myself black. The melanin in my blood was evident through the colored pigmentation on my skin tone. My hair was also very thick, course and kinky. Therefore, I considered myself black, even though I knew I was biracial.

I grew up being told that white people were the "enemy" and Dad was a "traitor" for being with a white woman. This sparked curiosity within me at a young age to question my own identity and who exactly I was. *"Where do I fit into in this world?"* I wondered why there was such hatred about differing races.

"Where do I fit in?" I often thought to myself. My white side may think I'm too "ghetto," "hood" or black. My black side thinks I'm too proper, light skinned, and not "black enough." *"Where can a line be drawn, that acceptance can occur on both ends?"* These were the questions that plagued my thoughts throughout my school years. Never truly feeling accepted by one side or the other, I often felt like an outcast and isolated myself from others, unless they were my friends.

I was also picked on and made fun of for how I dressed at school. Since Mom was the only one employed, at typically non-high paying jobs, we never had enough money. Corduroy pants and turtle necks that did not match were the attire which caused my embarrassment, not to mention my shoes were usually rather rugged and not in the best of shape. There were times I had a hole at the top of my shoe. My big toe often pressed against the top of the shoe, as my feet grew too big for them.

"You got a hole in your shoe!"

"Why do you have that on?"

Seeing kids point and laugh at me were taunting experiences I was forced to tolerate. As I got older, I knew if I made my own money I could purchase my own clothes. I began babysitting kids from around the neighborhood for cash when I was around eleven years old. By the time I was in late middle school/early junior high, I purchased my own school clothes and shoes.

I did not take offense to what Mom could or could not do. She was the only one working with five mouths to feed. Seeing her work ethic taught me if I wanted something or needed something, I needed to go out there and find a way to make it happen. Fortunately, babysitting came first, which gave me the opportunity to earn money until I was old enough to get a real job.

When I could wear the clothes I purchased with my earnings the remarks about my attire slowed down and eventually ceased. Like most kids, however, they found something else about me to pick on that I felt I needed to fix. Next it was my thick and coarse red hair.

Dad usually did our hair, unless Ebony did it, which was not often. They hardly ever allowed anyone else to do our hair. I don't think Mom knew how to do our type of hair, especially my hair. Even though I am biracial, my hair took after Dad's side more. April had the stereotypical –biracial-wavy hair. She had red hair like me though, and people often mistook us as twins. We called Crystal *Pocahontas*, due to her long, dark and silky hair. Her hair was the easiest to manage between the three of us girls, even though it grew all the way down to her waist.

A high pony tail which sat on top of a wad of thick hair was my trademark for others to make fun of. "You need a perm!" kids often told me about my coarse hair. "Who does your hair?" or "You need to get your hair done!" Black women relaxed or "permed" their hair to make it more manageable and straight. I did not have a relaxer though. My hair was in its natural state. I began to slowly hate myself more. Not only did I have to deal with the effects of being abused physically, sexually, emotionally and mentally; but I had to suppress more negativity from being bullied and picked on by my peers at school.

Eventually Dad decided it was time to relax my hair. Not only to make it more manageable, but also to allow me to do my own hair. A part of me wanted my hair straightened anyway. I wanted to fit in with the rest of the black girls who had slicked back edges; and the white girls who had hair which flowed with the wind. Either way, my natural hair was not fitting in with either side of my ethnicity and I was fed up with being teased and bullied over the texture and color of my hair.

As Dad parted my hair off into sections, I squirmed and squealed in the chair - my scalp felt like it was on fire! Not only was I tender headed, but also had a head full of hair that was difficult to comb through. My hair literally looked like red wool, and Dad was not being very gentle either. His large hands made my head feel as if a free weight were sitting on top of it as he continued to apply the relaxer. He raked the comb through my hair as if he were trying to comb sheep's wool. It was a painful and intense process. I endured it though, to fit in.

I continued to wear ponytails in my hair after the relaxer. I wasn't too "hair style savvy" back then. I was just happy my hair wasn't frizzy and was straightened. I figured if my edges were slicked back like the black girls, and my red ponytail was long like the white girls, I could fit in with both sides of my ethnicity.

Ms. Rice was one of my favorite teachers of all time. She was a positive woman who truly had a passion for teaching. She was very pretty and nice. She wore colored socks pulled over her footed leggings. I admired her style. "Never stop smiling, Casandra. You have a beautiful smile." Her kind words never left me.

Ms. Rice never knew how grateful I was for her kind and generous words she mentioned to "little ol' me" at such a tumultuous time in my life. I never thought my smile was *beautiful*, let alone looked at myself as *beautiful* period. My self-esteem had never been built up. I knew I was sort of smart, because my report cards reflected that. I was also on the honor roll at times. However, I never looked at myself in the mirror and thought *beauty* was the reflection. I suppose I absorbed the annihilating names I had been called by Dad and peers, and accepted them as my identity.

Although I never thought I was attractive, the boys in my class must have. Sometimes I received random letters which were passed to me asking if I "liked them" and to circle between three options; "yes," "no," or "maybe." At the time, the friends I did have and played with did not talk about having a boyfriend. These letters gave me pause. I usually did not respond because I did not know what to say.

My interest in boys really did not develop until I began to see more "couples" at school and hear friends talk about a boy they liked at the time. My mind was consumed with my personal experiences I kept a secret from the world, or the next school assignment or project I had to work on. I never gave having a boyfriend much thought. Not to mention, I wasn't too enthused about having a boyfriend after witnessing the way Mom was being treated and the unfortunate experiences I had up until that point. Boyfriends seemed to be bad news.

Inevitably, this changed. I began to take an interest in boys during middle school. Justin was a white boy I liked who was a hopeless romantic. He caught my attention when he called our house one evening on a school night. I picked up the phone and heard Whitney Houston's "I will always love you" playing on the receiver. As I felt my skin getting warm from blushing and the hairs on my arm stand as the goose bumps protruded through my skin, I smiled. I thought it was a very sweet gesture. The feeling caused me to think, "*Boys may not be that bad after all.*"

Justin was the only white boy who tried to catch my attention. Going forward, the black boys were the ones who made advances toward me. Not to my benefit, the black girls seemed to not care for me too much. Yet, the black boys showed appreciation for my appearance. They made me feel more accepted by half of myself, by giving me the attention I craved.

As school years progressed, smiles down the hallway and notes passed in the classroom turned into holding hands during recess and hugs before everyone got on the school bus. I liked the attention because I was not getting it from anyone else. For once, I felt wanted and liked. It felt good. Since they were black, and my negative experiences were coming from the black males in my family, it made it even better.

"Psssst." The boys were also annoying when attempting to catch my attention in the middle of class. I did not care for nor responded to these annoying gestures. I often ignored them, in fear of getting called out on it by the teacher and getting a poor report sent home for my behavior. As much as I was beginning to like the flirtatious attention, the fear I had from home trumped it. I did occasionally whisper with friends during class and even got caught a couple of times. However, it did not compare with getting caught whispering with a boy. I just did not do it.

I wondered why the girls were extremely self-conscious about their hair, attire and overall appearance at school. Neither Mom, nor Dad really taught us about going to school looking stylish. They couldn't afford new clothes. I wore hand-me downs and then April and Crystal wore my hand-me downs. I was taught to be bathed, wear clean clothes, and keep my hair somewhat combed. They didn't teach us about hygiene in great detail either. When I started my period, I was at Aunt Carol's house. Ebony was the one who told me about why I was bleeding down there, what to do and how to keep myself clean. Mom was never home to tell me any of that.

When I finally realized the other girls in my class were doing things to impress the boys, I began to become more self-conscious of my own appearance. I wanted to continue receiving the attention I was getting from the boys. If I looked rugged and homely, they wouldn't dare look my way. I soon became overly self-conscious of my own appearance. I picked out flaws on my body while staring in the mirror observing myself. I browsed through magazines, studying the photographs of the women who were called "stunning" "beautiful" and "gorgeous." I did not feel like I fit into any of those categories. The self-hatred I had toward myself deepened.

Julie was a friend who lived a few blocks down the street from me. When we were in junior high school, she began eating salads at lunch. By this time, we had more options and choices as to what we wanted to eat for lunch. I loved food and was far from a picky eater. I usually ate whatever main course was being served. However, if you did not want that as an option, students could go to the cafeteria during breakfast and request a salad for lunch.

"I noticed you've only been eating salads for lunch lately, why?" I asked Julie.

"I'm trying to lose weight and I read somewhere salads are what models and movie stars eat to keep their figures."

Something triggered inside of me.

"I want to look like that too!" I thought to myself. It seemed everyone loved models and movie stars. I figured if I looked like them I would receive just as much love and attention.

For breakfast, I ate a piece of toast and ordered my salad for lunch. This lasted all of two days. Although I wanted to be skinnier, I was not willing to sacrifice my appetite, nor my cravings for good food. I gave up on the "look like a model" mission, and went back to eating squared pizzas and tater tots for lunch.

Food was comforting. I stuffed myself to the point of vomiting sometimes. Appeasing my palate and filling my tummy made me feel better when I was upset, angry or just feeling down about myself. Unbeknownst to me, it was an attempt to suppress the pain I felt inside. It did not matter if it was a delectable dessert, a snack or a main dish. If it tasted good, I wanted more.

"Slow down, that food isn't going to grow legs and run." Dad often told me as I rushed through dinner. Resources were scarce. If I saw there was any bit of leftovers, I made sure to be the first one finished with my plate so I could get more. I liked eating vegetables, unlike my sisters, so it was easy for me to beat them to the race for second helpings. I never sat and processed if I was content or not. Rather, I put more emphasis on the pleasure my taste buds were getting from various flavors. I did not have as much control over my portion sizes and food choices as my friend Julie did.

Julie was a white girl with red hair like me, and an attitude like a black girl. Her attitude was so fierce that we fought at the bus stop one year after she called Mom out of her name. Everyone found out Mom worked at a Hardees' fast food restaurant and Julie was teasing me about it. I hit her and kicked her after she fell into the ditch as the school bus arrived. Her dad was beyond furious and went to my house to tell my parents about what I did in hopes I would be reprimanded for it.

"Your daughter beat my daughter up!" Julie's dad shouted at Dad.

Mom was at work and Dad was the only adult home, by default. He seemed to not be concerned about what I did, because he shut the door in his face.

"Don't go around starting no fires. But if someone starts one with you, you better put it out! And if I ever find out you get your ass beat, I'm going to beat your ass again when you get home!" I didn't say a peep. I allowed those words to marinate and was so grateful that was the gist of my reprimand.

Other than fighting my siblings and/or cousins, I did not get into a lot of physical altercations after that. I did not want to risk the chance of losing and having to get an even worse beating at home by Dad. Even though I was confident in my abilities because I was more defensive toward blocking Dad's hits, I still did not want to risk the loss. I chose my battles wisely.

CHAPTER FIVE

The Man Upstairs

The atmosphere changed when Mom's parents came to visit. It was full of love and we were happy. Mom's side of the family was the only time I recalled hearing "I love you." Although they were only able to visit during certain holidays and blocks of days they took off from work, their presence was most certainly welcomed and wanted. I even wanted to leave with them. It was amusing how Dad seemed to disappear whenever they visited. I figured he didn't want them to see what was written all over his face, his true character and how he had been treating all of us.

Grandma and Grandpa were very positive, loving and happy. They also were members of a church. It was obvious they loved God. They were giving, kind, loving and seemed to not mind that our skin color was different from their own. I loved to see the surprises they brought us, the special places they took us, the creative projects and games we played with one another; but, best of all, I loved the yummy food!

Since money was tight for us, the only time we really got to eat at a restaurant was when Grandma and Grandpa came into town and treated us all. They gave so freely and appeared to get enjoyment out of our joy from their generosity. Whether we were going to a restaurant or having a meal they prepared themselves, it was delicious and fulfilling.

I especially loved when Grandpa Frank visited. His smile lit up a room. Grandma said we shared the same smile. Grandpa's mustache felt like whiskers as it tickled my face whenever he hugged me. He was a heavier man. It was evident he loved food. I loved food too, so I didn't see anything wrong with it! We had something in common, which made me feel connected to Grandpa.

Grandpa was an educated, wise and intelligent man. He had a Master's Degree and worked at various educational institutions. Grandma was educated and had her Master's Degree as well. She substitute taught for various subjects and grades, amongst other jobs. She also worked for an insurance agency for many years. Grandma was the 'grammar Nazi,' as she called it. She corrected one of us if we mispronounced a word or used it in the wrong grammatical context. Of course, as a child, that became rather annoying. I did not understand the importance of speaking proper English. Growing up around Dad's side of the family, I had become accustomed to African American colloquialisms and not using proper English when conversing. That was my normal. It was not until I grew older, when I learned to appreciate Grandma's love for sharing knowledge with others that I put into practice what I was taught.

For a few years, Grandma and Grandpa only visited us, rather than us going to see them. I questioned Mom why we never got to go back with them, or go on a trip ourselves to visit, since they lived out of state. I wanted to see where Mom was born and raised.

"I promise, one day I will take you girls to Iowa." Mom must have gotten tired of me complaining about never being able to visit them and felt obligated to declare we would visit her old stomping grounds. Due to Mom's parents living out of the state, I knew then there was another world outside of Springfield, Illinois. I was eager to see it!

My first experience traveling to another state was during Thanksgiving. I may have been eight or nine years old. We went to Huntington, Indiana, where my Aunt Katie lived, Mom's younger sister. Grandma and Grandpa came to pick up Mom and the three of us girls. Dad didn't go, which did not surprise me.

We slept in their SUV while they drove to the next state during the night. I smelled my first skunk while we were on the highway. Grandpa told me what the raunchy smell was which burned my nostrils. It seemed like it was taking us years to get there. "Are we there yet? Are we there yet?" Were the chants we repeated when getting anxious about arriving to our destination.

I had seen pictures of my Aunt Katie holding me when I was a baby. But, I couldn't recall the last time I had seen her in person. She lived out in the country on a farm with her "roommate" (as Grandma referred to Molly) Aunt Molly. They had horses, goats, dogs, cats and sometimes other animals. When we arrived, they were as loving and fun as I had imagined them to be. They smiled often and gave us big hugs. We ate cookies for breakfast and played with all their animals. We each wore a pair of their slippers and played dress up too. We had the best of times with them!

Since the long miles separated all of us, we opened Christmas presents early after we ate a huge Thanksgiving feast. Aunt Katie and Aunt Molly sent us the best Christmas presents. One year they sent us a T.V and a stereo for our room to share. That was, and probably still is, one of my favorite gifts.

Before we left, they took us around town to see all the decorative and festive Christmas lights. My eyes lit up as I gazed at the décor and all its glitz and glamor. The scenery was very appropriate for that time of year. Then, Grandma and Grandpa took us back to "hell-field" (what I began to call home). I hated when it was time to go back home. Not only was I going to miss my loving family, I was going back to the world which I loathed.

Everyday wasn't always hell on earth at home. There were those moments when Mom tickled me to the point I laughed so hard tears rolled down my cheeks and my belly ached. Mom also engaged in cooking projects with us. She taught us how to roll dough for baking and decorate holiday cookies. Waking up to the smell of hot cinnamon and sugar rice cooking was a pleasantry as well. I enjoyed it just as I did any other meal. Mom knew how to do everything. She was the epitome of a well-rounded woman.

I wanted to mimic anything Mom did, other than being in an abusive and unhealthy relationship. Mom shared stories of how she played the piano for a short time and the clarinet when she was younger. I decided to try and play those instruments myself when I was around eleven years old. One Christmas, Mom got us a used keyboard to share. I took up more of an interest in learning how to play than my sisters. I told my music teacher at school I was interested and she was kind enough to teach me some of the basics of the piano. She taught me hand placement, how to stroke the keys and the difference between the white and the black keys. I was even able to memorize a few songs.

I didn't stick to playing the piano for very long. I soon developed an interest for playing the clarinet. Mom talked about the days she played, which contributed to my sparking interest in learning how to play the clarinet. Mom went to a local music store, and rented a clarinet. By this time, she was making a little more money as a manager of a fast food restaurant.

I didn't do a good job at retaining the lessons I had on reading music. Don't get me wrong, I knew the notes, but I wasn't very good at putting them together and reading them accurately. Though, I was very good at hearing music and repeating verbatim what I heard. I mastered "playing by ear," as the music world calls it. I listened to whoever sat next to me and watched the music instructor direct, as my fingers began to move and played the song which sat in front of me in print.

I became so good at playing the clarinet, I earned 1st chair. I continued to earn 1st chair for most my musical career, even through high school. Music was another tool used to escape my reality and go into a world that was peaceful and calm. I loved any genre of music, but particularly classical and jazz. Music was not only relaxing, but it did something for my soul. It was like drinking a cold glass of fresh lemonade on a hot summer day. It was a soothing remedy which refreshed my inner being and calmed my stressed nerves while they were in a state of frenzy.

My interest in jazz came from Dad. It was very seldom that we caught him in one of his good moods. He blasted jazz on the stereo as he jammed to the tunes being released from the speakers. Dad had all kinds of old records. My favorite out of his collection was Prince's "*Purple Rain.*"

Before any of us were even thought of, Dad played in a band with friends. I suppose my interest and love for music emerged from both Mom and Dad. My love for music deepened after getting involved in the church choir and hearing various hymnals. The words and melodies were extremely inspiring and lifted my spirits each time.

Dad decided when it was time for us girls to go to church. Dad referred to God as, "the Man upstairs." He taught us how to pray for our food. "Say your grace," he said in his deep, firm voice. We obeyed, "God is great, God is good, let us thank Him for this food, Amen." This turned into my daily ritual prayer before eating meals. It was strange how Dad enforced religion and prayer upon us, yet the only time I recalled seeing him inside of a church was for a funeral.

Mom walked with us a few blocks down to a neighborhood church they picked out for us to attend. She sat with us throughout the services. Mom was quite the entertainer during service. She snored as her head nodded frontward and backward. Before waking Mom up, the three of us girls usually got a quick giggle in. Then one of us poked her. She opened her eyes, sat with her posture erect and pretended as if she were never asleep.

After a while Mom discontinued walking with us to church. When the weather permitted, the three of us girls walked together by ourselves. On nasty, cold and snowy days or even rainy days, the church van transported us. Going to church had a positive impact on me.

I learned about God - my Creator. I discovered someone I could talk to; someone I could trust to never tell a soul. What a relief, to know there were ears out there to hear me! I didn't have to wish upon my white seeds anymore. There was a Higher Being who not only listened, but could answer me too. I did not have to worry about being judged for the experiences I had. It was so relieving to have that during a pivotal time in my life where I felt my world was nothing but pure torture and my life was pointless and meaningless.

The daily meal prayers were not the only prayers I recited. After a while, I cried out to God as if my very life depended upon it, begging for His help.

"Why is my life like this?"

"Please God, take me to be with you!"

"Take the pain away!"

"Make it stop!"

I cried out often from the pain I felt day in and day out. I especially cried out that specific prayer after Dad beat me or Mom. Dad made me feel unloved, unwanted, and a useless member to the family. Despite all of that, I still prayed for Dad. I prayed that he would become "saved" (as it's considered when speaking of the Christian faith). I often asked God to make Dad stop drinking and to make him "nice." God was who I continued to call upon for the rest of my life.

I was very active in the church. I sang in the choir and acted in plays. I even led children's church. I went to a few Christian youth camps. I became a youth group leader. I was a member of *The Missionettes*, amongst many other duties I assumed while a member. We had several fundraisers, pot lucks (which I loved), kid's camps, and many other fun and exciting activities and outings. Going to church was the first getaway I had when trying to find an excuse to get out of the house.

Contests during Vacation Bible School were my favorite. I went out of my way to invite more kids than everyone else and win all the other contests. I was beginning to become very competitive. I loved the praises and accolades one receives after winning first place, regardless of the prize. The only time I felt worthy and accepted is when I won. I felt I had to be the best at everything and win every competition I entered. I suppose I generated a competitive spirit after living in a household where I did not have a voice and nothing I did, rather positive or negative, seemed to influence the conditions at home. The attention I received from others after an accomplishment felt so good and new to me. Winning became an intense adrenaline rush. I was addicted.

I felt good going to church and being involved with various ministries. Everyone was so kind. I felt like I mattered, but without having to suffer for it. We all had something in common, we loved God! I had never met God, or heard an audible voice, but somewhere inside of me I knew God existed. I was comforted each time I cried out. I knew God was real.

Having a good night's rest was rare. The night terrors frightened me so, I was unable to go back to sleep. Waking up to Dad shouting at Mom as Mom pleaded for Dad to leave her alone was another norm. Hearing Mom scream as Dad beat on her were familiar cries to my ears. Either way, I knew God was real despite what was occurring in my world. I slept like a baby after praying to God. My Creator calmed me and gave me peace during my storms.

When Paw-Paw died, Madea was very sad. They had never parted until his death. I had been to a funeral before, but it was so long ago I could only recollect pieces of when another one of Dad's family members passed away. Crystal was still in diapers when that happened. Mom had to walk out in the middle of service because Crystal had been crying. Dad did not show any emotion at his father's funeral. He was as stiff as a board as he sat in a pew in front of the casket. *"Does he ever feel anything?"* I asked myself. It appeared as if nothing got to Dad, not even death.

When Grandpa died, the Pastor from the church we had been attending stopped by unannounced. At the time, we did not have a telephone. The Pastor came by to tell Mom her dad had died. Grandma Cassie had called our Pastor since she was unable to reach Mom. Mom immediately burst out into tears.

"Hold her, embrace your wife!" The Pastor urged Dad.

I thought *"how pathetic,"* Dad had to be told by another man to hold his wife after she was informed her beloved father had died! I wanted to run off and burst out into tears myself, but someone had to be strong for Mom. Inside, I ached. I felt like one of my organs had died inside of me and I could not function within my full capacity. I held in all my grief and despair for losing Grandpa, because Mom was so devastated. Both of us couldn't fall apart at the same time. That would be too much power for Dad to have.

Grandma flew Mom to Iowa for a few days to attend the funeral. I was beyond upset that I couldn't go with Mom. However, I tried not to let it show and be more understanding that Mom lost her dad. I loved Grandpa dearly. He was the only male in my life that made me feel loved. His positive energy was contagious. If he smiled, I smiled and if he laughed, I laughed. I could not help but to be in good spirits whenever he was near. His aura was infectious.

While Mom was away, I reminisced about the good times when Grandpa visited. When I was in the third or fourth grade, he picked me up from school and took me to get McDonald's for lunch. He even introduced me to the peanut buster parfait at Dairy Queen. Grandpa Frank was the best man I had ever known. I still miss him dearly.

Even though he was gone from the world, his spirit was still alive. After some time had passed, I had dreams about Grandpa. Initially I thought I was just mourning the loss of a loved one. However, I began to recognize a pattern. Grandpa encouraged me in my dreams, during some of the toughest moments in my reality. Upon awaking after having one of these dreams, I felt as if he were right there beside me. It was as if he was right there to tell me that "everything will be okay." Grandpa told me these same words as I slumbered. This was one of the first signs I had that God was with me. Grandpa was my first angel.

Another death in our family occurred. Madea died when I was in junior high school. I was upset she never got the chance to see me perform in any activities. "Your granny died." Dad casually mentioned on a Sunday morning as I was in the kitchen ironing clothes for church. I didn't respond. Silence overcame me as I meditated. Family members said Dad closed her eyes in the hospital after she released her soul from the vessel she was residing in. I wondered how he felt at that moment and if he expressed any emotion.

Sadness covered Dad's countenance at the funeral. I did not see him shed a tear, but his overall appearance differed from Paw-Paw's funeral. That may have also been due to the fact this was a "double funeral." Dad's cousin had passed away the same night as Madea. To save on costs, the family decided to mourn the loss of our beloveds on the same day. The weather was conducive with the circumstances. Clouds, gray skies, and occasional spurts of showers covered the atmosphere. Sorrow was all around.

I sat in a church with two caskets in front of me.

"Is this all life is about?" I pondered.

"Going through hard and difficult times, feeling sad, hurt, angry, belittled and confused, and then poof! - your life is over!"

I wondered, *"Where do the happy moments of life fit?"*

"Will I ever be happy?"

"What does it feel like to die? Is it better than living on earth?"

When Madea died, Dad's side of the family fell apart. She was the piece which kept us all together. After her passing, everyone went on about life without any efforts to bring everyone together for occasional reunions or family gatherings. Everyone had gotten consumed with their own respective families. There were no more summer gatherings at Madea and Paw-Paw's house, or barbeques or games. Since being molested by my cousins had stopped, I no longer had to worry about that. Despite all of that, I still missed smelling Madea's cooking or hearing her funny stories. I'm grateful she too speaks to me during difficult moments in my life. Just like Grandpa, Madea was my angel.

I never quite understood or grasped the concept of what an angel was. I saw pictures of what most would identify as an angel. The human figure with a halo around their head and feathered wings on their back, but this was not how Grandpa and Madea appeared to me in my dreams.

They looked like their normal selves as I remembered them, but in spirit form. No one else could see them but me. I knew they were deceased in the natural life even in my dream. Each time I asked them how they were talking to me and how I could see them. They always assured me God was with me and "everything would be okay." They gave me hope when I wanted to give up on life.

Dad introduced me to God, but Mom introduced me to religion. Dad taught me how to have very basic interactions with God until I could establish a relationship on my own. He knew then, regardless of his own demons he battled, the importance of having a relationship with the Most High. Something as simple as a meal prayer initiated my first encounters with the Most High.

Mom took us to church and made sure we learned about God in a Biblical sense. She knew how paramount it was for us to be exposed to the historical stories in the Bible, which revealed who and how powerful God was. Mom and Dad made sure I had a spiritual foundation in God. Without that, I don't know how I would have survived.

CHAPTER SIX

Friends, Fun & Fast feet

We got new neighbors often. Mostly everyone in the neighborhood rented like we did, but moved once their leases were expired. I was the tomboyish athlete, who jumped off roofs, played video games with the neighborhood boys, played in the rain and mud, and made the largest snow balls around. My snowballs were so large; all of us could sit on them without it tumbling down. They were also way too big for our scrawny little arms to lift and throw at one another!

One summer the three of us girls took a walk around the block. We saw two girls roller skating in their driveway. They were clearly sisters. They both had pretty hazel eyes and long dark hair. Seeing unfamiliar faces caused me to stare hard when trying to figure them out. Eventually we all introduced ourselves to one another and became good friends.

Elizabeth and Jessica lived two houses down from us. Jessica was about a year older than me and Elizabeth was about a year younger than me. Elizabeth and I hit it off the best and became very close friends. We all hung out together, Elizabeth, Jessica and the three of us.

We did everything together. We collected cans, washed cars and babysat neighborhood kids for money. We also went roller skating and to Six Flags often. Our friendships were interesting. We were eager to have fun, yet understood our financial circumstances and created ways to earn money to fund our activities. They even started going to church with us and were involved in various ministries.

Elizabeth and I ventured off into our own little worlds from time to time. We had something in common, her brother and my dad had weed. On a hot summer day, we got bored and decided to conduct an experiment. We wanted to see what the big hype was about with them smoking weed. We both took some weed from their stashes. As we rolled the weed up in a piece of notebook paper, we had no clue what we were doing. We found a lighter, lit the stuffed paper and smoked it. We got high for the first time in our teenage lives. As soon as we were finished, we walked down to the corner store to purchase some snacks for the effects of being high. We wanted munchies!

Elizabeth and I also tried cooking projects together. On Thanksgiving Day, we attempted to make baked macaroni and cheese. Elizabeth's mom was at work. I hung out with Elizabeth all day so she wouldn't be by herself on the holiday. I did not want to be at home anyway. We decided to make our own Thanksgiving meal. Unfortunately, neither one of us knew what we were doing. We put the hard, uncooked noodles in a baking dish, then poured a small amount of milk, butter, and cheese in the pan with the uncooked noodles and put the pan in the oven. It did not turn out well and was far from edible.

After the catastrophe, I told Elizabeth she was coming to my house for Thanksgiving. My parents generally cooked on most of the holidays. Elizabeth came over and had Thanksgiving dinner with us. Unfortunately, my family proved themselves to be dysfunctional, even when company was over. Elizabeth was the first of my friends to witness it.

Dad had already been drinking and was muttering to himself as he usually did when intoxicated and in one of his moods. Elizabeth and I were in the kitchen eating and chatting with one another.

Dad began yelling and shouting at Mom. I was beyond embarrassed. I assumed by having a friend over, Dad would behave himself, and not act how he usually did, especially since he constantly harped about, "what happens in this house stays in this house." Elizabeth, however, never judged what happened and even seemed to understand. Our friendship began to grow into a sisterhood from this point on.

As our bond, flourished and we became closer, her house turned into a haven for me. I ran there often when running away from Dad. They did not remain on the same block as us for long and moved a few times. I ran to wherever Elizabeth was, regardless of the distance. With all the running, I had developed some endurance. The further they moved away, the further I ran.

When I was in middle school, I heard about cross county tryouts for the forthcoming junior high school year. I had no idea what cross country was, I just heard it involved running. I figured since I was already used to running away from Dad, it was surely a task I could tackle head on. The first day of practice taught me what cross-country was. We ran for approximately 2 miles, nonstop. I was more than able to keep up with the pack and found it to be a liberating experience.

Running - for the fun of it, it was different in my world. It was a sport in which I quickly developed an interest in. It was a mindless activity. Running became my heart. I fell in love with running and how it made me feel. It allowed my mind to wonder freely in the fresh air, an experience I never wanted to let go of.

My first season of cross-country turned out to be a great undertaking. I learned breathing and running techniques, and increased my endurance. My legs ran for miles and miles. Each breath felt like an alleviation that cleared any negative feeling my body held on to.

Others thought I was insane for running like I did. I ran in rain, sleet, or snow. It didn't matter to me what the weather conditions were. If I had the proper clothing attire for the weather and my health allowed me to do so, I was outside running. In fact, this was a requirement when it came to running cross country. The ability to run in different climates determined how good of a runner you were in this sport.

Soon I was convinced to try out for track & field. I ran sprints when I first began running track. The coaches took advantage of my cross-country training, the endurance I had built and taught me how to become a power sprinter. Track was like cross country, in the aspect I was still running. Yet, sprinting gave me an adrenaline rush which caused me to be addicted to the sport, not to mention I became very good at running as well! All in all, running reaped many benefits for me.

Unfortunately, Mom and Dad did not get to witness my running successes. I can only remember Dad being at one or two of my meets and Mom being at none. Mom was always at work earning a living, and I just figured Dad did not care.

I used to catch rides with different friends and their parents to get home after practices and meets. If I couldn't get a ride with someone, I rode on the city bus home. Sometimes I even walked home, usually with a friend. Nevertheless, I was ecstatic to have found something I was good at which allowed me to get out of the house for long periods of time, even if that meant I did not receive a lot of support from home.

When track season came rolling around, I got pumped up and ready to perform. I had come to love sprinting and doing well, even sometimes winning. By the time I reached my eighth-grade year in track, I was training at Southeast High School with the high school girls. I learned the better I got at track, the more meets I would be able to run in, which meant less time in the house. Once again, I was creating another outlet to free myself of the barriers I was enclosed in at home.

The summer after junior high school was going to be one of the most memorable times of my life! I joined the Springfield Strider's track club, a summer track program. I had the same coach who took me to Southeast to train, who would also be my forthcoming track coach in high school. I met new friends, trained harder, got better, got great tans, and best of all - I got to travel across the country to compete.

This was also a time in which I was out of the house a lot due to the practices and meets! I sweated profusely, ran as hard as I could, and would breathe until my lungs felt as if they would soon collapse. That, however, was not pain to me, not compared to the pain I felt dealing with my family. It was more of a liberating experience that cleansed the inside of my mind, body and soul.

The first year I ran for the track club, I ran the anchor in the 4X100 M Relay. Our relay team made it to the USATF national meet in Baton Rouge, Louisiana! The only time I had ever left the state of Illinois was to go to Indiana with Mom and her parents for the holidays. Now, I was leaving the state off my own natural and God given talents. It made me feel good inside.

The following summer, I went to the USATF national meet in Seattle, Washington. This was the first time I flew on an airplane! I advanced to this meet in the 400 M. hurdles. Coach felt it was time for me to try something new. He convinced me to try the hurdles. I had no form at all. In fact, it looked as if I were hopping fences and running away from dogs rather than hurdling. It was quite amusing to watch. What caused me to win the regional track meet and advance to nationals was the running I did in between the hurdles. This was one of my prouder moments in my track career. I had an article or two in the local newspaper, which praised me for trying something new and excelling at it. I was beginning to feel better about myself.

During summer track, I met new friends. Monique and I both went through similar experiences as children, not loved by our parents. We both experienced abuse and neglect in different forms. Yet, we found humor in everything we did.

We were known for playing practical jokes on people and constantly laughing about things no one could figure out nor understand. When we were out of town for a track meet and in a different city's mall, we pretended to be from another country. We spoke in a fake mumbled jumbled language! We always had fun no matter what and enjoyed one another's company. Even though we used to annoy several people at times! Laughter was our common denominator. It felt like all my sorrows were being washed away to the shoreline as my belly ached from laughing so hard. It was a euphoric feeling.

It was so nice to have someone as a friend who understood and accepted me. Monique was more than a friend, she was like a sister. Our friendship felt how interactions should be with family members. We had a good time, understood each other and loved and accepted one another for who we were. Having these types of relationships in my life helped carry me through amid facing difficult and trying times at home.

Cross country wasn't fun for me anymore. I developed more of a liking for sprints. I could get myself involved in activities that allowed me to stay away from home more often. The need for me to run miles upon miles away from Dad was no longer necessary. The miles required for cross country caused a decrease in my interest in running. Hanging out with friends became more of an interest and priority. It felt good to be around people who wanted to be around me and treated me nicely. I felt like I mattered.

Once I reached my high school years, all I cared about was track and field. I was focused on getting so good I would have my ticket out of Springfield. I wanted to get away from my dysfunctional family and experience a new world.

I often dreamt about running in the Olympics. Flo Jo, Jackie Joyner Kersee, Carl Jones, Marion Jones and Michael Johnson were a few amongst many professional track and field athletes I admired and loved to watch perform. During the 1996 Olympics, I sat in the living room, on the arm of the couch, while casually asking Dad a few questions about the Olympics. I wanted to know how they got there and what would it take for me to get there. "Hard work" was all Dad said, and I accepted his response while continuing to watch the races. Dad was a man of few words when you tried to have a decent conversation with him. He managed to say just enough though to get his point across.

I guess Dad took me seriously about wanting to go to the Olympics. 5:00 a.m. was around the time he woke me up in the morning to go running. Dad took it upon himself to be my "personal coach." We jogged up the alley to Iles Park with his two dogs; one was a Rottweiler, the other a half Rottweiler and half pit bull. I had to run multiple laps around the park, with the dogs running alongside of me. Dad held their leashes, as I ran lap by lap. The dogs gave me a challenge. Dad sometimes jogged on the side of me too.

The training I received at 5:00 a.m. improved my running for the forthcoming season. These moments were awkward. The man who did all these things to me and Mom, and whom I despised, took an interest in me and something that was important to me. We were actually having a positive interaction and forming a healthy bond. I really did not know how to take it, so I kind of just went with the flow and reacted accordingly.

Ribbons, medals, trophies, and certificates are what I collected from running over the years. I kept them inside of a shoe box. I used to count my medals daily and feel so proud of myself. I loved the sound of the medals clanging against one another as I counted them one by one. "Clank –clank, clank-clank." It was such a beautiful sound to my ears. I cherished my awards so much that I hid the box I put them in. They were so dear to me, I would have been devastated if anything happened to them. My accolades were all I had.

As I progressed through high school, both athletically and academically, I began to have more friends. I developed friendships through similar interests. Most, if not all, of my closest friends were athletes who were dedicated to their studies as well. I began to learn that old saying Dad used to say, "birds of a feather, flock together," was true.

Boys. That's all I heard about, who likes who and who wants to go out with who. This wasn't a new topic to my ears, it was just more prevalent in my teenage years. During track season, Monique shared stories with me about the boys she liked and had been sexually active with. At that point, I just listened. I was not sure if I was ready to like boys in that manner yet. I most certainly was not ready to have sex.

I occasionally had crushes here and there, but never put much thought into having an actual boyfriend. In my former years, I held hands with a boy that may have displayed an interest in me or even hugged a couple of times before getting on the school bus. That was the extent of it. The boys were more aggressive in high school, especially the older ones. They smiled at me down the hall or gave me compliments on how pretty I was. Sometimes, they even grabbed my hand to catch my attention down the hallway. At first, I didn't pay it any attention. However, the more often it occurred, the more I began to like it.

They weren't tearing me down, or talking down to me, or trying to beat on me. They were simply smiling and giving me compliments, no harm in that, right? It made me feel good and wanted. *"They don't want anything from me. Maybe they really do like me."* Soon, I let my guard all the way down and was all about having a boyfriend.

My first official boyfriend was during my freshman year. He was a sophomore, so that was cool of me to have snagged a guy who was older. It was very short lived. The most we did was hold hands down the hall and hug each other after school. I liked it. I didn't feel hurt or feared I would get hurt. I felt good about the attention I was getting. So, I got another boyfriend.

The next boyfriend was a little older. It was the summer after I completed freshman year and would be a sophomore the following school year. Chris was going to be a senior. He ran track as well. We both ran in the summer track program. He smiled at me just like the rest, but approached me and wanted to get to know me. Another short-lived relationship, but we did a little bit more than the last.

We not only held hands and kissed, but he kissed me on my lips and used his tongue. He also kissed me on my neck and gave me my first hickey. I tried to cover it up with a band aid, but that did not work. Coach still saw it and scolded me for it. Chris also caressed areas on my body that had not been touched since I was a kid. This time though, I consented to it. It wasn't the same. He wasn't a family member. He wasn't forcing himself upon me. He was my boyfriend. I figured it was okay. If we didn't go *all the way*, I didn't see any harm in my boyfriend showing me affection.

I learned in church having sex before marriage was wrong and that we should wait to be married. I agreed. After experiencing a family member molesting me and another one playing her *game* with me, I didn't think I would ever want anyone to touch me again. I had never thought about the emotional aspect of it all. You know when you like someone and they express how they feel the same way and for once in your life you feel wanted? What about that? Curiosity settled into my mind as I was experiencing an attraction for someone and not minding them being affectionate toward me. *"Is sex with someone you have feelings for really that bad?"*

I never had sex with Chris. He wanted to, but never pressured me. I simply wasn't ready. I was curious, but did not have the guts to go through with the act, unsure of how I would feel afterwards. Not to mention, I had heard enough horror stories out of Mom and Dad's arguments of having me at a young age. I feared being a teenage mother.

The first time I had consensual sex, I was a sophomore in high school. I had been conversing with a boy who attended a different school than I did. Ken was older than me. We weren't actual 'boyfriend and girlfriend,' but I liked him and he told me he liked me too. His dad was a pastor at my good friend Pam's church, one I visited often.

I met Pam freshman year in high school, through a mutual friend. She had been in private school, so she transferred over to public schools in high school.

Pam and I's friendship grew as we both discovered we shared similar interests. We both played the same instrument and had music class together. She was also a track manager for one season and traveled along with us. As our friendship developed, I became open with her and expressed my situation at home. I didn't share every intricate detail though, just enough to make it known I did not like being at home.

There were several occasions where Pam's mother took me to school after I missed the city bus from over sleeping, or allowed me to stay in their basement and sleep on the couch.

"Pam, you leave that girl alone and let her sleep!" She would direct her.

"She doesn't have peace, let her rest." Pam's mom believed in the Lord, and I felt she may have sensed my unrest.

I went to church with Pam a few times. She taught me to turn my music down or off when driving by a church, out of respect for the Lord. Sometimes when we were joy riding and listening to Tupac she turned her radio down whenever we passed a church.

I saw Ken at church when I visited with Pam. We passed notes back and forth to each other during services. Eventually we started to meet each other to hang out outside of church and school functions. We met at friend's houses when their parents weren't home. By this time, with Mom always being at work, Dad seeming to be glad he got one more kid out of the house and all the activities I was involved in, no one questioned my whereabouts.

The night I lost my virginity, we were at Ken's friend's house, whose parents were out of town. It was just us teenagers there. He took me into a bedroom, and kissed me how he usually did. I liked the way he kissed me; it was different from the other boys. But this time was different. He began to touch me and caress me in a way he had never done before. I knew what was going to happen next. We already had conversations prior about sex. Rather than fighting it, I succumbed to his lure and laid down on the bed. We had sex; my very first time.

Several days later, I wrote him a letter to explain how he was my *first* and inquired about what was going to happen between us going forward. He told me how he had a girlfriend and that I was lying because he did not 'pop my cherry.' I never bled that night, so he assumed that was not my first time having sex. I wasn't going to tell him about what happened to me at Madea and Paw-paw's house, so I never attempted to plead my case.

This was the first time I truly felt rejected by a guy I liked. I wondered if I didn't "do it right." What was wrong with me, or my body that he didn't want me to be his girlfriend? I didn't stick around long enough to figure it out. I just moved along to the next boy who showed an interest in me.

Benny was one of the star basketball players. He was funny, charismatic, down to earth and most importantly - single. We had fun when we hung out together, but I had made up my mind to not have sex with him. I figured if he was going to be my boyfriend, I couldn't have sex with him because then he wouldn't want me anymore.

We dated most of our junior year in high school. We attended high school dances together, I went to his basketball games and watched him play to cheer him on, and we hung out at each other's houses when our parents weren't home. We were friends, but also in a relationship at the same time. Despite everyone in the school assuming we were sexually active with each other, we never had sex during our relationship.

We did what I had done in previous relationships; we kissed, hugged and he touched me places that usually lead to sex. But my mind was made up. Benny wanted to have sex, but he never pressured or forced me. This made me like him even more and eventually, I fell in love with him, or so I thought.

Benny was the first boy I told "I love you" to. I was devastated when our relationship ended. The demise of our high school love affair began when he first started dodging me during the day. We usually met up at each other's lockers and chatted before our next class. When he wasn't meeting me and it went from one to three days, I knew something was wrong. He wasn't answering my phone calls or returning them either. I began to hear rumors that he was intentionally dodging me because I was too "clingy."

I had heard this statement before - me being too "clingy." I suppose it came from the deep yearning and desire to be loved by a man. The moment a boy showed me some attention that felt good, I got emotionally attached to them without even realizing it. I was flustered that everyone in the school not only thought I had been having sex with Benny, but also labeled me as the "clingy girl." I felt like a fool.

After some time passed, Benny and I became friends again. The dynamics of our relationship were different. We were not in an actual boyfriend/girlfriend relationship, but began being sexually involved with one another. We were "friends with benefits." We had a mutual understanding that we would have occasional sex, without any commitments or ties to one another and to keep it between ourselves. Of course, we both ended up sharing our secrets with our friends.

Eventually word got out about Benny's "package" and girls at school became curious about having sex with him. Once I caught wind of this, I stopped being sexually involved with him. Even though we had an agreement, I still did not want to share Benny with other girls. Once again, I felt like a moron.

After that last failed relationship, I decided to not get serious about a boy again. I hung out with friends more and dissed any boy who demonstrated any form of interest in me. I was tired of boys telling me they liked me in the beginning and breaking up with me after they got some sort of physical interaction with me. I noticed that was all they wanted, and finally decided I wanted no part of that. I just wanted to hang out with my friends and focus on being better at track.

During summer track, I met Ray. He ran track too. Once we discovered we lived near each other, we walked home together after practices. Ray became a special friend to me. We hung out just like I would with Monique or Pam. Occasionally we played video games together, or just talked on the phone about life. There were even times Ray sat on my front porch, and listened to make sure Dad wasn't giving me a hard time by shouting at me or beating me. I had entrusted Ray over time with secrets about my life at home. He told me he knew something was "off," because I asked to walk slowly when heading home. I dreaded to go inside of the house. Ray sensed my unease.

Ray was so dear to me because he was a male who wasn't after anything. He didn't try to touch my body or have sex with me. He didn't cut me down with his words or make me feel worthless. He just walked with me, listened to me and watched out for me. Having a male in my life, in this capacity, gave me a glimpse of hope that all males weren't horrible. He was another person in my life who accepted me and didn't ask for anything in return.

I had my first drink as a kid. I sipped Dad's beer one day when he was in the bathroom. I wanted to see what was so good about this drink that he had to have on a near daily basis. It was absolutely disgusting and I spit it right out. The next time I had a drink was at my friend Steph's house.

Steph and I played volleyball together in junior high school. She also threw the shot put and discus during track and field season. Steph was another friend whose home was an escape for me when trying to get away from Dad. When not intentionally running away from home, I went there after track practice. I did not go home until it was late at night and I knew Dad was asleep. All my friends seemed to have a sense of normalcy in their homes and I enjoyed the peace while there. It was unlike anything at home.

Steph's house was also the party house for her friends. Her parents let us party all night long, if everyone turned in their car keys and spent the night after drinking all night long. Apple pucker was the drink Steph had me try. This was the first time I vomited after consuming too much alcohol. I hated that Dad drank and the person he turned into when he was drunk, yet at the age of 16, was beginning to drink myself.

Hannah and I knew each other from the Boys and Girls Club. She was another friend who shared my pain of not feeling loved by her parents and experiencing abuse from her dad. Hannah also ran track. After obtaining her driver's license, sometimes Hannah drove her dad's car. One weekend when her dad was gone, we decided I would spend the night at her house and planned to get our pictures professionally taken together the next morning. We drove around Springfield with nothing to do.

I had some cash on hand from getting paid at one of my jobs. I worked two part-time jobs. I worked at Hardees fast food restaurant as a cashier and as a surveyor at a telemarketing company. As soon as I was old enough to work, I did. Mom was the manager at Hardee's, so it was easy for me to get employed there. I became employed at the telemarketing company after passing their required entry exams. I decided we should get some alcohol to have more fun.

Hannah drove through the liquor store drive-thru window and ordered a pack of Hooch, per my request. I opened a bottle as soon as Hannah pulled off. We returned to Hannah's house and she decided to call her boyfriend and his friend over. I didn't think anything of it. I was too busy enjoying my hooch and listening to music while sitting in her bedroom.

When the boys arrived, I began to feel uncomfortable. It was obvious Hannah's boyfriend wanted them to have some privacy and his friend was trying to get more acquainted with me. I, however, was not interested. Despite efforts to display my disinterest, he insisted we at least talk since Hannah and her boyfriend left us alone.

We went into one of the spare bedrooms. I still felt uneasy about conversing with him. He had a poor reputation for being a hustler and a lady's man. In the back of my mind, I wondered if conversation was enough for him. I was right. One moment he was touching my hand, the next he was on top of me.

I squeezed my legs together as tightly as I could, to no avail. His force was more powerful than my will. He unbuckled his pants, pulled my panties to the side and forcefully inserted himself inside while holding me down and covering my mouth. I went numb. I knew this feeling; someone invading my body without my permission and taking control of me, out of their own lustful greed.

My mind went blank until he was finished. I had mastered not being mentally present when in the bathroom with Brian as a little girl. It was like a light switch was turned on, and for that moment, I disappeared. He got up and left as if nothing happened. I lied there, numb, feeling used and didn't say a word. I convinced myself I probably deserved it because I had been drinking alcohol and should have never went into a bedroom with this person. I went to sleep and woke up the next morning, pretending as if nothing happened.

I never told anyone at home what happened outside of the house. Enough had happened in our own house that I did not see the need to compound more problems on top of that. It was just easier to push everything away in a secret place inside of me rather than to regurgitate it all. I already had plenty of trouble in coping with the hell we all lived in.

As we all ate dinner one evening, what began as a normal dinner time discussion turned left. Dad began cussing Mom out. He called her stupid and beat her down with his words. By this time, I was beyond tired of the dysfunction I was forced to reside in. I said something.

"Why don't you just leave Mom alone?!"

I was bold. If no one else was going to stand up for Mom against Dad, I would do it! And I did. Infuriated and without saying one word, Dad jumped up from his seat. He came behind me while I was sitting at the table, wrapped his large hands around my neck and began choking me in front of everyone.

"What did you say to me?!" Dad began shouting at me in anger.

"What in the hell did you say to me dammit?!" Dad's grip got tighter.

I could not say a word, and was beginning to lose my breath. I realized no one was going to say anything. Fear was all I saw in Mom and my sisters' eyes. They were afraid of him. I saw a butter knife at my place setting. I grabbed it and began swinging it around. Dad immediately loosened his grip from around my neck, and said to Mom, "you better get your damn daughter!"

Once again, I felt like an outcast by my own dad and family. No one protected me or helped me, and Dad refused to claim me. I was amazed no one noticed the marks that covered my light-skinned body when I was at school, or anywhere else for that matter.

At this point I hated my life. Yes, I was a great athlete and student. But being at home was hell and I repeatedly ran away from home in search for some sort of peace. I began running away from home often. I stayed at whichever friend or family member's house would have me. Usually the rotation was Aunt Carol, Pam, Steph, and sometimes Monique. I could not stand being at home any longer. There was so much hurt, anger and hatred brewing on the inside of me that I wanted to escape my own self. Running away from home seemed to be the only reasonable solution.

"Don't come back this time!" Dad told me as I walked out of the door with my backpack stuffed with clothes and hanging from my shoulder. It wasn't a secret to those at home what I was doing, and it wasn't like I was trying to hide it either. I felt like I was grown – an adult. I felt I could come and go as I pleased. I was earning my own money, buying my own clothes and hygiene products, funding other miscellaneous expenses such as movies or restaurant food and supporting myself in my activities. I felt like I did not need to be home. I came home when there was nowhere else for me to go and the stay was brief. Long enough to take a bath, eat and sleep. I arose as the sun came up and returned after the sun set. I did any and everything to stay out of the house.

Regardless of any good I attempted to do, terror seemed to be riding on my coattails. After being raped at Hannah's house, I determined it didn't matter where I was. If I was still in Springfield, happiness would never be within my reach. Running on the road, on a track or in a park was not the only form of running I knew.

At this point, I began to run from myself, my circumstances and those who were in my world – the catalyst for the pain I endured… I mentally disappeared as Brian had his way with me in the bathroom. I tried my hardest not to use the bathroom at Madea and Paw-paw's house to avoid Brian invading in on me. I ran away from home to escape Dad's beatings. I ran as a sport to release the pain that was encaged inside of my soul. Running away from Springfield did not frighten me at all. It sounded like the only option I had to finally live a better life.

CHAPTER SEVEN

Fight-or-flight

Senior year, I was involved in a teacher's assistant program for a class at an elementary school across the street from the high school I attended. I was assigned to work under my friend Cynthia's mom, Ms. Smith. The children were pre-k aged. My duties were to help and document what I observed. Since an early age, I enjoyed working with children. It was more of an enjoyable experience for me, rather than a requirement for a grade.

Sometimes when the children were watching a program, I checked my email. I was eager to see what Aunt Katie had written me. She and I had been corresponding back and forth through email. I emailed her out of nowhere one day, asking about where she lived and what was it like. I inquired about the population, the schools, the atmosphere, and even the majority of which race lived there. I later found out, it was a predominately white town. I became curious and inquisitive about what was in her world.

Aunt Katie appeared to be happy and enjoying life. I wanted to know what was that like and how it felt. I arrived to a point in my life where I realized I had never been happy and wanted to experience happiness. I lived in a world full of turmoil and war. Everything in my life seemed to be about defending and fighting for oneself.

I looked forward to the emails. They enabled me to flee a malfunctioned world and imagine a new and different place where tranquility and peace existed. I desired for that world to become a reality - *my* reality. I was beyond sick and tired of the abuse and dysfunction. I couldn't take it anymore. I often felt like I was on the verge of killing myself. I wanted to rid myself of the awful pain I felt inside. Something deep within me wanted to live – the part of myself that always fought throughout my life to find the light at the end of the tunnel and hold on to a shimmer of hope for a better tomorrow.

I caught Mom home during the day for once. It was a day Dad was not present. I didn't have a practice of some sort either. I took that moment as an opportunity to express what I had been holding deep inside of my being. I sobbed. I told Mom how tired I was of the environment I was forced to live in.

"Every day I want to kill myself!" I cried out.

"If you don't get rid of Dad or I don't get outta here, I'm going to take a whole bunch of pills and kill myself, I can't take it anymore!"

Mom just looked at me in shock for a moment as we sat on the couch in the living room. There was a moment of silence before Mom responded.

"Well I can call your Grandma Cassie. I'm sure she wouldn't mind if you lived with them for a while."

I knew that would be Mom's initial response. She had been with Dad all this time, why would she bother leaving him now? Despite my pleas for Mom over the years to pick us and our well-being over being with Dad, she picked him again.

I felt rejected, by my own mother. *"It has to be me then right? Something is wrong with me!"* I could not help but feel that if Mom chose Dad over me, that had to of meant I was the poison in the house which needed to leave. I had, in a way, already come to terms with this and was preparing myself mentally to leave once and for all.

I didn't have anything against Grandma, but I felt I had already developed a good rapport with Aunt Katie. If I was the one leaving, I wanted to live with her and Aunt Molly. Grandma was older, plus Katie and Molly always seemed to be fun! I knew they had foster kids at one point. Therefore, I figured they loved kids and in a way, wouldn't mind taking a kid like me in. You know, one with a troubled background.

"I don't want to go to Grandma's," I told Mom.

"Aunt Katie and I have been emailing each other. Could you see if she and Molly would take me in?"

I felt, at that moment, I never wanted anything so badly in my life. I was full of hope and disappointment at the same time. I wanted so much to leave and experience a new life; yet, didn't hold my breath for the dream to come true. I was disappointed and hurt Mom chose to stay with Dad and preferred me to leave instead. Once again, feeling unloved by my parents.

Running track was not only a great way for me to release the negative tension it was a temporary distraction where I didn't have to fill my mind with endless thoughts and questions. As I patiently waited for Mom to talk to Aunt Katie and get her response, I continued to stay focused on training for the upcoming track season. I figured if she said yes, by the time I graduated from high school I could be there for the summer and get a job. If she said no, I considered the option of living with Grandma. Either way, I had a plan for both answers.

"Looks like you'll be going to your Aunt Katie's," Mom told me when I got home from practice. I was stunned. Honestly, I did not expect that answer. I mean, Aunt Katie always seemed to be nice and all, but I never imagined she would take me in. Mom already had the suitcases out for me to pack my clothes. She told me Grandma Cassie

would be here the day after the next to take me to meet Katie and Molly halfway. I couldn't believe it. "*Already?*" I thought to myself. I still had track, friends, and graduation. I didn't anticipate they would have me leave so soon. I was upset again. To someone else, I was on an emotional roller coaster and entirely too indecisive. I could not make up my mind as to what I wanted to do. I thought the common-sense thing to do was to send me *after* I had graduated and finished my senior year season of track.

My friends, teammates and coach were all devastated. They couldn't believe I was leaving and moving to another state within 48 hours. I still had a season of track to finish, two more quarters of school until graduation, and months to make more memories with my friends. Coach talked to Mom and Dad to see if I could live with him and his wife just to finish the season out. They didn't budge. I had to turn seven to eight months into 48 hours. I had to say goodbye to track and my friends, which was the hardest thing for me to do. I knew there was a track team at the school I was going to, so I did my best to not let that part affect me as much.

I didn't know what to expect out of this experience. Aunt Katie and Aunt Molly lived in a predominately white town. They had a farm and lived in the country. That was a lifestyle I was not familiar with. Surprisingly, it didn't bother me. I looked forward to being able to break out of my nightmare and *finally* have peace.

The day Grandma and Gary arrived, I was dressed in pajamas with a head scarf on. My bags were packed and I was ready to leave. April and Crystal stood downstairs to wish me farewell. Friends had come over to do the same. I don't know where Dad was. Obviously, Mom was there, probably reading a book while she waited. I said my expected "goodbye's" to everyone and jumped in the back seat of Grandma's car.

I wasn't quite sure what exactly Mom told everyone. Therefore, the ride was rather quiet as Grandma and Gary took turns driving. The scenery consisted of the usual fields, small towns and animals. This made falling asleep a piece of cake. I already was beginning to feel a sense of peace as the miles increased that separated me from my old life of misery.

"We're here," was the familiar phrase Grandma Cassie said in her singing tone. I sat up. We were in a small town that had a Dollar General and gas station on the same street, which ran through the entire town. Aunt Katie and Molly were already waiting on us. "Hi," Katie greeted me so cheerfully with hugs and kisses as I got out of the car. We loaded my bags into Molly's SUV and headed northeast to Huntington, Indiana - my new home.

Like the ride with Grandma Cassie to meet with them, I was quiet and listened to music. However, there was a brief interruption. "So, what made you want to come with us?" Aunt Molly asked. I nonchalantly shrugged my shoulders and continued to gaze out of the window. I didn't know what exactly to say, and figured the gestures I used would speak louder than any verbal response I could ever give. There wasn't anything to say really. I didn't know if they knew where exactly I was coming from. I surely was not ready or willing to reveal it either.

I never had my own room before. There was a bed, dresser and a closet that connected my room to Aunt Katie's room. It was refreshing to sit in a room that I didn't have to share with anyone else. As much as I loved my sisters, I never experienced solitude, peace and true time to myself. I unpacked my belongings and quickly got settled in. I laid down on the comfortable bed with my hands tucked under my head and feet crossed, stared at the ceiling and wondered what else was in store for me in life. I knew I had come to a place where I didn't have to fight, worry, or live in chaos anymore. However, I was soon going to hear my own thoughts, remember my experiences and begin to feel the pain.

My first day of school at Huntington North was unusual. It was the first time I was known as "the new kid" and the first time being one of the only black kids in the school. Since Huntington was a predominately white town, the only high school, of course, was predominantly white. Everyone appeared to be friendly. They smiled at me and occasionally said "hi." It wasn't long before my bubbly personality took over my shy countenance and I made friends!

Just like back home, I made friends of all sorts; the athletes, band members, geeks, popular crowds and the regulars. I quickly settled right in. I began training for the upcoming track season, tried out for band and was seated 2nd chair and became a natural social butterfly. Hanging out on the weekends with some of my closest girlfriends became my favorite pastime. Although we didn't share the same background, we all shared the commonalties of wanting to have fun, be happy and be accepted and loved. We did everything together, from camping, dancing at the nightclubs all night, to jet skiing at Molly's family's house out on the lake. Whatever we did, we had a blast and I soon forgot about my own tragedies I left, at least for the time being.

Soon the nightmares began. I often woke up in cold sweats as I fought to be awake, while recalling the tortuous memories I thought I left behind. I was frustrated and confused. I thought by leaving that I somehow had magically erased my past and was given an opportunity to create a new future. I was sadly mistaken. The nightmares started to become so unbearable, I preferred to stay awake throughout the night rather go to sleep.

I never discussed this with Aunt Katie or Molly. I was unsure what all Mom had disclosed when asking about me living with them. I surely did not want to bare all. I chose not to divulge any information and kept the nightmares, the memories and thoughts to myself. All the pain, self-hatred, bitterness, resentment and anger I kept inside. It was like poison seeping out of my heart, and into my veins, contaminating my entire being. Again, I wanted to die.

This is when the cutting began. Although I had friends, they weren't like the friends at home. See, they only knew what I told them about myself. They didn't know the harsh reality I escaped, or why I was even there. When they asked, I just brushed it off, "it was just easier for me to come here." And I said nothing more or nothing less.

The first time I cut myself, I found a razor in the bathroom. I was taking a bath and the only one home. Sadness consumed me and I began to sob. I was tired of hurting. *"Why do I still feel this way and I'm not even there anymore?"* I questioned myself. I was so sure by me leaving Springfield, all my pain and worries would remain there. I was desperate for the pain to go away.

I pressed the razor against the inside of my forearm and slowly applied pressure. As soon as the razor broke my skin open, I felt relief. It was like removing a splinter out of one's flesh - just enough relief to go back to what you were doing prior to when the tiny sliver of wood decided to find a home in your skin. The pain subsided and for a brief period I felt better. However, the alleviation did not last long. Every time I had a bad thought, a nightmare or a painful memory I cut myself to lighten the burden and temporarily release the anguish. Admittedly so, the razor hurt when cutting into my flesh. However, it did not compare to the pain which burned the inside of my being.

Scars and marks on my arms began to surface. I didn't contemplate the aftermath of cutting. I only saturated my mind with my own rationale for the moment, not thinking about the evidence. Aunt Katie and I were sitting at the dining room table. I must have had my arms positioned to where the tracks from cutting were visible.

"Are you cutting yourself? You better not be cutting yourself!" Aunt Katie appeared to be flustered, and I was embarrassed. I ran upstairs, went to my room, shut the door, cried and cut myself again. She didn't know the pain I felt or the reasoning why and I couldn't gather up the nerve to tell her. So, I suppressed it all, harbored every negative thought and emotion, and continued cutting.

I didn't want to die like I did when I was in Springfield. I merely wanted the pain to subside. I made sure to not cut too close to any veins nor too deep, just enough to break open the flesh and allow a little bit of blood to surface. This symbolized pain leaving my body, or at least that's what I convinced myself.

As my final year of school was reaching its end, excitement grew as graduation celebration planning was in full force. Everyone was so excited I graduated from high school. A feat that's expected by most, but considering what I had endured up until that point, I felt darn proud of it. Aunt Katie and Molly planned to have a nice gathering at their home to celebrate my accomplishment. This was the first gathering I ever had in my honor, I was beyond thrilled!

As the days approached closer to the ceremony, I talked with April and Crystal often, trying to figure out who all was coming. They were coming with Mom. Elizabeth indicated she was going to ride along as well. However, no one mentioned if Dad was going to come or not. Although I resented Dad for what he had done over the years, I still wanted him to come to the graduation ceremony and celebration. The little girl who still yearned to be daddy's little princess was crying out, but he didn't hear her.

"Sweetie, you know your Dad has a bad back. It just wouldn't be comfortable for him to ride all that way in that position for too long." It never failed; Mom always had an excuse for Dad and managed to sugar coat everything in attempts to make it sound better than the truth. I was heartbroken, to say the least. As Aunt Katie, Molly and I were in the living room watching T.V., I grabbed the phone and called Dad.

"Dad, why aren't you coming?" I was not used to speaking with Dad, let alone over the telephone. We had not spoken to each other in quite some time. Yet, I was desperate and thought I'd express myself one last time in an effort to plead my case and convince Dad to watch his firstborn daughter graduate from high school. He didn't have much of a response, just an awkward silence.

Aunt Katie and Molly saw the look of despair take over my demeanor. They were so positive, encouraging and loving. They reminded me of all the fun that awaited us during the celebration. Although appreciative, I still wanted Dad to be there. It mattered.

Graduation finally arrived. When Mom pulled up, April, Crystal and Elizabeth jumped out of the car. I still held on to a thread of hope. Maybe Dad's heart would suddenly become burdened with guilt, he would change his mind and opt to tag along. He did not.

Elizabeth came up to my room. I did not feel like going downstairs to socialize with guests who arrived on my behalf. I was trying to figure out what exactly was wrong with me, and why Dad did not want to see me walk across the stage. He went to Ebony's high school graduation, his favorite niece, but could not attend his own daughter's? *"Something must be wrong with me, then, right?"* The self-defeating thoughts surfaced as I tried to understand why Dad hated me so much. I wanted to cut, but with Elizabeth right there and others downstairs, I knew I would not have enough time to cover it up. I quickly pulled myself together and decided not to allow that glitch to ruin such an occasion as this.

From that point forward, my heart grew cold toward Dad. I began to hate him and openly expressed it to whoever listened. I wished for horrible things to happen to him -even death. I proclaimed if he died I would not attend his funeral. Feelings of bitterness and resentment evolved as the grudge I held against Dad intensified. I never wanted to see or hear from that man again.

CHAPTER EIGHT

College Girl

Grandma Cassie, Katie and Molly all contributed their time, money and efforts to ensure I continued my education. Grandma even went as far as to drive from Iowa to Indiana to pick me up and drive me down to my college of choice in Carbondale, Illinois for registration. Southern Illinois University was known for having a good criminal justice program. I decided last minute on attending this institution, but Grandma, Katie and Molly backed me 100 percent on this.

Grandma and Gary got a hotel room for us in Carbondale, while we toured the campus, registered, and signed up for classes for the fall semester. Grandma then drove me back to Indiana and continued home to Iowa. If it weren't for her, I don't know if college would have been in the picture for me.

Mom did not have any involvement with my decision to go to college. Grandma made sure Mom was the one who drove me and my belongings to Carbondale. "That's the least you can do for her," Grandma Cassie expressed to Mom.

When it was time for me to depart from Indiana and embark upon a new journey in my life, Aunt Katie and Molly drove to the usual halfway point to meet Mom. We all exchanged many hugs, kisses and goodbyes as we departed.

I wasn't bothered by having to be in Springfield for a few days before Mom could drive down to Carbondale. My mind was preoccupied with daydreams of my highly-anticipated college experiences. I was going to be alone for the very first time. No family or friends, just me and the world. I was more than ready to see what it had to offer.

While in Springfield, I went around and did the conventional "hi's" and "bye's" with friends and family, ensuring everyone knew I didn't forget about them and was going to venture off into a new journey. Mom borrowed a co-worker's truck for the heavy load. It was impossible to fit all my bags, bins full of the typical dormitory supplies and the TV Katie got for me into Mom's sedan

My last night in Springfield was a night to remember. As I gathered the remainder of my belongings to put in the truck, Mom and Dad began to argue. Initially, I ignored them and finished packing my bags in the truck. I was so used to their arguing it was not hard at all to drown their voices out and fall into an abyss of thoughts. However, that familiar cry I heard as a child rung like a bell in my ears. Mom was screaming and Dad was hitting her.

"You're a worthless motherfucker!" I screamed to Dad.

"If you don't take your hands off my mom I will kill you! Leave her alone!"

The hitting was something I was never able to drown out. Although I never could understand Mom's reasoning for staying with Dad and allowing him to abuse us, I still felt a need to watch out for her.

Surprisingly, Dad got silent and disappeared. Mom went outside to make sure everything in the truck was secure and packed properly. I sat in the front room to catch my breath and pull myself together. I was leaving in the morning, and would be damned if I let him take that away from me.

Dogs barking and cussing was all I heard next. "SICK, SICK, SICK," he said repeatedly as he instructed the dogs to attack me. In beyond a state of shock and completely confused as to why a person, who was my father, could do such a thing, I quickly calmed down and talked to the dogs, petted them, and reminded them of who I was. "Hey Bandit, it's me!" I knew those dogs since they were babies, they were the same dogs I trained with at 5:00 a.m. and there was no way in hell I was going to let him brainwash them. As the dogs licked my face I felt a sense of relief cover my flesh as the hairs on my arms stood down. I knew he did not win and was even more determined to prove him wrong.

I jetted out of the front door, and ran as quickly as I could. I felt like the 11-year-old girl again, running away from home. The rain was pouring down as my feet stomped through the puddles. I ran down to the corner gas station and hid behind the payphone. This was the very payphone I used growing up when there was not a landline phone in our house. I called a friend and let her know what happened. She was more than willing to pick me up.

"I can't believe this," I thought to myself as I stood in the rain. I was supposed to be leaving in the morning and this monster was trying to steal that from me. I watched him drive back and forth, yelling my name, as I hid behind the payphone. He never saw me, but I saw him. I wondered why he was looking for me and why did he even care?

It wasn't long before she pulled up. I was drenched from head to toe by the rain, distressed by what just occurred. She took me to her house, gave me some dry clothes and the two of us laid in her bed. She was asleep, but I lied there fully awake staring at the ceiling, wondering what was going to happen next.

I made sure to be back to the house before sunrise. I still wanted so very badly to leave and go to school. I assumed my belongings were still intact in the truck as well. Mom answered the door and I asked her was she still going to take me to Carbondale.

"Yes, let me tell your dad we'll be leaving here in a minute, "she responded.

"Okay, I'll just wait outside," I told her.

After last night, I did not want to step foot in that house again. I was so glad we packed my things the night before. Mom came outside with her book, ready to take me away from "hell-field." The ride down was a rather quiet one. I gazed out of the window most of the three-and-a-half-hour trip, as Mom focused on the road.

When we arrived in Carbondale, there were people everywhere moving into their dorm rooms. It was beautiful outside, not a cloud in the sky. More senior students were there already to help us "fresh-meat" move in. Thompson Point was the side of campus I moved into. There was a lake and a wooded area. It was a very serene environment.

As I unpacked my belongings and got settled in my room, Mom set up my new lap top that I purchased for myself with some of the money I had earned from working at a car wheel factory all summer. "Are you sure there's nothing else you need me to do before I leave?" Mom asked. Of course, a trip to Walmart was needed. Walmart was jam-packed full of new and returning students. The aisles were filled with school and dormitory supplies. It was evident I had just moved to a college town.

For some reason when we returned to my dorm, Mom didn't seem as if she was quite ready to leave. She looked through my lap top one more time to be sure all the programs I needed were downloaded correctly and it was ready for my use. "Mom I don't need anything else, you can go!" I was ready to start my college experience and wanted to have some time to myself to let everything marinate before it got started. I was not sure why Mom was lingering around, but I did not care. I just wanted her to leave. Mom and I said our goodbye's and she left to head back to Springfield.

I laid in my very neat and made up bed, crossed my legs with my hands tucked under my head, just like I did when I first moved to Indiana. I gazed at the ceiling and took a deep breath. I smiled. *"Finally, I'm free!"* Going to college just seemed to be the natural step of life, the next thing to do after high school. I never thought of going prior to moving to Indiana. However, once there, my peers had shared which prospective colleges they were attending in the fall. Originally, I planned on doing what a few friends at home were going to do, enlist into the military. No one at home really talked about going to college. Mom and Dad never instilled higher education in us either. Aunt Katie, Molly and Grandma were the individuals to thank. They got my mental wheels turning to think about obtaining a degree.

It wasn't hard to meet new friends. In fact, the first week on campus I met Lynette, who later became a lifelong friend. Mandy and I had already met through mutual acquaintances. I was friends with her cousin, Chad. Chad and I went to high school together. Mandy's family made sure we got connected so each of us knew at least one person when we got to college. Lynette, Mandy and I eventually became close friends. We called ourselves the three musketeers!

I vowed to remain focused while in school, this meant no boyfriends! The boys were everywhere: athletes, fraternity men, intellectual men, and the locals. I already had some adverse experiences so I was not going to give in to the smiles and compliments this time. Being studious was the focal point.

I was a walk-on on the track and field team at SIU with a partial scholarship. The original intentions were to just go to school and obtain a bachelor's degree to enable me to work in my field of study. However, after walking past the stadium several times, the itch for running consumed me like wildfire.

I contacted the head coach for the team, explained my situation and gave a summary of my track and field history. The coach advised me of the practice times and suggested I begin attending the practices if I were serious about running again. They would decide from there if I was a good fit for the team.

It was still strength and conditioning time. Luckily, I hadn't missed much in terms of training. I was not in the best of shape, but hadn't completely lost everything. I also had a few pounds to shed. With running, the lighter you are the easier it is to carry your own weight, which undeniably makes one faster.

Without hesitation, I went to practice and immediately became a part of the team. I felt right at home, my "comfort zone." I don't know what possessed me to not respond to the plethora of inquiries I received during high school and pursue a track and field scholarship. Maybe it was the injury I incurred my senior year that caused me to doubt myself and just give up. Whatever the reason, I returned to what was most familiar to me and what I knew how to do best, run.

I redshirted my freshman year, at the advice of the coaches. They realized my potential as a collegiate athlete and felt if I trained hard for one year, I would be stronger, faster and obtain more endurance for the forthcoming season. This in turn, would make me a competitive division I athlete. I followed their recommendations and trained hard. Running stadium stairs in 90 plus degree weather, interval training, sprints and early morning runs became a part of my collegiate routine.

I also got a job on campus at the local dining hall. Since I had begun working in my near pre-teens, I was accustomed to working if I wanted money. I also did not have anyone sending me money so I knew I had to get a job to start earning my own money quickly. I went to class, trained, worked and hung out with my friends. I also partied, which was to be expected. One night maybe a little too much, or at least that's what I convinced myself of.

On a Saturday night, Lynette and I went to a fraternity house party. We had met some of the guys on campus, and were invited to hang out at their fraternity house. We did not know them, but figured with it being a college party it would surely be fun. When we arrived at the house, there were only a few females and several men. That uneasy feeling, like the one I had when at Hannah's house in high school came over me. I ignored it.

They handed us red plastic cups, with an alcoholic concoction of some sort - their fraternity secret. We began to drink. What started off as a night of laughs and feeling slight affects from the alcoholic beverages we sipped on, turned into a morning of confusion and devastation. I woke up, in a foreign place, unable to recall what occurred. As I sat up, and began to collect my thoughts, flashbacks of the night prior glimpsed before my eyes.

"Did they rape me?" I whispered to myself as I headed back to the dorm. Images of my arms being held down, me saying "no," and voices saying "you know you want it," was all I could remember. It was a blur. Once again, someone had their way with me, against my will. This was becoming all too common. I decided to tuck it away on top of the pile of secrets inside and pretend it never happened. Lynette was gone, and I could not remember when she left. I pushed it back because if I asked questions it would bring up pain. I preferred to add it to the pile of hurtful mess I already had stored away inside of myself.

The summer following my freshman year, I went back to Indiana to work at the car wheel factory again. After surviving freshman year of college, I knew I had better save some money and the factory was where a 19-year-old college student could earn the most money. I did not even consider going back to Springfield; especially after the episode which arose between Dad and me. I only returned a couple of times to visit old friends, and the last visit was one I wish I did not have to take at all.

The first time I went back to Springfield during summer break, I made it my mission to visit Ray. We had been conversing over the phone and I missed him dearly. He was a great friend, someone I could call on when needing an ear to hear. I am beyond grateful I went home and saw him for the last time.

Mom dropped me off at Ray's mom's house and I spent the night. We watched T.V., talked about old times and even questioned why we never took our friendship to the next level and tried to date one another. I cherished our friendship too much to ruin it. After failed attempts to have a boyfriend, I preferred to maintain the one and only healthy and positive relationship with a male I had - my good friend, Ray.

The next morning, Ray walked me to the bus stop like old times. I took the city bus back to Mom and Dad's house. We hugged and promised to stay in contact with each other. Ray enlisted into the military, so he was leaving soon. I was so proud of him. After seated on the bus, I turned around and looked at Ray. I smiled and waved, and continued to look at him as the bus drove off. I felt like I was seeing him for the last time.

A month later, I received a phone call from Cynthia, "Ray just got shot at Juneteenth!" I paced back and forth while in the dining room. Aunt Katie and Molly were gone, I was home alone. "He's okay though, right?" I sat down, patiently waiting for a response. There was a moment of silence, my heart raced as tears welled up in the ducts of my eyes. "He's dead, Casandra."

I hung up the phone in disbelief. I did not want to hear my good friend was dead, the one male in my life that was there for me and didn't treat me with disrespect nor harm me. I was in denial. I called my friend Christy to confirm. After getting off the phone with her, I wept. Word spread quickly through Springfield as people lined up at the hospital Ray was at, and I was not even there.

Molly was kind enough to allow me to drive her old red pickup truck to Springfield by myself to attend Ray's funeral. Each cemetery I passed on the way to Springfield brought down a sense of reality of what I was going to have to face. I was going to see Ray in a casket, unresponsive. Just a vessel with no soul residing in it.

My friend Jennifer, and April and Crystal came with me to the funeral - a day I will never forget. Ray had a fraternal twin, Adam. He paced up and down the aisles of the sanctuary, shaking his head and sobbing, "He shouldn't be in there, man! He shouldn't be in there!" He continued to repeat this as loved ones mourned Ray's passing. I turned around and went back into the vestibule of the church. "I can't do it! I can't go in there!" I was overwhelmed with sadness.

Jennifer, April and Crystal each grabbed my arms, lifted me up from the chair and escorted me back into the sanctuary. As I approached the casket, my knees got weak. "I just saw him!" I belted out as I buckled in front of the casket my dear friend was lying in. Jennifer and my sisters held me up and walked me to our seat. I sobbed the entire service, not wanting to accept he was gone.

The first time Ray came to me in my sleep reminded me of how Grandpa Frank and Madea came to me when I was going through something. I asked him what was he doing, and wasn't he gone? He reassured me he was watching over me. I knew then he was still with me, my third angel.

It took some time to snap out of the grief phase and to begin enjoying life with friends again. My friends in Indiana were still there. I shared my first year of college experiences with them. Everyone wondered if I had a boyfriend yet. However, I told them I was focused and was not concerned with having a boyfriend.

Unbeknownst to me, this was my last summer of fun with the girls. We danced often at the nightclubs. I went jet skiing at Molly's family's cabin at the lake, and went joy riding with friends whenever possible. It was one of my most memorable summers, the last spent in Indiana.

CHAPTER NINE

Love Child

Upon returning to SIU to begin my sophomore year, I was in the best physical shape of my life. My abs were coming through and I was toned from head to toe. I trained all summer long in preparation for the upcoming season. I ran early in the morning before work to ensure I did not get out of shape or lose any endurance that was gained during training freshman year. I was ready to perform and show the world of Division I athletics my capabilities. Practices and training became even more intense. I trained with the best SIU had. I competed daily to prove I had what it took to be ready for the season which was right around the corner.

Training, class, and working was my only focus at the time. However, soon my heartstrings got tugged by an unexpected visitor. I met Lucas freshman year in Psychology class. He mentioned he needed help with the class. We met with each other to study and work on assignments together. Soon our conversations advanced from academia related, to sharing bits and pieces of ourselves. I fell for his charm and smile. Every time anyone saw Lucas, he had the biggest smile on his face. He consistently appeared to be in a good mood. He was so sweet and kind.

Those qualities alone drew me to him, because for me that was not customary. After a short period of time, Lucas revealed to me he was the same guy on the football field who had been trying to talk to me during my track practices freshman year. Because football season collided with track and field conditioning, there were times we were on the track while the football players were practicing on the field.

I was upset at first, only because I told myself I would never date any athletes or fraternity boys; and partially because I began to like Lucas. However, I was focused on school and track and he had a girlfriend back home. Exploring anything as more than a platonic relationship was not an option.

During sophomore year, a transition took place where a platonic friendship was not enough. As Lucas expressed the stresses of being in a long-distance relationship and how it was not working out, I saw a window of opportunity. Soon our friendship grew into love. We began dating each other.

I loved Lucas to the point I began to wrap my identity into him. Everything I did and most of my conversations revolved around him. I had never experienced this mutual feeling and never wanted it to end. Growing up and never truly feeling loved by a man, I yearned for it desperately. So, when I finally got it, I attached to it like a leach attaches to its host.

Walks on the wooded path through campus, dancing all night at parties, long talks and studying were how we spent many days together. We grew closer together and developed a close bond. As his football season approached, I supported him by attending as many games as I could, even some away games. I was proud and in love with my man.

Initially we weren't having sex while just friends. I made sure to stick to my guns on that, even after I recognized my feelings for him had changed. However, once we started dating, we had sex. I knew I wanted to wait until marriage to be intimate again, but I loved this man. Once we began having sex, the feelings I had for him magnified.

As Lucas's season was on the cusp of ending and my season was just beginning, I became ill. What I thought to be the flu or a bug, turned out to be another being living and growing inside of me. Lynette and I were roommates sophomore year in the dorm. "Red, I think you need to get a pregnancy test," Lynette urged me. Since she was several months along in her pregnancy, I believe her intuition kicked in and knew something was off with her roommate.

I went down the hall to Olivia room. Olivia was a year younger than I and lived in the same dormitory. We hit it off right away as friends. She was one of the few friends I had in college who had a vehicle. In a panic, I asked to use her car. I drove to Walgreens and bought a few pregnancy tests. I called Lucas on my way back to the dorm. "Lucas, I need you to meet me at my dorm as soon as possible." He sensed the urgency in my tone, and said he would be on his way. Lucas lived across campus from me, but had a car. He drove to my dorm quickly.

As soon as I got back to the dorm, I expressed my nervousness to Lynette. I was a 19-year-old sophomore in college, on the track team with a whole future in front of me. I never planned on having kids, let alone in this type of situation and this young. Two pink lines appeared on the first pregnancy test, indicating I was pregnant. In disbelief, I took three more pregnancy tests. They all had two thin pink lines appear, revealing once again I was pregnant.

As soon as Lucas arrived to my dorm, I threw the pregnancy tests at him, ran to my bed and began to cry hysterically. I never believed in abortion. I didn't want to be a hypocrite. But, I was only 19 years old, in college and trained to have a successful track season. I was not ready to be a mother and give all of that up.

"What am I going to do?"

"I can't keep this baby!"

"What about school?"

"What about track?"

I continued to weep. Lucas was his usual and calm self. "Children are blessings and you know how I feel about wanting kids. Everything will be alright. I'm here and my family will help too. Everything will be alright. I promise." I continued to weep until I cried myself to sleep that night.

I was on birth control, and thought I was being cautious by using preventative contraceptives to avoid pregnancy. Yet this situation forced me to recall how in the world I could have possibly conceived a child. During late October, I was ill with a virus of some sort and had been prescribed an antibiotic. I was unaware that I needed to be extra cautious when having sex because that very antibiotic could cause the birth control to be ineffective. I was not only disappointed in myself, but also mad at myself for allowing my emotions to take over my decision making.

I decided to keep the baby. I prayed about it and it just didn't sit right with me to have an abortion all because of my irresponsibility and selfishness. I also knew that I would have an opportunity to feel genuine love, an unconditional love I had yearned for my entire life. I had to tell the coaches. I was so upset. I trained vigorously for this season. The first meet was approaching and I couldn't perform because I was pregnant. The head coach was empathetic and understanding as she consoled me. "You know, women come back all of the time after having a baby; some even faster and stronger than before their pregnancies." It was so comforting to hear. I was worried I was going to get chastised and looked down upon, but it was exactly the opposite.

Unfortunately, I didn't receive the same response from the sprint coach. I never really cared for him too much. He always seemed to be gawking at us during practice and was flirtatious with some of my teammates. The sexual abuse I endured in the past heightened my sense and awareness for potential predators. Something was off about him and I didn't like it. I had one of those intuitive, gut feelings which alerted me something was not right.

"What am I supposed to do, huh? You're supposed to run in relays too. What happened? Did it feel good?" I was absolutely disgusted by his remarks. Without even responding, I turned around and walked away.

The head coach was kind enough to allow me to keep the partial scholarship I had, in exchange for coming to the track meets and helping; which I did. I had other grants and loans to help pay for college and was extremely grateful for my coach's generosity and being understanding.

I was heartbroken. I felt my dreams had slipped between my fingertips. As I cheered for and watched my teammates perform and excel, I felt shame and disappointment consume me each time. *"I should be out there! This wasn't supposed to happen!"* Disgruntlement settled in as I watched my lifelong dream to advance into a higher level of athletics dwindle away.

Before I could finally accept I was pregnant, I mastered hiding it for as long as I could. It was nearly winter time when I found out I had a baby growing inside of me. I felt ashamed because I was only 19 years old, a sophomore in college and not even married. I didn't want anyone to look down on me or judge me. I had done enough of that to myself. I criticized myself to the point where I decided to hide the pregnancy as I long as I could get away with it.

Despite the fact of knowing perfection does not exist, I wanted to exude a façade of perfection to convince not only myself, but to others alike that my world was just fine. I did this for several years. I often daydreamed and imagined myself living in a fairytale where everything was perfect and nothing was wrong. I wanted those daydreams to become reality. I did any and everything to cover up flaws and imperfections. At this moment, hiding my baby bump was one of them. Although I was slowly growing to love the being developing inside of my womb, I was still embarrassed of the circumstances surrounding my pregnancy.

Oversized hoodies became my go-to attire. I even had moments where others asked if I was pregnant. Rumors shuffled fast around campus. With Lucas being on the football team and me on the track and field team, it did not take long for the rest of the campus to hear the news. I denied it out of guilt and shame. I presume my baby bump was becoming more visible than I had cared to realize.

As time progressed and my belly grew out further and further, I knew it was time to tell my family and friends. I went back to Springfield to share the news with everyone. April said she already knew, because she had a dream about me. The three of us girls shared the similarity of having prophetic dreams. They both seemed to be more accepting of me being a pregnant teen. Mom, however, like most moms expressed concern for my future.

"So, what are you going to do about school and track?" I began to tell Mom about the programs I found for single parents and how my track coach was going to allow me to keep my partial scholarship for the remainder of my pregnancy, in trade to help at the track meets. "I'm not going to stop going to school and I plan on going back to track after I have the baby," I explained.

"So, what happened to keeping a nickel between your legs?" Mom asked. "What nickel?" I responded. Mom was referring to the nickel I was supposed to keep between my legs, to not have sex. However, the only conversation Mom had with my younger teenage self about boys was brief. She basically told me not to let them take advantage of me because I was pretty. Unbeknownst to her at that time, I already had sexual experiences, some against my will and some consensual. Mom was 20 years old when she had me. I repeated the same cycle of bringing another being into the world outside of wedlock and not ready to financially care for a child. I did not have an answer for Mom. I became quiet.

Further along into my pregnancy, I found out Crystal was pregnant too. I was infuriated because she was still so young at the time and in high school. I went back to Springfield to investigate the circumstances. Something I typically did when I got news of Crystal doing something unfavorable.

At the time, Crystal worked at Hardee's and was behind the cash register. I marched right in there, walked behind the counter and began shouting at her. "So, who did it?! Who got you pregnant?! Who's the dad?" Shocked to see me, Crystal really didn't have an answer for me, just a blank stare across her face.

I was upset that I was not around to prevent her from getting pregnant. Being the oldest, I felt this overwhelming sense of duty to protect Crystal and watch after her. I beat up boyfriends for her, told her when a boyfriend was being unfaithful and/or tried to talk to me or April. I felt I failed her by being gone. I felt like I was more her mom, than her sister at times. It pained me to see she was pregnant.

I didn't want to appear as a hypocrite for chastising her and her pregnancy because after all, I too was pregnant. However, I felt because I was a little bit older and going to college, my circumstances were different compared to hers. Concerned that the path she was about to head down was not going to be promising, I begged and pleaded with Crystal to come with me to Carbondale. I told her of the assistance which was available, how she could have a new beginning, and help with the baby. Consequently, the pleas landed on deaf ears. Crystal remained in Springfield.

April also got pregnant shortly thereafter. All three of us were pregnant as teenagers, and not married. The effects of our dysfunctional and abusive upbringing were becoming evident. It was disheartening to see all three of us had succumbed to searching for love through men, which entailed having sex prematurely and irresponsibly. Our acts out of brokenness landed us with seeds growing on the inside of our womb. The three of us were soon to be single, unwed mothers at the same time.

I had a couple of friends who were pregnant at the same time. Monique, was one of them. We talked about how our kids would grow up together, shared pregnancy stories and encouraged one another throughout our respective journeys. We eventually passed along hand-me-downs to each other when our children grew out of their clothes. Sharing the experience with a friend helped tremendously. I did not feel alone.

Lynette referred me to her OB/GYN. She was a nice white lady who genuinely cared about her patients. She never looked down on me for being a young, unwed soon to be mother who had to live on public assistance. She often encouraged me to continue going forward with my education and shared stories of her own with me. She helped in making my pregnancy experience a tad bit more bearable. Lucas didn't come to all my appointments, but he came to most of them with me. He was the perfect boyfriend. He often rubbed his hands on my growing belly while talking about our future together… marriage… coming up with baby names. I was beginning to live my fairytale out in real life.

Not at any time did I ever imagine Lucas would cheat on me. I thought he was in love, happy and proud to be my man. As Lucas drove and I sat in the passenger seat, a little red car almost ran right into us. At first it appeared to be an accident. However, after I saw the scowl on the girl's face who was driving the little red car, I knew it was intentional. I immediately looked at Lucas to see his response. I was perplexed. He looked back at her and had this "what the hell are doing?" look upon his face. I asked him did he know her and what was going on. He was too engaged in this girl's behavior to respond.

The girl parked her car in the middle of the road, got out of it and began yelling and screaming at Lucas. She answered my question for him. That's when reality hit me. My perfect world did not appear to be so perfect after all. Nonetheless, I believed what Lucas said, "that girl is crazy! She's just mad because she tried to get with me and I turned her down." Not wanting to raise our unborn child alone, I left the incident in the middle of the road and focused on being a family with Lucas.

Eventually I discovered Lucas lied. The girl was upset because Lucas had slept with her and promised to leave me for her. When she saw me, pregnant and all, sitting in the passenger side of his vehicle, she knew he lied to her. Despite knowing this, I still decided to stick by Lucas. I was determined to not be a single-mom. I also did not want to be alone.

Lucas was in the hospital room when I gave birth to Amari. Mandy was in the room as well, while other friends waited in the lobby. He held my hand, coached me through breathing exercises and tended to my every need. He was the perfect boyfriend - supportive and loving. When it was time for me to push, Lucas held one leg, while Mandy held the other.

When Amari was born, Lucas called his dad with tears running down his face and joy in his voice tone. "Dad, he's here! She just had him!" It warmed my heart to know he was as happy as I our son had entered the world. At that moment, I felt I had everything one could ever ask for in life. A boyfriend who was right there with me through every step of the pregnancy, a beautiful and perfect baby boy and friends who genuinely cared for me.

Lucas was in the middle of football camp, and had already missed a day when Amari was born. The coach did not count it against him, but he could not miss any more trainings. In support of his dreams to go to the NFL, I did not give him any fuss about not being able to take baby Amari and I home from the hospital. I accepted that sometimes he would be present and sometimes he would not, all for the sake of the betterment of our family.

My roommates brought Amari and I home from the hospital. After the spring semester, before Amari was born, a classmate and her friend approached me about being roommates. It would save all of us on living expenses, in addition to having the luxury of living off campus, something every college student wanted. Lucas was roommates with his teammates. The arrangements worked out wonderfully for the both of us.

After Amari was born, I only had a couple of weeks left until the fall semester started. I developed a new determination to continue with my education, knowing I had one more person to care for other than myself. Since I went back to school before Amari was 6 weeks old, I was unable to put him in daycare. Lucas and I developed a system in the beginning to enable me to go to class while he kept Amari. My roommates and friends also assisted in caring for Amari so I could attend classes.

I was a working mother and a student. I tried to train and go back to track, but the drive wasn't there. I allowed fear and doubt to take over. I worried about how long I would have to train to get back at my peak level. The drive for running was not in me. I knew with a baby I needed to be able to provide for him, so I focused on excelling in school and getting a good education so that I could do just that for Amari.

I supported Lucas by going to almost every football game I could possibly attend, even if they were out of town. Friends and I packed everything up and drove to games that were not too far away. I loved that man with every ounce of my being. I got excited each time I watched him play and help the team win. I had bragging rights to be able to prance around campus saying my man was the 3-time All-American football player. The football team was very good and a lot of the girls wanted to have a football player as their boyfriend. And, if they could not get them as their boyfriend, they would settle for sleeping with them.

Consequently, Lucas fell into the hype and began sleeping with random girls around campus who gave him the extra attention which caught his eye. After the incident with the girl in the red car, I had a sense of suspicion I kept tucked away about Lucas. I knew this girl had a reason for trying to hit us and Lucas had to have showed her some type of attention to cause her to express herself in such a volatile manner. She was the first girl I found out he had been sleeping with. I found out about the others when I snooped through Lucas's phone. Despite knowing this, I stayed with him. I was scared that my identity would be lost if we were no longer in a relationship and I would not find another man to love me. Not to mention, I did not want to raise Amari alone.

Eventually Lucas and I decided it would be ideal to live together. We got an apartment together to co-parent and begin practicing being under one roof for our future. If no one else knew of Lucas's affairs, I kept it to myself and pretended what we shared was perfect. I did what I thought a future wife was supposed to do, stand by her man no matter what. I encouraged and supported him in the best way I knew how. I even cooked dinner for Lucas and some of his teammates because they could not go home for the holidays.

I arranged my work and school schedules around Lucas's schedules under the understanding that we would be co-parenting. One day, Lucas refused to watch Amari. I had no other choice than to pack my baby boy up in an infant backpack, walk to campus and take Amari with me to class. Amari did exceptionally well. He either slept during the classes or was so quiet you could not hear a peep out of him. My professors were impressed with his demeanor as well. I knew God was with me at those moments by keeping Amari calm.

This was also the same day I heard rumors on campus about Lucas sleeping around with random girls. One of the girls even lived right in our apartment complex! I felt sick to my stomach. What I thought was my secret, was now public knowledge. Others on campus knew Lucas was sleeping around with other girls. It was not until his infidelity became public knowledge that I acted. I refused to be embarrassed and made a mockery of. I did not want to be perceived as the naive girlfriend who took his mess.

I confided in a few girlfriends what I had been keeping buried away inside. I decided to kick Lucas out of our apartment. I had it all mapped out. I packed all his clothes into trash bags, stuffed his truck with his belongings and parked it at the football field. I removed his car key from my key ring and returned it to Lucas as he came out of the locker room. I quietly told him I knew about his affairs and walked away. Mandy followed me there to give me a ride back home. At that moment, I felt I did what I always wanted Mom to do – walk away. I felt empowered.

That moment of empowerment lasted just as briefly as the sky does when it turns from dusk to dawn. I could not make up my mind as to what I wanted. One minute I loved Lucas with every fiber of my being. The next, I loathed him and despised the day I fell in love with him. I felt as if my heart were in constant battle within me. I battled between logic and emotions. I could not make my mind up as to what I wanted. Yet, my heart kept whispering that I loved him. My heart and mind both, struggled to balance one another. The game of tug-of-war within me was exhausting.

Despite wanting to stand up for myself, I still loved him. I did not make the best of decisions when it came to Lucas. I made many impulsive and emotionally-driven decisions. One minute I wanted to leave him because he was a lying, cheater and I wanted him to pay for it. The next minute I wanted to be with him because he was Amari's dad and my first true love. I was constantly torn.

Drama seemed to be my nickname, figuratively speaking. Everyone on campus was pretty much aware of Lucas cheating on me, me creating public scenes of embarrassment out of the pain I felt and still wanting him in the end. I was very much a fool who was in love, but in fact, I was *in fear*. I feared being a single mother. I feared another woman having the man I spent a piece of my young life with. I feared I would never have a man again because I had a baby. I feared I would never feel love from a man again and would be alone. I feared I would lose myself if I lost Lucas.

I did whatever I had to do to hold on to him. I used his phone to call the women he had slept with. I harassed them as I threatened them to leave him alone. I showed up unannounced to his apartment or to parties I heard he was at, trying to make sure he was not with another woman. I even smelled his underwear to see if he had slept with anyone. I caught him with this method before. Whatever woman he had last slept with reeked of catfish. The raunchy odor was evidence on his boxer briefs.

When I was upset enough I became physically aggressive. I pushed and shoved Lucas during heated arguments when he was caught being unfaithful or questioned our relationship. I even threw a block of concrete at him when he admitted to cheating on me. Anger and frustration dominated my thoughts, words and actions as I failed to properly articulate the hurt and confusion I felt. I even offered sexual innuendos in attempts to seduce Lucas into staying with me.

I began to explore my sexual side by wearing lingerie and dancing for him. I aimed to bait Lucas into only wanting me. I thought sex and seduction was how you keep a man. At least those were the unspoken lessons I learned from Mom. Not only did I grow up hearing them, but when I went through Mom's stuff in her room as a little girl, I found lingerie. I did not know at the time what I was looking at, but I remembered when I was trying to think of ways to keep Lucas. Regardless of how dysfunctional Mom and Dad's relationship was, they still stayed with each other. I just wanted Lucas to stay.

I literally became obsessed with *keeping* this man that did not want to be kept. Deep down in my heart, I knew he did not want to be kept. We were only 19 years old when I got pregnant with Amari, and I was asking this man to give up his early twenties, the prime of his partying escapades while in college, to be a father, a man and a future husband. Simply put, Lucas was not ready and I did not want to accept that.

Granted, other guys on campus tried to pursue and date me, but Lucas was the only man in my eyes. He was the first man whom I truly fell in love with, opened my heart to and could envision a future with. I even shared with Lucas my history of abuse during my childhood. I never shared this information with anyone other than close friends. In fact, I never shared with anyone that I was even molested as a young girl. Unfortunately, Lucas used this information against me to defend himself for not wanting to be with me, rather than telling me how he truly felt.

"You're crazy as hell! You need help! Everything you've been through has messed you up!" Rather than trying to understand my pain and talk to me sensibly and reasonably, he spoke down to me. He reaffirmed the negative image that was taught to me by Dad each time he tore me down with his words and judgements. When I heard this enough, I began to believe it and felt I finally needed to address the issues of my past.

I sought out a counselor on campus. Lucas respected that I decided to get help for the emotional and mental issues I suffered because of my dysfunctional childhood. He encouraged me to continue going to sessions and to get peace for the pain I was harboring. Not even realizing how deep my pain went, the first few sessions did not do as much as graze the surface. I had dozens upon dozens of layers to unravel and was completely unaware.

I mainly shared with the counselor the abuse I endured at home from Dad and domestic violence I witnessed between Dad against Mom. I offered some detail, but not in its entirety. I held back. I lacked trust. I was unfamiliar with counseling, but was not opposed to it. Yet, I still was not sure if I could trust this total stranger with some of my deepest and darkest secrets. These secrets that shaped and molded me into the drama filled, emotional wreck of a person I turned out to be. The counselor wanted me to retract those white seeds. I did not even know where they floated off to. That's how I felt about the pain I had tucked away somewhere inside of my heart.

To face who I was and how I got there, I had to address those hidden secrets I cared not to remember and kept stifled inside me for several years. Although my counselor at the time provided me with excellent advice and tools to do such a thing, I did not want to disclose everything. That meant I had to remember how it made me feel. Truth be told, I was tired of hurting.

I was not ready to face my own demons. I continued as the dramatic, raging and crazy in love "baby-momma." I was often provoked by Lucas's lying, cheating and scandalous mannerisms which hurt me immensely. It made me want to try to *keep* him more. It was as if I saw his resistance as a challenge. If I could convince, or even seduce him to stay, I felt I "won".

I suppose Lucas got annoyed with me questioning him about his unfaithfulness. He became infuriated and began shouting at me. The shouting escalated. Lucas grabbed my arms, and lifted me from the spot in the bed I was in as he tossed me against the wall. My back hit the floor lamp pole that was in the corner beside the bed. I was more emotionally hurt than physically hurt. Although my back did hurt and I was frightened by Lucas's aggressiveness, I was more hurt inside that he did this to me, knowing my former experiences.

I left the house and ran to Amari's old babysitter to explain what had happened. She suggested I call the police because I had just experienced a form of domestic violence. I called and made the complaint. Lucas was at my apartment that night. When we returned, he was sitting on the stoop of my steps, in handcuffs with officers surrounding him. I was devastated. "I did not want this! I'm not pressing charges! Can you let him go?" I pleaded with one of the officers, but it was too late. Lucas glared down at the ground as the officers read him his Miranda Rights.

I felt that it was my fault. He would have never thrown me against the wall had I not continuously badgered him about sleeping with other women. Out of guilt, I went down to the State's Attorney Office and dropped the charges. But this tragic event was not erased from *our* records.

I was conditioned to live in a chaotic, dysfunctional and dramatic environment. I was oblivious of how unhealthy and draining this way of living was. I watched Mom and Dad argue, Dad beat on Mom, Mom retaliated a few times, and it was an endless cycle. I thought this was how relationships were supposed to be. No one taught me that romantic, intimate and loving relationships were meant to be healthy, full of trust, communication and respect. I only displayed what I was taught at home.

My gut knew that this was not right for me. Yet, I still loved him. My insecurities and fear of being alone interfered with my decision-making when it came to Lucas. My inability to follow through and stick to those decisions became obvious each time Lucas and I got back together. I not only disagreed with the way Lucas treated me as a girlfriend, but I also felt that he was not a present father. He lied about days and times he would get Amari. The financial burden to care for Amari was becoming solely my own. It seemed Lucas did not want to be a father.

When I finally came to this realization, I confronted Lucas about it while he was driving. "I don't feel like you're being a good father to our son. I can't be with someone who is not a good father to my son." Lucas got upset. As we approached a bridge on the outskirts of Carbondale, Lucas swerved his SUV toward the edge. I panicked and grabbed the wheel, fearful of what he was trying to do. "Are you nuts?! You're going to kill us!" I screamed as Lucas drove erratically. "That's the point!" He shouted back at me. Thankfully, Amari was not in the car with us. Eventually Lucas calmed down. However, I knew our time was winding down to its catastrophic end.

I fought it tooth and nail until Lucas finally decided to leave. I had just graduated with my Bachelor's Degree not too long preceding this moment. Lucas did not get drafted into the NFL as anticipated. He blamed me and said it was because I called the police on him. He accepted no accountability for his actions. In less than 24 hours' notice, Lucas informed me that he was moving back home to Florida to try to make something of himself. He led me to believe that everything would work out just fine and that he was leaving for the betterment of us all.

For some reason, my heart told me to brace myself and prepare for the journey that beset me. I was going to be a single mother to a black boy in America. I had a history of abuse and had not faced or addressed the hurt, pain, guilt and shame. At this moment, I felt my world was crumbling apart right in front of my face, and there was nothing I could do about it. "What about Amari? What about us?" were the only words I managed to utter between my lips. Distressed, I could say nothing more. "Everything will be ok. Everything will work out." He attempted to assure me. Yet my heart told me otherwise.

CHAPTER TEN

Something New

After Lucas moved back home to Florida and forsook his responsibilities in assisting me raise our son, I fell into despair. I did not follow him in hopes of rekindling an old romance or force him to be the present and consistent father I knew Amari needed. I did do my fair share of begging and pleading with him to stay and be with me.

Moving to Florida without him initiating it would have caused even more heartache for me in the long run. I let Lucas go and stayed in Illinois, while unknowingly holding on to rage, bitterness and resentment toward him. I added yet another layer of hatred toward men to my heart, and eventually went into a wilderness phase of my life which lasted several years.

My curiosity about women began to emerge in high school, while I was living in Indiana. I occasionally glanced at women, found some attractive, exotic, and even stunning. Yet, I never realized I was beginning to look at them in a different manner until I began finding women sexually attractive. A desire grew inside of me to have a sexual experience with a woman.

The summer of freshman year in college, when the social network site Blackplanet.com was the current frenzy, I curiously roamed the lesbian pages and began to frequent them quite often. I found women to chat with and opened a door I was unaware would take me years to close.

Not knowing if this desire was something that I was born with or forced upon me plagued me for quite some time. It was also a recipe for disaster; not knowing who I truly was and what I truly wanted. I attribute this to the experiences I had with Ebony as a young child. I don't think these thoughts ever quite left my mind; rather I pushed them back to a subconscious place that remained dormant until something triggered them to resurface into my consciousness.

Living in a predominately white town and never having dated a white boy before, my mind was not quite open to the option of exploring that. Of course, I had crushes on the charismatic guys who made the girls laugh and had the Hollywood sex appeal that most girls admire. However, being a biracial girl, I automatically assumed they would find no interest in me, so those crushes quickly vanished. Nevertheless, I began to reach out to random women on Blackplanet.com and expressed thoughts and feelings I had never shared with another soul.

"Red, would you have sex with a woman if your man was right there?" Mandy asked me this in a room full of other women. It was sophomore year in college, as usual, we were chatting about sex.

"Hell no! I'm strictly dickly," I defensively responded.

"Did she see the picture of her breasts in my phone? Did she read my text messages?" I thought to myself in guilt while wondering why she asked me this.

I just knew she came across something in my cell phone that gave it away. I wanted to have sex with a woman. One of the girls was looking at me, or what I thought at least, like she knew this about me and was keeping it a secret for me. I was paranoid. For the last year, I maintained contact with one of the women I conversed with on Blackplanet.com. We never met in person, but continued to text, call and e-mail each other periodically. Although I was dating Lucas, in the back of my mind I still wanted a sexual experience with a woman. It would be a few more years until I could finally turn my fantasy into a reality.

Tyreese was a smooth, and handsome educated hustler who had his way with the ladies. The night we met, we were at a mutual friend's small gathering. Our encounter was brief, so no lasting impressions were made at this moment. We made each other's acquaintances again at a night club. As he played pool, I sipped on a cocktail and admired his attire. He had on a neatly pressed blazer; button up collared shirt that was left unbuttoned at the top, jeans, and shiny square-toed dress shoes. I had not seen a man dressed as sharp as he anywhere in Carbondale. Intrigued by his debonair, I wondered what he did. Did he have some fancy job where he turned his business attire into something more casual for the evening? Or, did he dress like this to impress the ladies? Possibly, he was one of those metro-sexual guys who liked to be fashionable. Whatever the reason, I enjoyed the eye candy in front of me.

As I watched him shoot the balls into the pockets, we made eye contact. A flirtatious smile and cocky head nod were the nonverbal gestures we exchanged as we acknowledged one another. After he won that round, he introduced himself. He brought out his right hand to shake mine, "how do you do?" I believe I paused for a moment before I could give him an answer.

"How do you do?" I thought. *"This has to be some kind of joke, I mean, who talks like that anymore?"*

I discovered by his own admittance, he always wanted to use the classic line borrowed from a movie, and saw this to be the perfect opportunity to do so. Uncaring if he used a line or not to grasp my attention, I still blushed like a teenage girl and cheerfully replied, "I'm Casandra, what's your name?" "Tyreese," he responded in his deep masculine tone of voice.

We chatted for hours. Being able to hold a decent conversation and keep my attention kept my interest piqued. I thought all hope was lost in the small college hick town called Carbondale for me and a man. Tyreese's first impression was quite staggering.

We had the time of our lives during our involvement with one another. We were both risk takers, willing to do anything at the drop of a hat. Impulsivity was our common denominator; the catalyst for our adventurous and sometimes scandalous moments. Casinos, strip clubs, night clubs, and spur of the moment highway trips were our versions of fun. We partied until the rise of the sun and did it all over again the next day. Bonnie and Clyde is what we called ourselves. Our love affair was short lived though. We recognized we were much more alike for the purposes of a platonic friendship, rather than a romantic relationship.

Tyreese was also quite the ladies' man. His phone often rang in the middle of the night. It was usually some girl looking for him. When I saw Tyreese display similar characteristics as Lucas, in terms of wanting many women, I decided this was not the man for me. However, I still enjoyed hanging out with him.

Tyreese advocated for me to have my first sexual experience with a woman. I once shared this desire with Lucas, but he neither acted upon it nor acknowledged my secret desire. I wondered if he had a fear I would no longer be his woman if I had a sexual encounter with another woman; the irony. At any rate, Tyreese seemed absolutely thrilled when I shared this long-hidden secret of mine. He even went as far as wanting to orchestrate my first sexual experience with a woman.

After a night of drinking and partying, Tyreese suggested I try to meet a woman who I was attracted to. I earnestly waited for this moment for a few years. Was I ready? Ready to consent and commit this act on my own, all because I wanted to? Or were these seductive thoughts that I only entertained through conversation without action, something I should leave in my mind and not act upon?

"When she gets into the truck, play in her hair, women love that." Tyreese scoped out the scene at the club we were at, and found a potential candidate. He knew I was looking for someone sexy, my build or smaller and the obvious, into girls too. I really did not have much of a say in the girl he picked. I was too intoxicated from partying and dancing all night to offer an opinion.

As I sat in this large, black SUV and waited for who may be my first female sexual rendezvous, I began to feel nervous and excited at the same time. Random thoughts scurried about in my mind, as I anticipated a moment I longed for.

"I wonder what she looks like."

"Is she pretty?"

"Is she sexy?"

"Does she like girls too?"

"Will she like me touching her?"

"What if she doesn't like girls?"

"What if she tells someone I tried to come on to her?"

When she got into the truck, I made up my mind I was not going to make the first move. I wanted to sit and have a casual conversation with her, read her body language and decide if she was down for this or not.

When she entered the truck, her long flowing hair was what I noticed first. She had on a little sexy black dress, black heels, and a black leather jacket. *"So far, so good,"* I thought to myself. Her smile could make any head turn. She smelled so good I wanted to kiss her softly on the nape of her neck, but I didn't. As the silence broke after our words filled the space, I discovered she was just looking for the next party to go to, or so I thought.

"So where are you guys going next, where's the after party at?" It was nearly three o' clock in the morning, and she was ready to party until the sun came up. I, however, was ready to either explore her naked body, or turn in for the night. I had had enough partying for one night.

"That's why I asked you did you want to come and kick it with us, we can make our own after party." Tyreese was not ashamed to assertively make our intentions known, without directly stating them. I began to feel embarrassed. I was fearful she would not be receptive to his offer or even interested in going on a sexual journey with me. Before finding out if she would go for it or not, I quickly impeded on the original plan by talking about how tired I was and maybe we should just take her home.

The young lady seemed a bit confused, however I was not about to reveal my true intentions so that the rest of the world could know my secret. I'd rather go to bed with my curiosity captivating me, than to be filled with humiliation after rejection. Assumptions and fear superseded spontaneity and courage on this night.

Tyreese didn't understand why I reacted this way.

"I thought that's what you wanted? What happened?" He was confused.

"I don't know. I guess I chickened out and got scared she wasn't down, so I hurried up and said something to save myself the embarrassment." I quickly and defensively replied.

We didn't discuss it any further; Tyreese didn't try to push this upon me. He allowed me to slowly become more comfortable with the thoughts and feelings I was having about women before making another attempt at my sexual undertaking with another woman.

Tyreese was determined to make sure he was the one who facilitated my first consensual sexual experience with a woman. He knew of a girl he grew up with, who had messed with women before. I suppose it dawned on him that night to call her and see if she wanted to indulge in a sexual escapade. I couldn't believe it was that easy for him. To call someone up, suggest this random sexual act, and they go for it? My thoughts began to roam and question him.

"Did he bribe her?"

"Were they secretly seeing each other?"

"Why was she so willing to do this? "

After another night of partying at the club, we went over to her house. He stopped by the liquor store on the way and bought a bottle of Hennessey, it was for me. I was so nervous that I needed something to take the edge off. I did all of that talking about wanting to sleep with a woman and explore her body and she explore mine, yet when the opportunity finally presented itself, I froze! It seemed this time I couldn't talk my way out of it and I had to roll with the punches. So, my curiosity and Hennessey were going to have to take over my skepticism and apprehension.

She was an average looking woman. A tad bit older than me. She also had a gap between her top two front teeth, just like me! She was calm, cool, and collected. I didn't know the contents of the conversation which transpired between her and Tyreese. Whatever it was, I figured she was ok with what was about to occur.

"You want some?" I figured if I needed a shot of whiskey, maybe she would like some too. "Sure, let me go get us some glasses." As she got up from the couch, she began to switch her hips from side to side in such a way I could tell she wanted to catch my attention. I relaxed and felt a little more at ease. Her flirtatious innuendo was appealing. I was eager to know what her touch felt like. When she returned with the glasses, I opened the bottle of liquid courage that was soon going to send us into a moment of bliss. She winked and smiled at me as the liquid poison filled her glass. I smiled back, while trying to maintain my composure.

"Maybe she found me attractive, or did Tyreese bribe her in some way or fashion?" I still didn't understand how she was willing and wanting to sleep with this perfect stranger all because of a phone call made. It was bizarre and I couldn't figure it out.

As we continued to have small talk and sip on the whiskey, Tyreese asked why we weren't sitting next to each other. She came over and sat with me. The chair I sat in was a one-person-seat. She was nearly sitting on my lap when she came to sit with me.

"You smell good," she whispered in my ear as she slowly grazed her lips across my neck and swiveled her tongue in a circular motion. She looked me in the eyes and smiled, and then she kissed me. She was a good kisser. Her lips pressed against mine felt just how I had envisioned a woman's lips should feel, soft and succulent. We kissed for several minutes before deciding it was time to move on to phase two.

I could not sleep for the next 24 hours. I was unsure if it was the sexual encounter I just had, or if I was running off pure adrenaline. I felt guilt and shame well up inside of me like an ocean wave touching the surface of land. I was ashamed of myself and a piece of me was starting to question my sexual orientation.

"Does this mean I'm a lesbian now?"

"Am I a gay person?"

"Am I bi-sexual?"

"What am I?"

"Who am I?"

"What did I just do?"

The puzzlement of the incident turned what was supposed to be something simple and spontaneous, into a complex maze causing me to hit several dead ends before I could finally reach an exit. This lasted for several years.

CHAPTER ELEVEN

The Wilderness

I did not care for the Master's courses I was taking. They were mundane and I was burned out from anything that was remotely close to school at this point. After giving birth to Amari, I rushed back into the classroom to finish my Bachelor's Degree in a timely fashion. I put more energy and effort into the degree than anything else.

Rather than buckling down and writing the 30-page writing assignments and reading the several chapters a night which were required of me, I decided to take a "break" from it all and try into entering the professional world. I rationalized this decision by convincing myself experience was more important than furthering my education at the time and I had a growing boy to feed! I made the excuse of not having time as a single mother and that I needed to put my energies elsewhere. I did not have the focus and willpower needed to complete a Master's Degree.

Obtaining employment in my field, in rural southern Illinois, turned out to be more challenging than originally anticipated. I thought I possessed the credentials most employers required, yet, I was not getting a single letter or a phone call for an interview. I continued to work for the University's campus daycare and picked up a part time job as well.

The pastor's daughter of the church I attended was the manager of a retail store in the mall. I inquired about working as a sales associate and was offered a position there. This was my first time working in a retail store, however not my first time working a cash register.

Since I wasn't getting any responses from the applications I submitted, rather than finishing my Master's degree, I picked up a second part-time job at retail store - Wet-Seal. Wet-Seal had the current albums playing in rotation to keep the customers entertained while shopping. It kept me entertained as well. I loved music and the capabilities and power it holds to transform one's mood, thoughts and emotions. I could be in a funk upon arrival, but within minutes ready to go out to a nightclub and party after the nostalgic sounds infiltrated my being, awakening a desire to dance. Sure, there's nothing wrong with dancing and having a good time with friends, albeit that usually included alcohol and possibly sex - not so good things. After some time, partying at a night club would not be the activity that caused me to engage in a random rendezvous - it was one of my managers at work.

Reina was a beautiful Puerto Rican and African American woman who was bi-sexual, which she quickly let me know once we began conversing. She had a way about her that was intriguing and mystifying. She drew people in with her charm and flirty giggles. At first, we just had casual small talk, the usual demographic stuff: where we're from, why we're in Carbondale and working there, etc. Yet, one evening, after just the two of us closed the store together, she suggested we go to Apple-bees and have a couple of cocktails. I assented and joined her. Our once previous casual talk turned into a more personal conversation. I don't recall specifically what or how we even got onto this topic, but out of nowhere we both expressed our attraction for women. I even shared the sexual experience I had with a woman.

I did not notice it then, but I believe Reina sensed this already about me and was trying to bring it out of me. Once you've had a sexual encounter with the same sex, you almost develop a sixth sense toward others who either have had one as well or maybe contemplated it. At least I did. I suppose I had sensed the same about her somewhere inside of me; hence why I joined her for cocktails and shared one of my deepest secrets. Speaking with Reina made me feel at ease. I no longer felt as if I was the only woman in the world battling with these thoughts and emotions. I had someone to share this similarity with and I liked it.

After we finished our last cocktail and it was time to go our separate ways, through the final minutes of our conversation we discovered we lived in the same apartment complex. How ironic I worked with this woman, and shared a secret intimate moment in my life over cocktails with her and she just so happened to live in the same vicinity as me! I did not know if this was merely a coincidence or the universe feeding me back the energy I had put out about women. Whatever it was, I was receptive and open to it. The night did not end at Apple-bees. Reina invited me over to her place where episode number two of an intimate experience with a woman occurred.

When I arrived to Reina's apartment, which resembled a similar floor plan as mine, I admired her décor and eclectic taste, particularly in the Japanese culture. She had a Japanese folding screen room divider in her living room. I wondered if she had ever undressed behind it like they do in the movies. Her linen was red with Japanese symbols and she had squared plates with Japanese symbols on those as well. With Reina's nationality being black and Puerto Rican, I found it peculiar, yet appealing, that she adopted an interest in a culture such as this.

Not only was her beauty and décor easy on the eyes, her cooking was sensational to the palate. Reina cooked an array of dishes which came from multiple ethnicities, my favorite being Mexican. Looking back, I can see how she lured people in with not just her beauty and charm, but her talented culinary skills as well. We both enjoyed cooking and eating. Sharing this commonality with someone else was quite an enjoyable experience.

As I admired Reina's taste and style, she came downstairs with only a bath towel on, after just taking a shower. I was not sure if perhaps she had forgotten something downstairs or what, but I tried not to gaze too hard and continued to look at her choice of décor. She sat on the arm of the couch right next to me, with her legs straddled on each side as if she were straddling a horse. I started to feel nervous, my flesh was getting warmer. She looked at me and said, "Come here, come sit up here with me." Without hesitation, or even asking any questions, I scooted over and joined her on the arm of the couch.

She gently placed her hand on my face and began to kiss me. It was a passionate and tender kiss. This kiss was different from the former, in that we had developed some sort of a rapport with each other. I had the opportunity to form a real interest in her. After that night, I came to the realization that the very first encounter I had with Tyreese's lady friend was not my last, nor was whatever was happening between Reina and me.

Casual and professional conversations turned into flirtatious remarks and gestures while we worked together. We both still worked hard and got our work done, but the energy between us shifted. We planned on what to do the nights we closed together, which usually consisted of a party or just going to each other's apartments and having cocktails. It was nice spending time with another woman who was attracted to women and had so much in common with me.

She was a single mother to a little boy too. The downfall - Reina never quite pictured herself being solely with a woman. I, however, was beginning to want to be *exclusively* with a woman. I was tired of men and being treated like crap by them. I was beginning to lose interest in men in general. Reina still wanted to date men though, and started to get interested in one. I slowly felt jealousy sit in the pit of my stomach as I decided to disconnect myself from having any type of an emotional attachment to her. I had to look at Reina as just a friend, nothing more and nothing less.

Reina and I still hung out together, but with the understanding that nothing intimate would occur between us. I met many of her friends and vice versa, particularly her best friend and son's God-mother, Sarah. Sarah was outgoing and had a magnetic personality. She got along with any and everybody. Her laughter was infectious. She made me laugh so hard my belly would ache. We also talked about music for hours. We shared a common interest in hip-hop music. She brought CD's over that we listened to and had discussions about the undertone of the songs. Eventually Sarah and I grew an attraction for each other. Rather than ignoring it, we acted upon it.

Sarah's flirtation toward me was becoming obvious. We started out by hanging out at Reina's house and all of us enjoying each other's company. However, Sarah began coming over to my apartment alone and that's where our bond grew. Sarah was more affectionate than Reina. I could tell Reina just wanted to *play*, but I was looking for love. I wanted someone to love me, be with me and want me for me, not to just have an experience with. Sarah made me feel like she was genuinely interested in me.

The first night we had sex, we took our time. There was no rushing. I felt intimacy with Sarah. I had not felt that in a long time. I desired to be wanted, needed and loved by another soul. Sarah was giving that to me and I leached on to her as I did with anyone else who showed me this type of attention and affection.

Sarah and I kept our love affair a secret, per my idea originally. I did not want to hurt Reina. Even though Reina made it perfectly clear she could not exclusively be with just a woman, I still felt that our actions would hurt her. I could not stand to be the reason for anyone's pain.

Sarah and I became inseparable. We cooked together, watched movies, went on outings and she was great with Amari. I was beginning to feel like I had what it took to be with a woman long term and desired to have a partnership like my Aunt Katie had. I wanted to be loved and treated right. The gender as to who could do that did not matter to me anymore.

Women seemed to get attached to me and want me more than men did. They also treated me differently, *better* I thought. Women made me feel wanted, loved, and I thrived from that feeling. As Sarah and I's relationship grew, I wanted to publicize it. One afternoon, while we were both on our lunch breaks, Sarah and I went out to eat and were having a great conversation. I reached for her hand. I wanted to show my affection toward her at that moment. She withdrew.

"What are you doing?" She asked with a puzzled look upon her face.

"What's wrong? We do this all of the time." I responded.

"Not in public though, Casandra." Sarah whispered back.

I was hurt. I felt I had finally found someone who wanted to be with me as much as I wanted to be with them, only under one condition, we had to keep it between us.

I suppose one could say I had this coming. I was the one who originally suggested we keep our relationship between the two of us. It was more of protection for Reina than the rest of the world though. For all everyone else knew, we had a great friendship and looked like we were best friends who were always with each other. If we appeared that way, Sarah was content. I was ready to break "out of the closet." I did not want my lifestyle to be a secret anymore. I was in love with a woman and I wanted the world to know. Sarah was not ready and expressed that to me.

"My grandmother would kill me, Casandra!" Sarah cried out to me as we had another discussion about her need to live "in the closet."

"I don't want to live in the closet, Sarah! What do you have to hide? I thought you loved me? I though you wanted to be with me? Why does this have to be a secret now? People that are in love don't hide it!"

Once again, I was devastated. My heart felt as if it was being twisted with a wrench and no mercy was being shown. I wondered what was wrong with me that I continued to be engaged in relationships that were unfulfilling and did not give me everything I needed.

We continued with our relationship at the cost of keeping it a secret. A couple of friends of ours knew, but they were sworn to secrecy. That was her way of allowing me to share what we had with others, but with limitations. Frustration and resentment soon smothered the love I had for Sarah. If I could not have it my way, I did not want to continue being involved with her. I wanted to be with someone who would hold my hand in public, kiss me in the rain and take away all my pain.

Sarah was quite devastated when I broke things off with her. She was even more upset when she caught wind of me sleeping with other women. I began a perpetual and awful habit of being promiscuous when in pain. It made me feel like I was in control to have one night stands with women. I fulfilled their sexual fantasies and then did not return their calls. I pretended as if they did not exist. I felt as if I was in control for once and no one had control over me or my heart. If I did not allow myself to catch any feelings for the other person, I could sleep with them and not think twice about it.

Sarah was floored! This caused her to break our deal - she exposed our secret love affair to Reina. Sarah did what any other woman does who is hurt by their lover. Reina called me and went off on me like a woman goes off on a man who gets caught cheating on them. I didn't understand why she was so upset since she had already made it perfectly clear with me that she slept with women for the fun of it and could never be in a committed relationship.

"I really liked you, Casandra! I know I did not do what you wanted me to do and I probably hurt your feelings, but I really did like you! Why did you have to go be with my best friend?!"

Reina was hurt and the only response I could provide was to shift the blame.

"Sarah wanted to be with me! She loved me! You didn't even want a relationship! You couldn't stop messing with men!"

I attempted to justify myself by placing blame on Reina for my actions. It was easier to do that, than to accept responsibility for the pain and hurt I inflicted on another person. Reina and Sarah both did not speak to me for quite some time, but like most female relationships, we later became friends again.

After things did not work out with Sarah, I decided to temporarily forsake relationships. I partied more and had one night stands with women, just because the opportunities presented themselves. When out at a club or bar, women approached me and flirted with me. That was all she wrote. I flirted back. I kissed them in the club while extremely intoxicated and did not care who was watching. Sometimes I even went to their place to have sex after a night of partying. I stopped caring, and just started doing.

Being promiscuous with women was not fulfilling for me. Yes, I felt the power was in my hands because I controlled the outcome, but I still yearned for and desired to be loved by another. Thinking that the next relationship would be better, I continued to jump from relationship to relationship in attempts to get over the previous one, while losing more of myself each time.

I attached myself to others to feel worthy. If I wasn't in a relationship, or having sex with someone, I did not feel closeness with another human. I needed this closeness to validate my existence. I did not know who I was, nor did I love myself. I needed someone else to love me, for me to feel love.

CHAPTER TWELVE

Toxicity

I began going out to night clubs and partying more for the attention. After so many times of hearing praises for my genetically given beauty, I finally started to believe it.

"You're sexy!"

"You're hot!"

"You look good!"

"You're bad!"

"You're gorgeous!"

"Damn, you're beautiful!"

I did not think I was getting negative attention, rather getting complimented on my good looks. I yearned for that my entire life and was finally receiving it, many of them in fact.

My self-esteem took a boost as I began to walk pompously. After dating both genders, I really began to feel myself. I was being told by both men and women I was beautiful, and I loved it! My self-esteem was not only boosted, but I also became more assertive, and at times aggressive. If I saw something or someone I wanted, I went for it without any hesitation.

Eva was not like the other women I had encounters with before. She had locs, gold teeth, was heavy set and dressed like a boy. I was still drawn and attracted to her nonetheless. As I began to walk toward her, different guys made their attempts at trying to talk to me and catch my attention. They reached for my hand. They were outspoken in their attempts. Yet, I continued to walk on as if they were not even present - my eyes were set on someone else. My drunken self saw someone attractive, made eye contact and took it upon myself to approach her.

"What's your name?" I asked "Eva." she replied. I flipped out my cell phone and asked her for her phone number. We exchanged phone numbers. As soon as I left the shack of a club we were in, I hopped into Pam's car and called her. I asked her to come see me at Pam's condo that very night.

I was only visiting for the holidays, and had been staying at my sister Crystal's house. Pam's place was the only one I knew of where we could converse at those hours of the night. Eva came out to Pam's house, and we sat in her dining room while I ate my fast food meal. As I was eating, Eva took off my high heel boots, and began to rub my feet. She gazed deeply into my eyes with this look upon her face that captured my heart from that moment on. It was something about her that was intriguing and caused me to want to know more.

Soon, she grabbed me by the hand, lead me into Pam's living room and we began to chat privately. She asked me why did I want her to meet me there and in so many words, what was my agenda. I didn't really have an agenda. I saw someone I was attracted to and walked up to her.

Eventually, we decided our night would not end at Pam's place with a foot rub and conversation. I followed Eva to a hotel. She gave me some lame excuse about why we couldn't go to her place. I didn't even question her any further.

I knew what was about to happen, and so did she. I had had sex with a stranger. I figured this would be like any other time. We would have sex. I would make her want me. Then, I would reject her like I had done with other women I had previous encounters with. I never imagined this one night stand would turn into an emotional roller coaster.

Eva and I began the most toxic love affair I had ever got involved in. At first, nothing seemed wrong. Eva drove, took the train and/or bus to visit me as often as she could while I lived in Carbondale. When she wasn't visiting, we conversed on the phone. We became inseparable since the first night we met. Amari and Eva also got quickly attached to one another. The bond they formed ultimately determined the longevity of the relationship and was the force that put such a hold upon my own happiness.

Eva spoiled me like no other. After only seeing each other for a month, she bought me diamond jewelry, took me shopping and we went on trips to other states I had yet to visit on my own. Eva showered me with gifts, love and affection. She made me feel special. *"She must really care about me! Why else would she buy me all of this stuff?!"* I began to equate love with monetary possessions. Growing up poor caused me to place a high value on monetary things. I connected gifts with love.

The best part, Eva held my hand in public. The first time Eva held my hand in public, we were in a strip club together in St. Louis, Missouri. She met me there, since St. Louis was a halfway point for the two of us. I had gotten so used to going to strip clubs with Tyreese, that I did not mind going with Eva. We didn't even watch the entertainment. She gazed into my eyes, gently grabbed my hands and softly caressed them as she told me how beautiful I was.

Eva acknowledged me in front of the world. That act made me love her even more. She was not new to, nor ashamed of living her lesbian lifestyle freely. I found her openness to be admirable. I desired her more. She was more affectionate and open with me than anyone I had experienced, even my encounters with men. I felt good inside. She made me feel wanted. I didn't see gender with her. I only saw someone who wanted *me.*

Eventually I saw and ignored all the signs which indicated this was not going to be good. The first time Eva and I went on a trip together, we went to Alabama to visit her family. We had only been seeing each other for a little over one month. I felt honored that she wanted to take *me* to meet some of her extended family. *"She must really be serious about me."* I told myself this when she asked me to go with her.

Initially, we had a ball! We ate good food, shared great laughs and danced in various night clubs. Her family was hospitable and kind. They accepted me as their own. However, one night, after me, Eva and her cousin left a nightclub and got inside of the car, I saw Eva nasty side. Her cousin wanted to know why I was doing most of the driving. Eva did not have her driver's license and I shared that with her cousin. I did not see the big deal. I thought this was only temporary. I also did not mind driving since I had not drunk nearly as much as Eva and her cousin did.

"Who the fuck told you to open your mouth?!" Eva shouted at me. I never heard her talk like this before. She usually had a quiet, yet raspy tone of voice. I got a flash back of being back home as a little girl. I had not heard words spoken out of such aggression in so many years. It alarmed me. I pulled over to the side of the road, parked the car and got out. It was late in the middle of the night. The sky was as dark as a fully ripened blackberry. I did not care. I needed to take a walk. I did not know what just happened and was hoping Eva just had a moment.

"Baby I am so sorry. Please come back to the car. My cousin is just nosey, that's all. I didn't mean to talk to you like that." I accepted her apology. We carried on with our trip as if nothing happened. We never brought it back up again.

Unfortunately, as time progressed, I began to see Eva was considered by many as a "ladies' man." Women wanted to converse or be around Eva often. She loved the attention they showed her. When Eva and I first met, I was under the impression she was getting out of a relationship and no longer involved with anyone; making her available to be with me. I did not want to experience any drama like I did when with Lucas. That was not the reality of the situation though.

One night my phone rang, "Where is Eva at?" It was another woman on the line. I had never received a call like this before. I was used to being the one who made these calls when Lucas and I were together. Yet, I had never received a call from another woman inquiring about the whereabouts of *their* mate.

"Who is this?" I questioned, even though I already knew who it was. Since I had been on the other end of the phone before, I already did the math and figured out it was the woman whom Eva claimed she was no longer in a relationship with. "This is her *wife*. I know she's down there with you. You know we still live together right?" My heart dropped down to the bottom of my gut and I began to wonder, *"Were these the lies Lucas used to tell when he was out doing his dirt?"*

Eva was possibly out with another woman, because she surely wasn't with me and she wasn't with her *"wife"* in Springfield. I did not know where she was. Within an instant, I decided not to speak with her anymore and cut her out of my life. I did not want to get involved with another individual who felt they needed more than one woman. I had been down that road once before and discovered it was a dead end. I tried to call her, but as expected, she did not answer. I sent her a text message stating why I could not continue seeing her and wished her luck with who was supposed to be her ex-girlfriend.

Eva was very persistent and convincing. She nearly begged me to continue seeing her and persuaded me to give her another chance. I fell for it. She made me feel wanted when she refused to let me go. I loved the feeling she gave me. Her love, attention and affection was like a drug to me. I became addicted to another human who desperately wanted me in their life. A person who felt they needed me in their life and professed that to me unapologetically.

I had never experienced that before. I figured she must had really cared for me since she expressed those specific words. I did not once consider if the connotation behind the words was genuine or not. I was just happy to hear them. I kept on with our love affair, knowing she was still living with another woman.

I interviewed for a position in Springfield at the county's Juvenile Detention Center. Since I was unable to find a position in my field in Southern Illinois, I figured I would try my luck with moving back to my hometown. I never wanted to return home, but Amari was growing up and I did not have much help in Carbondale. With Lucas living all the way down in Florida and being an inconsistent father, I knew I needed my sister's help. Nearly everyone I was close to moved away and started their lives. I felt it was time for me to do the same.

I also wanted to be closer to Eva. I had every intention of making sure she stayed with me and only me. The only way to ensure this would happen was to reside in the same space. Eva did not seem too thrilled I was planning on moving to Springfield, pending a job offer. She was not totally opposed to it either. She seemed to be on the fence about me moving to Springfield. I began to question if she truly wanted to be with me or not.

For it or against it, I decided I was moving back to Springfield. I was offered the position at the Juvenile Detention Center as a Treatment Specialist. I was beyond ecstatic and finally felt my hard work was not in vain. I had a place lined up for Amari and me to move into. I was convinced I was going to steal Eva right out from that other woman and make her live with me. Although I had a victory in one area of my life, I began to go through a bout of an emotional downfall once I finally moved to Springfield.

Any time we were in public together, Eva watched me very closely, as if she suspected me of looking at other people.

"You like niggas!"

"You're looking at them niggas, ain't you!"

Eva was not educated. She did not even have her GED, so listening to her obscenities was beyond annoying. It was like listening to a child who had not learned how to manage their emotions. Her raspy, child-like voice tone was a nuisance to my ears. Although she was older than me in age, her mentality was very juvenile. Despite the annoyances, she continued to berate me.

"You want to fuck with them niggas, don't you?!"

In confusion, I often responded defensively, "Eva what are you talking about? No one is looking at anybody!" The backlash worsened, it was like living at home with Dad all over again. "You ain't nothing but a hoe!" She always shouted back at me when I tried to defend myself.

I honestly was not looking at any men during the times she hollered these vulgar and demeaning obscenities towards me. After Lucas, I never allowed myself to heal so the last thing I wanted to do was scout out a man. Nonetheless, Eva felt otherwise and had no regard for where we were. Public outburst and embarrassing public scenes became common between us. It was absolutely humiliating and horrifying, but I never stopped her, nor did I leave her. I simply gave my usual response and walked away from her, trying to spare some sort of dignity for myself.

Walking away generally exacerbated the tension that was already present. One night, as Eva and I walked out of a bar she began on her accusation rampage again about me "looking at niggas." This time, I completely ignored her and did not respond. I was tired of defending myself and realized at this point she was doing this out of her own insecurities. I was a beautiful woman, and she feared I would be with a man.

At this point, I wasn't even attracted to men. They disgusted me. I felt all men only wanted one thing, sex. Or, that they were just abusers, cheaters, womanizers and abandoners. When with Eva, I even tried my best to look down at the ground. I wanted her to see I was not looking at anyone else, regardless of their gender. I'd rarely lift my head up to even acknowledge anyone. I was worried I would get accused of "looking at niggas."

I thought by not responding she would stop. I was wrong, it got worse. When I got inside of the car, she pulled my hair and dragged me out of the car from the passenger side. I kicked, screamed, scratched and did whatever possible to get her off me. Finally, one of her friends came and pulled her away from me. A large chunk of my hair went with her. As I threatened to call the police, Eva quickly hopped in the driver seat and pulled off; leaving me in the parking lot stranded and destitute.

Calling the police on Eva was a major threat. Not just out of her own fear of going to jail, but it would expose her "business." When I met Eva, she told me she worked for her mom and babysat for her sister. Her mom was disabled. Therefore, Eva got paid to care for her through a state agency. She also got paid through a state agency to care for her sister's children when her sister was at work. I did not know she was "flipping" checks though.

When I dated Tyreese, it was obvious he sold drugs. He was not employed, but had monetary possessions which required some sort of income to obtain and maintain them. It was not so obvious with Eva. Due to her having two different sources of income, I never suspected her of being a drug dealer; mainly because she was a female. It was not until I started paying more attention to her behaviors and actions that I became suspicious.

Nearly every weekend, Eva had someone rent her a different rental car. She also had very brief and discreet phone calls, always ending with "I'm on my way." There were times where I even accompanied her as she drove to different apartments and houses. Sometimes she stopped at several within a matter of only one hour.

One late afternoon, when I returned to my place after getting off work, Eva was upstairs in my room. Although we were not actually living together, she had a key to my place. Eva had a large amount of cash spread across my bed. I asked her where she got all the money from. She continued counting as she ordered me to "get out" until she was finished. As I began to piece things together, I suspected she was selling drugs. She just tried to hide it from me.

I had all intentions of leaving Eva. Especially when I discovered she had been sleeping with a hammer underneath her pillow. I feared for my life. She told me she put it there just in case she caught me trying to leave her. I then filed a temporary order of protection against her and had her arrested. I finally reached out to some family and friends and told them some of what had been going on. Everyone encouraged me to leave her alone and reminded me of my worth.

This was the first time we broke up for longer than one month. Whenever she was not in my world, I felt like a different woman – a better woman. I regained my will power and strength. I felt my independence return to me and I was on my way to having a better life. I even gave my phone number out to a couple of girls and entertained conversation with them. However, Eva did something I was never used to - she apologized. Again, and again and again.

"Baby, you know I love you."

"I'm so sorry!"

"Please don't leave me, beautiful. I got issues and need help."

"I'm sorry." Out of all the names she had called me to tear me down and the times she was physically violent and abusive toward me, all I heard was, "I'm sorry." The words I yearned to hear my entire life - words of recompense. *"She must really love me, if she's telling me she's sorry. I never even heard Dad say that."* I was slowly beginning to excuse her behavior in exchange for empty "I'm sorry's" and "I love you's."

I felt sorry for her and thought maybe she really did love me since she always came back for me. No one ever apologized for hurting me at this point. I carried these wounds that had never been kissed or bandaged. She bought me jewelry, took me shopping and bought bouquets of flowers to make up for the damage she had done. I continued to place more value on monetary things, identifying them as expressions of love. At those moments, I felt loved and wanted. I was so used to a lifetime of abuse and pain that I held on to the false moment she gave me when she pretended to love and care for me.

This same cycle often repeated itself over and over. One night, when Eva was supposed to come spend the night at my apartment, she never showed up. When she came strolling in early the next morning, reeking of booze, I instantly accused her of being with another woman. She then pointed her finger directly at me, and accused me of being with a man the very night in question.

"Who were you fucking last night?" Her breath reeked of alcohol. It was as if she had just stopped drinking liquor the moment she walked into the door. It was a familiar scent. It reminded me of Dad. "What nigga you have ova' last night?" Her speech was so slurred, she sounded as if her tongue was swollen and she was fighting to properly enunciate her words.

Unable to realize she was trying to shift the blame, I became defensive and told her I was alone and waited on her. She continued with her accusations as she pushed and shoved me around. Worried I was going to be late for work; I quickly grabbed my car keys and ran to my car. Eva chased me down, and told me she was going to drop me off.

When Eva did not have a rental car, she often dropped me off at work and used my car. However, on this day, I did not want her to drop me off. I wanted to drive alone. I wanted to be in peace and pull myself together so that no one at work knew the mess I just came out of. Eva started to yell at me and pointed her finger directly in my face again as I drove down the road. I pushed her hand away from me, asking her to not do that as I drove. That's when the fighting began.

Eva violently pushed my face against the window on the driver's side door. I immediately pulled the car over and parked it. I did not want to get into an accident. Eva pulled the keys out of the ignition. "Now you're not going anywhere, bitch!" I threatened to call the police as usual. Eva got out of the car, threw my keys over the viaduct where we were parked, and began yelling obscenities toward me as she walked down the street. I dialed 911 and waited for them to arrive. I then called my job to inform them that an emergency had arisen and I was going to be late for work. I sat in my car, without any keys, and wept.

Eventually, the local law enforcement got frustrated with my phone calls against her and the fact I never obtained a permanent order of protection against her. They felt I was inflicting this pain upon myself and I should not call them anymore if I wasn't going to leave her for good. I felt maybe one day, she would have gotten arrested too much, and would eventually stop. I was living in denial. These were our patterns. Fight, I'd call the police, break-up, I entertained someone else briefly and then Eva would come begging and pleading for my forgiveness. Then, I took her back. I always took her back.

I even took Eva back after a time she spit on me in my face right in front of Amari. By this time, I knew deep inside I should not and did not need to be with her. I was tired of her treating me like I was worthless. Eva asked me to come pick her up from her mom's house. When I arrived, I could tell she had been drinking. I refused to let her in the car and locked the doors. I had the window rolled down far enough where we could hold a conversation. Eva spat on me after she became so agitated because I refused to let her in the car. "Fuck you bitch! I don't want to get in your car anyways hoe!" I pulled off. I kept a straight face as I used the sleeve of my shirt to wipe her spit off and began singing along with the music on the radio. I did not want to give a reaction for Amari to be overly concerned. He had seen enough.

Not only did Eva verbally, emotionally and physically abuse me, I found out she was cheating on me as well. She was still seeing her ex, whom she had supposedly left to be with me. As foolish as I felt, I stayed. I figured out where she lived by my recollection of Eva going there one day when I first moved back home. She had me stay in the car.

At the time, I did not think anything of it. She was always running in and out of various folk's houses while I sat in the car. I didn't ask any questions. She never had me wait in the car alone for very long at all, literally just a few minutes of a wait. I figured she was just making an exchange. Yet, this apartment stayed on my mind for some reason. I remembered staying in the car longer than usual. Eva was nervous when she returned and defensive when I asked about her taking so long. My intuition hinted to me something was different about this place.

Recalling those memories, one night I decided to drive by to see if the rental car Eva had been driving was parked there. Eva did not answer her phone, and I had been waiting on her for a couple of hours. Eva and I had not established that we were living together, but she spent the night at my apartment quite often; nearly every night. She had some of her belongings at my place and some at her sister's house. One night, I cooked homemade lasagna, garlic bread from scratch and a dessert. She usually came right over as soon as I called letting her know the food was done. This time she was not answering nor returning my phone calls.

I drove over to that very apartment we were at when she had the look of guilt written all over her countenance. My heart was beating so hard I could hear it. I thought it would burst out of my chest and right onto my lap as I was driving. I recognized this feeling. I felt this before, when I was with Lucas. It was déjà vu all over again, except this time I was with a woman.

As I turned the headlights off, and slowly crept around the parking lot of the apartment complex, I saw the rental car Eva had been driving that week. *"Maybe that's a car that just looks like the one she was driving. Rental companies always have duplicate vehicles."* I was trying to convince myself she was not at another woman's house before I assumed anything further. I walked up to the car to peek inside and see if maybe she left anything inside. *"A ball cap! She just had that on the other day, I know that's hers!"*

I became infuriated when I saw her cap sitting on the passenger seat. I quickly ran to the same door she went to, and knocked and banged on it as hard as I could. I had one hand on my hip, while my foot was tapping against the concrete, and muttered every cuss word I could think of under my breath.

"Where's Eva?" *SHE* answered the door with a purple silk robe on. I knew Eva was inside her apartment. "She's not here, she just left." She had a grim smirk upon her face as she appeared to have complete joy in watching me turn red and become even more infuriated with the shenanigans the two of them were playing.

"I just saw her rental car, where the hell did she go?!" I shouted back at her. "I don't know, but she went out the back." She continued to stand in the doorway, smirking as I stood there waiting for Eva to pop out of hiding. I walked off, got in my car, and decided to not contact Eva anymore. After experiencing several similar episodes with Lucas, I did not have the energy or the desire to fight with the girl she was cheating on me with. I just did not think it was worth it.

I had never truly gone without a significant other since Lucas. I managed to hop from relationship or fling to another to keep my mind and heart occupied from the previous situation that did not work out. Eva, however, had this hold on me. It did not matter how bad she hurt me or what she did which defiled every meaning of being loyal and respectful in a relationship. She made me feel wanted and loved each time she repeatedly came back for me, no matter how bad things were or had gotten.

I knew Eva drove rental cars various people rented on her behalf for her, and I seemingly was ok with that. On this day, she was not driving a rental car. The license plates were all too familiar to me; the name of her ex-lover. She fed me a story of how she could not get a rental car because it was too last minute. I knew she was lying, but I did not want to face the truth at the risk of being alone. I also did not want to fight with her. Whenever she was in the wrong, she had a way of trying to turn things back around on me. She loved to accuse me of false things. This usually was followed with being talked down to and her putting her hands on me.

Instead, I went along with it - hurt and all. She continued to drive her ex lover's car sporadically. She had a newer car than me at the time. I felt less than her. I had identified my self-worth through material possessions and if I had a significant other, regardless if they were good to me or not. If someone was there, I felt worthy and loved.

What I considered normalcy, a healthy person would consider chaos and dysfunction. I allowed myself to become content in being disrespected, physically and verbally abused, controlled, manipulated, treated less than my worth and brainwashed. I succumbed to daily put-downs, mind games and antics which kept me inside of a box and isolated from the world. I convinced myself that at least I knew what I was dealing with in terms of Eva. Nothing was coming as a surprise after a while. At least I knew Eva was always going to say she was sorry and come back.

I often felt as if I had to walk on egg shells around Eva. I was scared to speak my mind or relax in fear if it would upset her or cause an argument. She even questioned me when I wanted to spend time with my friends, asking if there were going to be men around or not. Eva was very suspicious of everyone I knew, friends included. She felt that my girlfriends were trying to "hook me up with some nigga." Anytime I went somewhere without her, I was accused of secretly "meeting up with some nigga."

One night, I went to hang out with Monique downtown. Somehow, Eva knew we were downtown as she randomly showed up outside of a bar we were about to go into. "You're going in there to fuck niggas!" She shouted as she sped off. I was beyond humiliated. The only response I could offer Monique was that "she was crazy."

Eva's strange behaviors persisted. She drove past my sisters' or friends' houses when I was there visiting them. It was as if she knew my every move, before I even knew it myself. Sometimes I walked into a store, and she was already there, staring at me. Looking at me in such a way as if she wanted me to know she was watching me.

If Eva did not know where I was, she texted and called repeatedly until I answered. She questioned me over the phone about my whereabouts and if there was a man around. If I did not answer, she left cruel and hateful voice messages and text messages on my phone. She told me I "wasn't shit" and that she was "going to get me" when she saw me. She was everywhere. My life was no longer my own. She owned me now. It had gotten to a point where it was easier to deal with her if I was at home and away from the world I had once known.

When I did try to hang out with my girlfriends, Eva ruined it by causing a dramatic scene which usually ran my friends off. One of my most horrifying experiences was on my birthday. One of my good friends I met in college, Olivia, came to visit and celebrate my birthday with me. The first night was fine. I suspect because Eva was at the same nightclub with us, making it easy for her to keep her eyes on me. However, the following night was awful.

By this time, Eva and I had moved in together into a small two-bedroom bungalow house. It was raining so hard outside; there was mud all around the yard and driveway. Eva had already begun drinking. I thought she was in a good mood. She was laughing and joking with me and Olivia. Olivia and I had gotten all dolled up and were ready to drive to St. Louis to have a great time. As soon as Eva saw me after I changed, her entire demeanor changed.

Eva glared at me as if I was her world's worst enemy. She had so much hate in her eyes I felt she was cutting straight through me like a dagger stabbing a heart. "Where the fuck you think you're going?" I was so excited to wear the new dress I had bought to celebrate my birthday. I hid it so that Eva could not find it. There were times she saw what I wanted to wear and hid it from me so I could not go out. Eva always acted jealous when I got dolled up. She accused me of either "looking at niggas" or wanting to "fuck niggas." I just wanted to look nice and feel good about myself.

This night was my worst nightmare. As Olivia and I ignored Eva drunken attacks, we walked outside to get inside of the car to leave. Eva suddenly came dashing out of the front door. She picked up a handful of mud and threw it at me. I was devastated. My dress had been ruined. My night was ruined. My birthday was ruined.

As usual, I threatened to call the police and Eva fled the scene. I sobbed and apologized profusely to Olivia. I was beyond mortified and felt stupid she witnessed one of Eva' rampages. Olivia did not once judge or ridicule me. She did not even want to talk about it. She encouraged me to change clothes. I cleaned myself up. I found a different outfit to wear and Olivia and I still went to St. Louis as originally planned.

I slowly began to convince myself that the abuse I received from Eva was not as bad as the abuse I endured as a child from Dad. I eventually told myself that Eva' abusive, manipulative and controlling tactics meant she really did love me. I told myself that she wanted me all to herself, because she cared for me and did not want anyone else to have me. I told myself this, to justify her actions and the reasoning as to why I stayed with her.

As time progressed, I began to fight back. Even though Eva was larger than I was in size, I was taller than her. I thought about the times I wished Mom defended herself against Dad. I told myself next time Eva put her hands on me, that I was going to defend myself. I did; repeatedly so. There was a time I was so tired of Eva talking down to me and putting her hands on me that I completely blacked out. When I came to, all I heard was, "Casandra! Casandra! I am not your dad! I am not your dad!" Eva had my arms restrained. She said we were arguing, and suddenly I began hitting her, as hard as I could.

Although I did not show this, I was glad I defended myself. The look of fear upon her face was priceless. She seemed to be confused that this pretty woman, who she thought was timid and gullible, had hit her. In a way, I felt as if I got some sort of revenge.

As I continued to fight back and defend myself, Eva began to lay off on being physically violent and aggressive toward me. The hateful words did not stop though. She also began running around town with different women. Just like I did with Lucas, I went through Eva' phone. She had been conversing with a few different women and even slept with a couple.

After a while, I became numb to the unhealthy nature of our relationship. I began to become financially dependent on Eva. Lucas was not only inconsistent in how often he saw Amari, but he was also inconsistent with financially helping me take care of Amari. All I had to do was ask and Eva gave me anything. I convinced myself I was not getting her drug money, rather her earnings from her paychecks. I let Eva buy my love. The cost for me was pain, as I relived the experiences of a little girl who once dreamt of the day she would be able to leave her parent's house. I was now living that same misery as an adult.

Not only was I in an abusive and unhealthy relationship, but also experienced scrutiny and ridicule from people who were supposed to be my friends, members of the community, co-workers and random strangers. Whispers and backlash about my sexual orientation were more prevalent at the onset of my relationship with Eva. It was obvious we were in a romantic relationship. She was very butch and dressed like a boy. I, however, still appeared like any other feminine woman.

Gawking, laughs, smirks, scowls, and other unfavorable gestures became expected and normal remarks from others. People glared at us when we were in the grocery store. I saw girls whisper and laugh at us when we entered heterosexual bars or other establishments. Family and friends continued to tell me how I needed to leave her alone. That I was, "too pretty to be with a woman."

I was judged for being in a relationship with a woman. *"They just don't understand. She loves me! No one else is going to love me the way she does."* I felt no one understood that I just wanted to be loved. Eva was showing me what I thought was love. I didn't want to let that go. I feared I would never find anyone else to love me.

Eva often told me that they were all just jealous of me because they did not have "true love" like we did. She caused me to believe that our love was real and that everyone else wanted what we had. Eva also constantly reminded me of my past and what I had been through. She reaffirmed how men would never treat me right so I shouldn't try to be with one.

"Your dad and cousins treated you like shit!"

"Your baby daddy left you to raise Amari by yourself!"

"All niggas want to do is fuck you. They don't even love you!"

"That's how they all are. No man will ever treat you right!"

By this time, I was in such a state of confusion, I did not know who or what to believe or think.

Restless nights and crying spells were taking over daily. As each year passed, I felt like I was diminishing from the person I once was and slowly turning into a woman I did not know. My life was slipping away from me, moment by moment, month by month, year by year. I had become so entangled in Eva' web she called love, that I feared no other would love me. So, I stayed. Though I loved her, deep down inside of my heart I knew this wasn't right or good for me. In fact, it was completely unhealthy, unethical and risked potential damage to my son's development.

Although Eva was more like a second parent to Amari, I did not want this toxic environment to have an adverse impact on his life. Don't get me wrong, Eva was very good to Amari. She treated him as her own. Amari was only 4 years old when I met her. They created a bond which seemed to be unbreakable. She felt bad for Amari not having his dad around. Eva was loving and kind toward Amari, and bought him anything he needed or wanted. Yet it was at the sacrifice of my own happiness

She babysat while I worked nontraditional hours at the detention center. I was never worried or concerned about Amari being mistreated by Eva. She loved kids and adored Amari more. She often referred to him as her son. I felt she loved him more than she loved me. At the time, I considered that a good thing.

Yet, it was made clear, quite often, how I did not want Amari to grow up the way I did. I never wanted him to feel the way I felt and ultimately end up scarred the way I was. I also did not want Amari to be in an environment which could ultimately subject him to things that could cause him to make poor choices in the future. Our morals and values just weren't the same.

Eva thought it was okay to sell drugs. Her family had done it, was still doing it and they even taught her how to do it. She thought it was a necessary means of survival. I often encouraged her to go back to school, get her education and possibly learn a trade. She promised she would "one day," but I think she was too caught up in the lifestyle. The lifestyle of quick money, flashy clothes and jewelry and getting with women she could splurge on seemed to be more important to her than the risk she was taking of obtaining those things.

I felt like a hypocrite. Here I was, going to mentor and teach troubled youth on how to stay out of the criminal justice system. I harped on the importance of getting an education and working so that they could become productive members of society. However, when I got off work, I went home to an abusive drug dealer.

I often asked myself why I still allowed this nonsense to go on? I was no longer the child stuck at home with no way out. I could make my own decisions and change my environment.

"What is this hold she has over me that continues to make me feel stuck with no way out?"

I began begging and pleading to God for strength, a way out, to help me and remove all fear within me. My soul desired peace. I had stopped going to church, because I got tired of being judged and ridiculed by members. As each year progressed, nearly everyone in the community knew I was with a woman. If I wanted to get my spirit strengthened and renewed, I had to call on God for myself, at home in the state I was in.

I told God I could not do anything without Him. I needed help and strength from the Most High. No one on this earth could help me or give me the right words to convince me to leave, but deep inside I desperately wanted to.

"God, please!"

"Please, God give me strength!"

"Help me Lord!"

"I need you to help me please!"

These were my daily cries and pleas to God. I didn't know what else to ask, but to plead for help. I knew I needed Him and Him alone to pull me out of the mess I was in. I needed Him to make me whole again. I needed God to strengthen me from the top of my head to the soles of my feet. I needed God to help me live!

I was reliving my childhood. The chains and cycles of abuse, dysfunction and chaos followed me into my adulthood. I was Mom now - a battered woman. One who was desperately seeking a way out, but fearful of the unknown. I was unsure if I would ever find love or be loved again. I dreaded the very thought of being alone and having to raise Amari alone. Eva had become such a financial crutch for me, I was scared I would not be able to care for Amari independently. I had been with Eva for nearly four years by this point and felt my life was already mapped out for me. I was a miserable woman in a horrible situation, feeling there was no way out.

CHAPTER THIRTEEN

Nervous Breakdown

Depression seemed to follow me throughout life. It was as if a dark shadow was forever present, planning the perfect opportunity to take over me. Once the shadow came upon me, my mind felt as if someone had a hold on it. Thoughts of self-hatred worsened. I felt less than and unworthy of love. This detrimental combination sent me down to a dark place that disabled my normal way of living. Sleepless nights, being unable to work and a lack of motivation to do anything other than lay around all day was all I knew.

These roadblocks caused a constant detour in the progression of my internal growth. I had come to the realization that one's outer appearance was just an illusion. One that individuals set upon a pedestal, to cause people to become infatuated with this false ideology to distract them from truth and one's inward self. I had been presumed as the one who had it all together; beautiful, educated, driven and having the strength of the Most High on my side. Yet, no one saw the internal poison that was eating away at my emotional, mental and spiritual state.

My primary physician recommended I take something for the recurring chronic depression I had been experiencing. I had frequent nightmares of my childhood which caused sleepless nights. I also wanted to spend most my time sleeping all day, to not have to live through or face that day. It was easier to sleep the day away, rather than face anything. She prescribed an anti-depressant, Celexa. This was a new medication I had never tried. I hoped this one would work; however, it was similar to most of the other anti-depressants I had been prescribed. I was in a constant state of unawareness; feeling like a zombie if you will.

It was early in the afternoon, Eva and I were arguing as usual. Arguing between the two of us was not the normal bickering of two sides wanting to be right. It consisted of hollering and yelling at the top of our lungs. Screaming out the most hateful obscenities one could blurt out in the heat of the moment in attempts to win the debate.

It was already embarrassing she did this in public, in front of strangers, with no regard for my reputation as a public servant. It was even worse when she did this in front of family or friends. April had just got out of the hospital from having surgery. She stayed with us for a few days since she had stairs in her apartment and my home was a small one story bungalow. Eva did not care though. The arguing persisted as she continued to yell degrading names at me.

I was frustrated and exhausted with the constant arguing between the two of us. She mentioned she was going to pack her belongings and leave. I went blank; mind, body and soul. Nothing of importance had the opportunity to enter my mind. Not even Amari. I didn't even think about the fact that I was a mother, a daughter, a sister, etc. I could not think, at all.

I began to take the prescribed Celexa, pill by pill by pill. As I continued to consume each pill, one after the other, the pill bottle was close to being empty. I succumbed to a distracted state of mind as I lied upon the faux cheetah fur blanket while dazing at the ceiling. Thoughts of death and escaping my lifetime of pain swarmed about in my mind. I replayed every negative experience, heartbreak, and disappointment as I wished and willed for my life to end.

Eva ran into the bedroom and realized what happened. She immediately began to search for the pill bottle, "How much did you take, Casandra?!" I heard her, but I was disoriented at the same time. By this time, April sent me a text message stating, "Let me know how it goes. Next time come talk to me. But I feel like I'm a kid at home again. Don't want this to follow the kids like it did me." I was disturbed by her response when Eva informed her I was going to the hospital.

Since it was below 20 degrees and snowy outside, Eva went outside to start the car, as Amari and I got our coats and boots on. We drove to Eva's sister's house and had Amari visit with her while Eva drove me to the emergency room. I am still shocked Eva did not get pulled over since she was driving so fast.

As soon as we arrived, the nurse at the front desk asked what my emergency was. "I-I-I took more than ten Celexa," I stuttered in response. The nurse immediately asked me to step behind the nurse's station and began to check my vital signs. By this time, I was becoming confused and unaware of my surroundings. One minute I was laying on a gurney in the emergency room, and the next minute I was waking up to an I.V in my left arm, bright lights shining in my eyes, a nasal cannula (in laymen's terms, an oxygen tube) in my nostrils and a strange voice calling my name. I was delirious and frightened, unaware of what was happening and why.

"You had a grand mal seizure," one of the nurses told me. Eva sat to the right of me as I saw worry and fear in her eyes. She had witnessed everything. "How bad was it? How bad was it?" I repeated until someone responded to me. The only piece of information that was provided for me next was that I was going to the Intensive Care Unit (ICU). I knew Monique worked there. That news was a relief. Someone I knew, was close to and grew up with could watch over me. That was unquestionably alleviation within itself.

I later found out Eva texted Monique to notify her I would be coming to the hospital and why. I was surprised by this, since Monique was one of my friends who disapproved of my homosexual lifestyle and made it quite known. She also expressed her dislike for Eva and Eva was aware. Nonetheless, Eva must had felt the urgency to put her personal feelings to the side and inform Monique of the news.

I repeatedly asked Eva "how bad was it? How bad was it?" I experienced seizures in the past; however, I never had a seizure that knocked me unconscious. I was extremely inquisitive about the details of the incident. I felt very loopy and it seemed everything I experienced at that moment was occurring in clips or scenes, as if in a movie. I could recall one of the nurses asking me if I had ever cut myself before. I assumed they saw the cuts on both of my wrists during my seizure. I began cutting myself again while in a relationship with Eva to make myself feel better.

I told them the truth, "yes, I've cut myself." *Why lie,* I thought to myself. I'm already in here for overdosing on Celexa, so what's the point of lying. "They saw your arms," Eva whispered to me.

The taste of the charcoal was beyond disgusting. The nurse told me it would coat my stomach. It was more like drinking a charcoal milkshake. My eyes became heavy and my limbs became weak; before I knew it, I was out of the emergency room and in the ICU. I felt delirious and wondered what exactly was going on. Soon I saw Monique. She was beginning her shift. She watched after me during my time in the ICU, or at least until her shift was over. She later informed me she pretended to not know me so she could keep an eye on me.

I slept like a baby. So much so, I was moved to another room, and completely oblivious to the move. I felt so absent-minded. Not feeling I was inside of my own body. It seemed as if I was on the outside looking in at myself and observing my actions. Eva never left my side, morning, afternoon, or evening, she was there. She watched over me, assuring I was going to get better. When she wasn't at the hospital, she cared for Amari. She made sure he was fed, bathed, and dressed. She took him to school and rushed back to check on my status. When Amari's school day ended, Eva left to pick him up and take him to a family member's house. She never revealed to Amari why I was in the hospital, she just told him "your mom is sick." And for that, I was truly appreciative for not infecting his mind with information he did not need to know.

When Eva returned, three doctors in white "SIU Psychiatry" jackets sat before me. Each of them had a clip board in their arms and a look of seriousness upon their faces. The older man with the gray beard did most of the talking. "Do you know why you are here?" He had little concern in his tone. "Yes," I replied. "I took pills." There was a moment of silence as the doctors and I starred at one another. "Do you know you scared your partner?" I sat silently with a blank look upon my face.

I really, truly did not know how to respond. I don't think it crossed my mind that she would be scared; or anyone for that matter. I think I was too consumed in how *I* was feeling. Before long, they informed me that I was going to the 10th floor (the Psychiatry unit), by voluntary admission. I honestly did not remember consenting to such a thing. I was so medicated at the time, they could have told me anything and I would have believed it.

Surprisingly, I was not nervous about going up there. Commonly, when one thinks of a mental institution or a psychiatric facility; calmness and a worry-free mind are not what originally surface. However, I felt maybe that was a place I needed to go for the time being to resolve some hidden issues or learn how to deal with those issues. Either way, I knew that checking into a psychiatric unit was not a determent for me and may even be beneficial.

My last day in the ICU, was to be my first day in the psychiatric unit. I was calm and curious. I wondered if I was going to see the stereotypical "crazy looney-tunes," as often portrayed on T.V, or if all of that was just a figment of my imagination. Clearly, I soon realized that these people were no different than me. We were all human beings, trying to survive in this cruel and unusual world, and make it without being deeply harmed or affected by the actions of others.

I was quiet and observant on the first day. I took everything in and did not divulge much of myself to be dissected. The gist of what I discovered was that people were either admitted to get a refill on their medication, depressed and lonely, or like myself, depressed and attempted suicide. Either way, all of us had something in common and possessed no reason to judge one another.

I only had a roommate my first day there. She was an older Caucasian lady who was probably old enough to be my grandmother. She expressed to me how she was there because she had severe depression. I felt sorry for her. Eva was constantly coming to visit me, while this poor lady had no visitors and sobbed often. She didn't say much to me and vice versa. Most of the time I spent there, I slept. If I wasn't eating, or visiting with Eva, I slept. I did not see the point in doing anything else. The entire facility had cameras, even in my room. I did not feel comfortable doing anything other than that.

My first night there, I was awakened by two of the nurses injecting liquid medication through my IV and putting padding and a bell around my bed. It was just in case I had another seizure. Luckily, I fell back to sleep. When I woke up in the morning I felt out of it and not in my right mind. I knew it had to have been the medications which caused my mind and body to suddenly feel this way.

A team of doctors came into my room to talk with me. The Asian doctor reminded me once again how frightened Eva was and did I really understand the seriousness of my actions. Some of the medication wore off and I could answer the questions with more of a sound mind. I briefly explained my history of abuse I experienced as a child and how it still affects me today. The doctor went on to explain how I took a large amount of Celexa, how bad the seizure was and wondered if I was in my right mind to go back home. Of course, I was not discharged to go home. However, I did inform them that I desired to go home as soon as possible for the sake of my son, my partner, and job.

By my second day in the psychiatric unit, I was sick and tired of the IV being in my arm. I was beyond pestering the staff of when they were going to remove it. Eventually, one of the nurses, who happened to be an African American, removed it. I had full use of my left arm again.

My last night there, Eva brought a new pajama set and hair products. She waited for me to shower so she could grease my scalp and comb my hair. As I got ready to get into the shower, I spaced out and forgot to take off my bra. I realized what I had done when I tried to wash under my arms and saw the pit of the bra blocking my way. I knew the medications caused me to have an altered state of mind. After the shower, Eva greased and combed my hair as she promised. She then left to pick up Amari from Crystal's place to go home.

That night I tossed and turned, with aches and pains roaming about my body. My back felt like a dagger was stuck inside of it and my legs were in excruciating pain. In the morning, I was awakened by a nurse telling me my breakfast had arrived. I did not have an appetite but, I knew I was going to try to go home that very day. Therefore, I ate the vegetarian omelet and took the medication as directed. I laid back down in my room and waited for the doctors to arrive.

The doctor already knew how enthusiastic I was about wanting to be discharged to go home. Unfortunately, he was not sure if I was ready or did I need more treatment. Considering I had overdosed on my depression medication, went into a serious seizure in the ER and had scars of cutting myself on both wrists were not good factors to support my case. Luckily, if I promised to go to therapy and take my medication, they promised to discharge me that afternoon. I called Eva as soon as I was aware of the great news. "I'm getting discharged today babe! Come get me!" I exclaimed in excitement.

The doctor that discharged me explained how imperative it was I go to therapy and continue to take my medication. I could tell by the look on his face he did not want to discharge me. However, I was not going to cooperate with the doctors and the nurses in the unit any longer. I was tired of being awakened out of my sleep while they injected liquid medications into the IV. I was tired of having an altered state of mind and I did not feel like my usual self.

When Eva arrived to take me home I was ecstatic. I had never been so ready to go home in my life! Eva was happy I was coming home as well. I was even happier about being able to see Amari soon. He was still in school, so I figured by the time he got off the bus I would have pulled myself together and wouldn't appear ill to my son.

When we left the hospital, I realized I had gotten paid that day. So, I had Eva take me around to pay bills and tend to other business matters that were neglected while I was in the hospital. Out of nowhere I began to weep and cry. I screamed out all the pain I felt and had been holding inside. I felt courage and strength consume me. These feelings were new and once seemed unreachable.

For most of my life, I was terrified at the very thought of spilling every emotion, heart break, and tear that was experienced over those several years. As Eva and I drove along, and I began to empty out everything I ever felt inside, tears began to wash away the pain that was buried for decades. *Ahhhh*, it was a fresh new feeling that overwhelmed my inner-self with relief.

"I want to go to my dad's house now!" I exclaimed tearfully. "Are you sure babe, you just got out of the hospital. Are you sure you're ready to talk right now?" Eva replied with a concerned tone of voice. "Take me now!" I yelled. If I didn't know anything else at that moment, or in my life for that matter, I knew I was ready to face Dad and everything that happened to me as a child. I knew God was with me and I didn't have to be afraid anymore. Dad was no longer the giant in my eyes that could beat me or terrify me. I was an adult now. I let my past haunt me for too long and it was time for it to stop. It was time to bury the horrific events that followed me for too long.

"Mom, is Dad at home?"

"I want to talk to him and no one is answering the door." Mom was at work as usual, so I called her to see where he was.

"What's wrong, sweetie?" I balled and cried out like a new born baby everything I had been holding inside and blew away on the white seeds.

I told Mom of the times Brian molested me and Ebony played her *"game"* with me at Madea and Papa's house. There was a moment of silence. "That's why I never wanted you girls to go over there unless I was there with you." She then gave me Dad's cell phone number and told me to call him. I quickly dialed Dad's number and told him I needed to talk to him. "Alright," was his shortened response. He told me he would be home in about 20 minutes. I told him I would come back to the house around then. Eva and I drove around and I told her everything I planned on telling Dad.

"It's time! It's time!" I kept repeating to her. I knew today was the day I could release everything and not hold anything back. I would no longer be bound by the afflictions of my past. I was going to be set free and able to move forward with the rest of my life. I allowed my past to eat me alive as I buried the memories, scars, and heartbreaks deep inside of me. Burying those issues only caused more difficulties. I knew within minutes, I was going to begin my process of healing and able to face my past and let it go. I wanted to live a new life.

Despite my optimistic attitude for an optimal outcome, I still let the negative thoughts creep in to contaminate the positivity.

"What if he's not receptive to what I have to say?"

"Or tries to deny everything and place the blame on somebody else?"

So many thoughts raced about in my mind. My heart was beating faster than a drum, and my palms were beginning to sweat out of nervousness of what was about to take place. I knew, no matter what the outcome, that I had to do this. It wasn't about him and his feelings, it was about me, my healing and learning how to let go, so I could forgive.

CHAPTER FOURTEEN

Loose Ends

Random thoughts endlessly raced about in my mind. I was unsure of what the outcome would be. I convinced myself to remove any expectations I had. I did not want to be disappointed by not receiving a desired outcome. I persuaded myself that regardless of how the conversation between Dad and I turned out, I was going to forgive, heal and move forward with my life.

As we drove up to the house, Dad paced back and forth on the front porch. I knew he was waiting for me to arrive. Eva walked me up to the house and sat on the porch while Dad and I went inside of the house. I was about to tell Dad everything I had ever felt and ask him, *"why"* in the very house I grew up in and where the abuse occurred. I never imagined this day would happen.

As I sobbed hysterically with tears running down the sides of my cheeks and snot running over my lips. In desperation, I asked why he did not come to the hospital to check on me.

"Why is it that Mom and Eva were the only people who came to see about me?" I continued to weep.

"What did I ever do to any of you, for ya'll not to come and check on me while I was in critical condition?! I had a seizure that knocked me unconscious and I was admitted into the Psychiatric unit on the 10th floor!"

I continued to cry out and expressed everything I had ever experienced, how I felt about it, and how it affected me still in the present day.

"I remember everything! How you used to beat on Mom and me! I used to be so afraid of you, but I'm not scared of you anymore!"

I recalled the several times I went to track meets and practices with band aids taped across my bruises and scratches he inflicted upon me, so that no one noticed. I reminded him of the time he picked me up by my neck and hung me eye to eye with the ceiling fan that was right above us, as it was moving in motion. I thought I was going to lose my head at that moment. So many scenes and emotions ran through my mind and inner-being. So much so, I was unable to grab a hold of them individually and verbalize them. I sobbed. Flashbacks of the painful memories which tragically affected my adult life continued to speedily run through my mind.

I told him about the times Brian molested me and Ebony played her "game" at Madea and Papa's house on Adams Street.

"See no one told me about it!"

"I know their mother didn't know about that, Jesus Christ!" He shook his head in shame and disappointment.

"I didn't know anything about that! I'm so sorry you had to go through that alone." He constantly repeated, like a broken record. Dad appeared to be devastated as I recalled the memories that scarred my mind and pierced my heart.

"I'm sorry. I thought you didn't want me around. No one ever tells me anything." Dad repeated these words a few times after I asked why he was never there.

"Track practice, meets, music performances, graduations, in the hospital...my life....it all mattered!" I cried out.

"I have cancer in my stomach." Dad belted out.

"I have a lot of health problems, but I can't fix any of them because I do not have any insurance." He attempted to use as an excuse.

I was not expecting anything out of this conversation. I figured if I went in with no expectations, I would not be disappointed. I was not complaining. Rather more in shock of the facial expressions and words that uttered through his lips. "I want to repair this," my eyes grew wide and I just stared at him with confusion. Something I've yearned for my entire life was being offered to me, right here, right now, and it wasn't me saying this. I was excited, grateful and at a loss for words.

For at least a minute there was nothing but silence that filled the room. I briefly stared at the ground and then would occasionally glance back up at Dad to see what the expressions on his face were. I never imagined in my wildest dreams, that I would have the courage and the opportunity to confront Dad with everything I had been holding inside of my mind and heart for all those years. Better yet, I never thought I would ever get an apology. I used to think I would be overlooking him in his casket after he died, devastated that I was never able to express how I felt, and just ask *"why."*

"I'm not scared of you anymore!"

"I used to be so scared of you, but I'm not now and I refuse to let my past continue to haunt me."

He continued to stare at me with an arid look upon his face. The fact I had the courage and the ability to stand before this man I once was terrified of and hated at the same time, felt as if something were removed from my soul that was trying to eat me alive. I stood up for myself in the best way I could ever imagine. It felt exhilarating!

I checked the time and realized Amari was getting out of school soon. Dad mentioned that he and Mom would stop by and visit more often, and try to be more involved in our lives. That was joy to my ears. He then hugged and embraced me as if I was his long lost prodigal daughter who had finally reunited with her family. I sobbed in his arms, as I felt closeness and love as one. At this moment, I forgave. I forgave Dad for being the first man to break my heart. I released the pain through the tears which landed upon his chest.

As I walked out of the front door and stood on the front porch, Dad looked me in my eyes, and asked me with concern "do you drink?" "Sometimes," I casually responded. "Don't drink, because your dad is an alcoholic," he proclaimed before me. "Okay" was the only response I could mumble out. I was humbled by his confession as I continued to walk down the steps and walked to the car.

Eva smiled, mostly because the conservation did not end up as WWIII. In that instant, I thanked God verbally and internally from the depths of my being. That was a moment of clarity in my life, where I felt with deep conviction, *"there is a God!"* God spared my very life; He gave me one more chance to change my life around; and for that I was truly grateful for His love and mercy. Most importantly, I was thankful God let me hear the words I yearned to hear my entire life… *"I'm sorry."*

I finally got to a place of humbleness and expressed myself to someone who tortured my mind, body, and self-esteem. I stood up to Dad, and he humbled himself enough to say "sorry." That was enough closure for me. From that moment on, I felt like I could literally touch the stars. I no longer had to wake up in cold sweats from nightmares of Dad beating on me or Mom. Or allow ancient thoughts to haunt my mind that affected my daily life. I was free, to say the least, and that was a feeling which remains indescribable.

I began journaling everything I had experienced. I wanted to get everything out in desperation to heal and change. I knew writing my thoughts, feelings, hurts, pain and everything in between down on paper symbolized me releasing my past. I was ready to take steps toward my future. Writing everything down was one of those steps.

One morning April came by and I decided to share what I had written thus far. As I sat and read aloud what I had written thus far, April had a stale look upon her face. I ignored the stares and continued to read on until I reached the point I last left off at. I thought reading to her would make her proud, or realize the obstacles I had hurdled and how I was still standing today –alive and well. This very situation is why I usually tend to hope for the best and expect the worst. Not only did she not apologize for not once coming to visit me in the hospital, she criticized me and boldly stated how I "fell off." {In reference to living like a Christian} I was exasperated!

"You know… me and Crystal were just talking about all of this."

"How when you were in Carbondale you were so saved and involved in the church."

"You made me want to get my life together."

I glanced back and forth from making casual facial remarks at Eva and looking at April confused. I was upset, but didn't dare let it show. I kept thinking to myself, *"shouldn't they be more concerned of what drove me to the point of wanting to take my own life? Or better yet, offer a positive, more uplifting conversation that may have helped me?"* I listened as she ranted and then announced it was getting late and time for me to go home to rest.

Eva defended me and my situation before we left.

"She was away from here, and didn't have to face anything while she was down there." "She made a new life for herself and had a new support system."

"She also experienced a lot of 'church hurt' while down there."

I was greatly appreciative of the defense she put up on my behalf. She also proved a point of mine, without me having to verbalize it myself. I was just another human being, who experienced trials and tribulations in life. I found unhealthy ways to cope with the pain. I felt judged by my own sister. It hurt beyond expression.

My conversation with Crystal went differently. She spoke of her and April's conversations about me in regards to the day I was hospitalized. "She told me you were reminding her of how it was at home." Crystal went on to tell me the rest of April's accusations toward me. I explained to Crystal everything that took place that day that I could recall; even when Eva reached out to April out of concern.

Crystal began to look at me with a twinkle in her eye, as if she were becoming emotional, and sat quietly while I finished telling her what happened that day.

"So, she knew all day?!"

"I had been talking to her all day, and she never said anything like that!"

"She is so stupid!"

"I can't believe her!"

"I can't believe she didn't tell me!"

"All she did was talk about you, that's it!"

Crystal was extremely upset about the news she just heard. She was left in the dark about the entire situation and did not appreciate the fact I was in such critical condition and she did not know as soon as everyone else knew. Crystal told me April called her that day and not once mentioned I had overdosed on my depression medication and was being rushed to the E.R. She was devastated about the news.

I was deeply hurt and once again felt those childhood feelings of *"no one cares"* and *"I'm the black sheep of the family."* I left shortly after our brief discussion. From that moment on, I concluded that I was no longer going to strive for success in my life to prove something to Dad and family. Rather, I was going to strive to grow stronger individually, internally, mentally, physically and spiritually. I was driven by anger and resentment most of my life. It was the fuel which propelled me into achieving things. I no longer wanted to be driven by hate and anger. I wanted to learn how to love and forgive, and use that as my new motivation in life.

I still had not talked with Mom. I called her to tell her I was home. She stated she would be on her way shortly. Eva offered to take Amari for a car ride to allow Mom and I some privacy to talk. Since I knew Mom read often, I felt compelled to have her read to herself what I had written thus far. I watched her read as she occasionally made minor grammatical corrections. Tears ran down the sides of her cheeks as she read what her first born daughter experienced.

"I'm so sorry honey!" she cried out to me.

"I never trusted anyone, that's why I didn't want to put you girls in daycare."

"You were always so precious to me."

"I thought your dad loved you and would protect you girls."

"I knew I was living in hell, but I had no idea..." She continued to weep as she held my hand and used her available hand to wipe her tears.

"I was molested by an older male cousin, so I never wanted you girls going to Madea's or Papa's because you had older male cousins."

"I just never felt comfortable or trusted any males around you girls."

She continued...

"I'm so sorry you had to go through that sweetheart."

"I hate you never felt you could come talk to me and tell me."

"I failed you as a mother, and all I can say is I am truly sorry." Mom went on to say how she regretted missing out on my childhood years, which is why she made attempts to stay more active in her grandkid's lives.

"I wish you would've told me, things would've been different."

"I wouldn't have stayed."

"I stayed and put up with your dad because he was you girls' dad and I thought he was protecting you." We sat quietly in my living room as Mom continued to hold my hand. Mom's face was cherry red and she had tears running down her face. I didn't know what to say, or to think for that matter. I never knew she didn't know. *"How could she not know?!"* I thought to myself. For so long, I blamed and hated her, all because I thought she knew without doing anything about it. It was hard for me to believe Mom *did not know*. I thought about the time we walked from Madea's house after the police took us over there earlier that day, or the times I begged and pleaded for Mom to leave to Dad. *"How could she not know?!"* I continued to ask myself.

I felt awkward as Mom kissed me and hugged me. She had never been so affectionate toward me and I didn't know how to react or accept it for that matter. My body was stiff as I sat with a confused expression upon my face. *"Is this really happening?"* I thought to myself as Mom cried out to me and held my hand as if she never wanted to let go. I never thought this moment would come. I felt like it was Deja vu all over again. First, I had talked to Dad and confronted him of how he treated me and made me feel. Now I was facing my mother and doing the same.

I cried out everything else I ever felt. I showed her my scars on both wrists from me cutting myself. "Do you know why you cut yourself?" she asked in concern. "Yes," I quickly responded. "It felt better to cut myself and feel the physical pain I inflicted upon myself; rather than to face the pain I endured for all of those years." I told her I wished she would've just left him. Yet after talking with her, I realized she didn't think she needed to. It seemed she truly felt she was staying with him for the sake of her children.

I still could not come to terms with what Mom said. It was hard for me to decipher if she was being genuine or not. I did not have the same feeling with Mom as I did with Dad. I felt Dad was genuine with his apology. I did not care anymore. I was no longer going to look to Mom for answers. I already made up my mind I was going to forgive her.

"Well I better get going so Amari can go to bed, I know he has school in the morning." Mom gave me a hug, apologized one more time, and let me know she loved me. "I will never judge you; you can always come and talk to me, okay sweetie." She then walked out the door. As Mom walked out of the door, I felt the rage and grief I once felt toward her leave out of the door with her. I forgave Mom.

Only God knows the emotions and thoughts which ran through Mom. As a mother, I could not imagine the pain that she felt; she unable to protect her kids. She did what any other mother would have done; trusted the father to help raise his kids. She never anticipated he would be an abuser who would scar his oldest daughter's mind and heart for years to follow. At that moment, I thought, *"I don't know whose pain runs deeper; me or Mom's..."*

"I FEEL FREE!!" I exclaimed after leaving the hair salon. For once in my life, I felt free. I had just gotten 6 inches of my hair cut and it felt great. I had all the processed and relaxed portions of my hair cut off. I had a little red afro. My hair had never felt so healthy and free. It was like the process I was embarking upon within myself. I originally thought I was going to have that butterfly feeling in my stomach and be scared to death of cutting the remaining portion of relaxed hair off, and only having my natural, God given strands left. But I sat confidently as the beautician cut each inch off.

I loved the results and loved even more the empowering feeling that I had. It was very liberating. I had a smile on my face that was genuine. My face had a natural glow which expressed unfolding freedom. I felt nothing could stop me at this point. I had confronted and talked with a few members of my family, which was very healing and topped it off with a new look. God was changing me for the better. Every drop of blood, sweat and tear I shed was worth the feeling I had at that very moment!

CHAPTER FIFTEEN
Running Toward Destiny

Running allowed me to escape the dysfunctional and abusive environment I was forced to call home. I was unsure as to why running became the means used to break away from the hand and words of Dad as a youth. It was a natural response, to fleet or fight. Tired of fighting back, I chose the former – to run. Running not only become a sport of interest for me, I learned to run away from my problems, fears, hurts and mistakes, only to later discover I had to face these challenges of life head on, address them and work through them to be able to heal and move forward.

I struggled with the heartbreak and betrayal I experienced from Monique. Our friendship began to deteriorate the longer I was with Eva. She particularly did not like Eva. The tension was high when Eva was present. Our friendship really took a dive shortly after my suicide attempt.

Monique did not seem to like the lifestyle I was living and often made snide remarks about it. Sometimes in front of me, and other times behind my back. It made me feel as though I did not measure up to her standards of being "good enough." I felt that she should have understood why I was with women. She out of all people knew me best. I felt judged and disliked by my own best friend. I thought she understood and knew my pain. Rather than expressing myself to her, I suppressed the pain.

During a time Eva and I were on one of our "breaks," I began to casually date a woman I knew from high school. She ran track in the next town over from Springfield, and admitted to always having a crush on me. I entertained her briefly, but eventually lost interest when I received a disturbing phone call one evening. She called to inform me her and Monique had recently began conversing on the phone while Monique worked the overnight shift. She told me how much she was beginning to like Monique. I was both furious and hurt. I thought,

"How dare she! How dare she judge me and talk about me! Then she goes off and does the same thing?! She's married! She has a beautiful family and a home, why would she do this?!" I was heartbroken and felt betrayed.

I tried to talk about it all to Monique, but I was just too hurt. Rather than talking things out with her, I ran. I blocked her from calling me on my phone and from social media – I blocked her out of my life. I was hurt and angry. I felt by cutting her out of my life, I could cut out the pain. I was wrong. I was tormented by the anger and grudge I held against her.

Writing was the best and easiest way for me to articulate whatever emotions and thoughts I had brewing inside. I often struggled with verbalizing what was inside of my mind and heart. But when the pen hit the paper, my words flowed like sap from a tree.

Several months later, I tried to reach out to her by writing her a letter. I was still angry when I wrote the letter, but thought I would put forth an effort in trying to forgive and at least be cordial with her. It was not well received. Monique responded with a nasty letter.

She told me how I was only with women because I was hurt by Lucas and I was "no Mother Theresa," far from perfect and could not judge her for what she had done. Although she was right about some things she had written, her delivery made me feel as if she hated me. I was even more hurt. She took the secrets I confided in her and used them against me in her defense. It was like we fell out all over again. Betrayal... again. I was beyond devastated.

I shut down after this. I fell into a deep depression. Crying spells, not feeling motivated to do simple tasks, (such as cooking and cleaning) and negative thoughts consumed my mind once again. I decided no one loved me and I needed to figure out why. I secluded myself from the world and often lived in complete isolation. I did not like who was inside of me. Therefore, I could not possibly stand to be in anyone else's company.

I was in an unstable, unhealthy, and abusive relationship which caused me to shut myself off from the world and live inside of my own mind. My friendship of over 15 years had ended dramatically and caused the most devastating heartbreak I had ever experienced. Ending my life was not an option this time. I needed an escape.

After not running for several years, and picking up a few extra unwanted pounds, I returned to my first love. Initially, I wanted to get back into shape and get my old track body back. However, I discovered while pursuing physical health, I also wanted and needed mental, emotional and spiritual health. Running was a tool which enabled me to accomplish those things.

I started running again after a long hiatus, and was determined to stop running away from everything; my fears, pain, disappointments, and my past. Having perseverance to face my past head on, face every obstacle I once avoided, and begin to revisit painful memories for healing were my new goals. I decided to shift directions and begin running toward my destiny, the reason for which I was created. I did not want to merely exist and survive. I wanted to live and fulfill purpose.

As my feet hit the pavement, and each breath became rhythmic, my heart rate rose and my body profusely sweated as my thoughts focused upon God - the Creator, the Most High, my all in all. I thanked Him for the ability of my limbs, for the dreams and visions He placed inside of me and basked in His Glory with a spirit of gratitude. There was something about inhaling fresh air, viewing the beauty of nature and hearing the outside clutter that was pure music to my ears. Running outside made me feel as if I was in God's embrace. Surrounding myself around His work of genius brought me the ultimate high. I felt one step closer to Him.

To become a better person, and live a better life, I had to let go of the pain, hatred, anger, resentment and bitterness that I allowed to leach on to me at an early age, take control of me and have power over my life. I was tired of allowing the past to dictate my present and future. I had gotten so used to everyone complimenting me on my attractiveness, education, drive, and career that I spent years covering up what was inside of me.

I partied and drank all night long to suppress the pain. I thought it made me look attractive to wear tons of make-up and dress in provocative clothing. It was an attempt to hide the mess that was brewing inside of me. I jumped in and out of unhealthy relationships, just to say I had someone.

I lied to myself and others about how I truly felt on the inside when in all actuality, I felt empty. I hated myself and everything about my life. I blamed everyone in my past that hurt me for my anger, having a poor attitude and having a sense of entitlement as if the world owed me something.

I finally got tired of feeling and thinking so negatively. I accepted responsibility for my own thoughts, feelings and actions. It was not easy looking into the mirror and not liking the reflection. It was hard and scary. I looked into my eyes and then turned away. I had gotten used to looking at the (my) surface. When I gazed into my own eyes, I felt the cries of my younger self. There was an excruciating feeling in the pit of my stomach. I glanced down and then with courage, looked again. I became humbled when I looked past my reflection and into my soul. I was broken. I saw my fallible ways and admitted I had work to do!

This is when the real work began. Not the work of building endurance, or strengthening my body to run harder or faster, but the rigorous steps needed to heal and cleanse my soul. I was all messed up on the inside and I knew it. Being aware is conviction within itself. I was faced with a choice to make; to either endure the pain of change or stay in pain of remaining the same. Either way, I was going to experience pain. One was beneficial, the other was detrimental. I desperately wanted to change.

After enduring abuse, heartbreaks, and other experiences alike, my image of men became faulty and distorted. I hated men. They were the enemy, the reason for my pain and heartache, suffering and struggles as a single mother. Men were the reason I felt I never measured up to being "good enough." I was convinced I was a case of *damaged goods* and no decent man would ever want or treat me right.

Having this mentality made it easy for me to continue dating women over the course of several years. Most of the women I was involved with were understanding, gentle, sympathetic and attentive to my emotional needs. This was something I never quite experienced with men. By being with a woman, I felt more secure, loved, wanted and important. I also felt more in control when with women. Typically, I was the one who ended the relationships when dating women. I did not experience rejection or not feeling loved or wanted with women like I did with men. Why would I want to trade that for a man? Dad was the first man to break my heart, and men after him continued to break my heart. I felt unloved, unwanted and rejected by men to the point I turned to women for love. I just wanted to be loved.

Despite those adversities, I still needed to face the reality of the relationship I was involved in. I experienced an abusive and unhealthy relationship while with a woman and needed to come to grips with that and see the truth. In fact, it was no different from being with a woman than being with a man. I sugar coated my relationship with Eva, to condone the lifestyle I chose to live in. I chose to live through hurt, in pain and bitterness. As I began to heal after experiencing forgiveness, truth began to surface within my being. I was with women for the wrong reasons!

Something interesting occurs when healing and restoration begin to take root on the inside of one's being. Old thoughts are replaced with new thoughts, you feel differently about situations and circumstances and learn to open your heart again and trust. Trust that not everyone in the world is out to get you or harm you and their motives are not always impure.

Through these changes, I began to open myself to the possibility that one day, a man may sweep me off my feet, fall madly in love with me and make me the happiest woman in the world when he asked me to be his wife. I felt differently about my circumstances and needed to stop comparing my present to my past. I was learning how to leave my past behind me, knowing it had no place in my future. The old negative way of thinking, the victim way of thinking, the old stinking thinking I had, was replaced with Biblical scriptures and positive affirmations to serve as daily reminders I no longer had to continue living in the past.

What good would it do for me, the mother of a growing boy, to have such strong, ill-willed feelings toward men? I knew I needed to let go of everything, remind myself of who I was and show my son what forgiveness and healing is truly all about. I knew Amari could sense the hurt and pain caused by his dad. He even asked me one day, "Mom, do you not like my dad?" He told me he asked because after he got off the phone with his dad, I rarely got on the phone to talk with him. I explained to Amari that adults are busy and being able to talk to his dad was most important.

I couldn't dare share with him the hidden grudge which had been living and eating away inside of me as I harbored old resentment and pain. With each year that passed and every new school the year approached, every haircut, each inch Amari grew, each tooth that fell out, each month that passed and I did not receive any child support or financial assistance consistently, anytime he was sick and every time I kissed my son goodnight, or how Lucas married another woman after she got pregnant with his baby and I was still struggling with raising ours - I was reminded I was a single-mother. I chose this path to give Amari life. It reminded me of the empty promises Lucas made to me in that I would never have to raise Amari alone nor struggle. Yet, I did just that. Struggled.

Despite it all, I still had to forgive. Not forgiving what Lucas did or the areas I felt he lacked in as a father, rather forgive for the sake of my own peace. I had to forgive Lucas because I was hurting other people because of the pain I suffered from him. And I did just that. I forgave him. I got in touch with him randomly on a Saturday afternoon, expressed how I realized how much pain and bitterness I had been harboring in my heart over the years. I never thought I would say those words to him, but I did. By forgiving another person, I unpeeled another layer.

I not only had to be honest with myself, but with those around me. I needed to be honest with Eva. I had to tell her about my convictions. I needed to tell her that I was with women for the wrong reasons. I knew I needed to leave Eva completely alone, once and for all if I wanted to truly change inside and have a transformative experience within my life. I spent too many years being involved in an inconsistent, back and forth love feud with her. It needed to end once and for all.

I knew this would hurt her, but it would hurt her more for me to continue living a lie. I was not quite sure if I was ready to date men again, but I knew my heart was opening to the possibility. I was healing and I needed to share that with her.

To my surprise, Eva was not surprised. In fact, she had experienced her own transformation during our on and off again 4-year relationship. She began to eat healthy and exercise, face herself and work toward becoming a better person. She even gave up the "street life" in trade for a restaurant job. She attributed these changes to the impact I had on her life. "It's your turn. It's your turn to face yourself and heal. I want that for you, for you to be free."

When Eva expressed this to me, I never realized I had such an impact on her. I was so caught up in my own mess, I didn't take the time to look up and see she had been changing right before my eyes. Despite her changes for the better, I still did not want to continue being with a woman if it was built out of pain from my past. I decided it was best to end the relationship so I could move forward and discover a new me.

Each time my feet hit the pavement; sweat drenched my clothes and cooled my skin. I was running toward healing, freedom, restoration and victory over my life. I declared I was no longer a victim of past circumstances, rather a survivor for overcoming every barrier and hardship that tried to take me out. I no longer wanted to be broken, miserable, depressed, and a bitter woman. I wanted to be happy, free and love as much as one possibly could.

It wasn't easy. I had to make a conscious effort each day to want to be better, and then put it into practice. It was challenging, but I knew it was possible and the rewards would be worth it. I felt the freedom to be who you are truly created to be was worth the temporary pain of changing, versus the permanent pain of remaining the same.

I never took mental health seriously until my failed suicide attempt. Not only is there a general stigma regarding mental health in society, but it is also taboo in the black community. I never thought I had mental health concerns until Lucas told me I needed to get help. Even then, I still did not put forth effort into ensuring my mental health or stability. From the moment of the suicide attempt, I decided to never take another pill to suppress the deep and hidden issues residing in the very depths of my being. I found a counselor, stuck with her, and dug away at each issue and unpeeled layers upon layers. It was a very painful and frightening experience, but also a liberating and healing one. It took courage to face my own demons, but I was determined to come out victorious.

By running again, even Mom was provided with a second chance to watch her daughter perform. I began training for a half marathon. I had never run so many miles in my life; however, when one has a lot on their mind and heart, the time seems to pass by without realizing 13.1 miles have passed right along with it! As race day approached, I asked Mom to come watch me run. If she came, this was going to be the first time she saw me run competitively. I wanted nothing more than for her to see why running meant the world to me.

I was thrilled when Mom watched me run in my very first half-marathon. She rode along with my sisters to Champaign, Illinois. They all stood at various mile markers to cheer me on. I wanted to cry each time I saw Mom. I thought about the times I wished she was there at a track meet to see me cross the finish line and win my race, or the times Dad woke me up to run in the morning, but Mom didn't get to see me train. Each mile brought back not only a flashback of the moments she wasn't there, but healing from the one moment she was there. I declared that each mile I ran that day made up for the sprints she missed out on in my youth. It didn't matter anymore, because she was there for that moment.

After the half-marathon, I decided to train for a full marathon and keep the momentum going. I ran all over Springfield to train. So many memories traveled through my thoughts as I crossed a street, ran down a familiar road, or passed certain houses. I was extremely grateful that this time, I was not running away from anything. In fact, I was running toward something. It felt different. I wasn't consumed with fear or hurt, rather I was filled with love and freedom. Each step I took released a shackle which kept me in bondage for many years. Complete and total restoration was within arm's reach.

Running appeared to help with my work performance as well. Not that I was a bad employee, but I had an attitude and was always defensive. While conducting evaluations, my supervisor at the time mentioned how she noticed a change within me. "I don't know if it's all that running you've been doing, but you seem like you're happier. Something is just different about your demeanor." I was thrilled to hear this. For someone else to notice the transformation begin to manifest was a miracle within itself. I knew something inside of me was truly changing. I told her that it was the running, but did not share the intricate details.

I knew running saved my life once before, and it could do it again. I was now going to run for myself, healing, and my future. I was going to run for my life. If I wanted to have healthy relationships and interactions with others, I first had to have a healthy relationship with myself.

CHAPTER SIXTEEN

Therapeutic Career

At a very young age I wanted a career in the criminal justice system. I had a desire to work with people who had resorted to committing criminal offenses out of fear, pain, hatred, poverty, low self-esteem, being products of their own environment, etc. I started my career working with juvenile delinquents at the Juvenile Detention Center in Springfield. This was the initial reason I moved back to Springfield. I saw my younger self in these youth - the stories they told, the struggles they had, and the abuse, neglect and abandonment they experienced.

I was humbled each time I worked with them as it reminded me that I could have *been* them. I could have been sitting in a green suit, answering to complete strangers, all because of an offense I committed out of the pain inflicted upon me by someone else's pain. Some of my colleagues viewed the youth at the detention center as "mess ups" and they were doomed to continue going down the path of being criminals. I, however, saw potential, hope and lost souls who only needed that one person to give them those encouraging and empowering words they had been seeking their entire young lives. I used to be them.

I facilitated cognitive behavioral based groups with the youth detained there. We covered topics that varied from Forgiveness and Healing, Restorative Justice, Social Skills, Rational Behavior Training and Anger Management. I enjoyed running the groups with the youth. It gave me the opportunity to reflect as I shared tiny bits and pieces of my story with them. I mainly shared how I ran track to stay out of trouble and deal with my pain. I never divulged too much information, just enough to show them I understood. Some of the groups hit home for me; particularly Anger Management and Forgiveness and Healing. Little did the youth and my colleagues know, I was healing as I facilitated the groups that were geared toward their healing. It was one of the most liberating and therapeutic experiences I had ever had, to be able to hear these detained juvenile's stories, be able to relate to some, and give them the tools they needed to heal and change. These were the very tools I needed for my own healing.

I was accustomed to receiving multiple praises from my supervisors on the way I facilitated these groups. They sensed the authenticity in my engagement with the youth and knew that I was not only taking my job seriously, but I had a genuine concern for their well-being. I went to work with the mindset, *"this could have been me in here. How would I want others to respond to my situation?"* It enabled me to see life through their eyes and understand their pain so I could look beyond their circumstances. I knew there was more there than the offenses they committed, the harm they caused others and the damage they inflicted upon themselves and their reputations. I knew these youth were hurting inside, and in turn, they were hurting others.

I worked every shift at the Detention Center, some of them twice. I did not care for the overnight shift, because I could not work with the youth. Although I got to spend more time with Amari by working while he was asleep, it was just not fulfilling for me. Fortunately, there were plenty of times some of the youth stayed awake until I arrived at work just to speak to me. It was a good feeling to have a positive impact on them.

Unfortunately, the inconsistency with my work schedule was beginning to take a toll on me. I missed being at home with Amari. I didn't want to be like Mom - always at work and never at home. I was beginning to feel like that was me too. I wanted to be home more with Amari. I also did not want him to feel unloved or unsupported, simply because I was trying to make a living.

I felt perplexed about the movement in my career. I was ready for new challenges and experiences. I did get some of those challenges and experiences I sought out when I was promoted to a new position. Yet, I was still hungry for more. I applied for an adult probation officer position downtown at the courthouse. It was this moment that I felt some sort of relief and gratification for the yearning that I had to do and be more. I had been at the detention center for a little over 5 years and running the same groups day in and day out. It was beginning to become a bit mundane. I wanted to have a one on one experience and get to know people on an individual level. I felt I would have an even greater impact on other's lives if I could have consistent one on one interaction with them.

I was offered the position as an adult probation officer after my second time applying. The first time I applied, I was the runner up; however, they went with a candidate who had a few more years of experience than I did and was the Senior Treatment Specialist at the time. It was her position that I was promoted to once she left for adult probation. It was interesting how the order of these events occurred.

At first, I was upset because I was beyond ready for a change and to move to the next level in my career. Quickly, I saw this as an opportunity to get promoted and to gain supervisory experience. It was a perfect setup and I acted swiftly. It was not long before another opportunity was present. I reapplied for another adult probation officer position and was offered that position as well.

I wrestled and tussled within myself over this decision. Since I had accepted a promotion at the Detention Center, I was faced with losing a considerable amount of money in my salary. The pay at the detention center was higher due to the nontraditional work schedule. The perks of going to probation were the case management experience, having a flexible schedule and paid holiday and weekends off. I had not experienced this in nearly 6 years! I accepted the position as an adult probation officer. I trusted God to cover our financial needs, so I could spend more time with Amari.

I glorified the adult probation position in my head. When I began to work, I was exposed to the naked truth. I spent more time pushing paper and less time with the clients. It was as if they were all just a number in the court system. It was not realistic to be able to spend a great deal of time with the clients. Usually when meeting with a client, there was another one in the lobby waiting to meet with you as well. Nevertheless, I spent as much time as I could with each one. I witnessed an even greater number of broken people in the community. I saw souls who had been hurt, broken, made poor choices in life and were forced to live with the consequences.

It was disheartening to look into my client's eyes. I saw lost hopes, dreams, failure and disappointment. Many of them appeared to have lost hope in themselves. The look of despair was written all over them. I wanted to pour into them all and tell them they did not have to accept their life the way it was! I wanted them to believe that they could change. I encouraged them to want more out of life and themselves, but there was a stipulation; they had to work their butts off to get it!

I was challenged in my efforts each time I tried to convince a client they had what it took to work hard and diligently toward changing themselves and creating a new life. Many clients felt they were either too old, had ruined their reputations, committed too many offenses or just simply felt they had failed at life. Redemption was not within their reach. Many had become complacent and content with living off the system and just counting their years down until their demise. Most of them were alive, but were not living.

I saw several probationers I had gone to school with or just knew from around town. "Red? You're a probation officer?!" was often the response I got when recognized. They appeared to be in a state of disbelief that "one of us" was not in the system, but working for the system. My hope was for them to see they too could become whoever they wanted to be, that they did not have to accept the life they had come to know – a life based upon past mistakes or circumstances. I wanted them to believe that they could change for the better. They *could* change their life.

After several months had passed, I still toiled with the feelings that I was meant to do more in life. I gained fulfillment each time I had a positive impact on someone; but I wanted to reach a greater population; I wanted to reach the masses! After working a short amount of time as a probation officer, I felt *"if this small town has so many broken and hurt people in it, then there are multitudes scattered throughout the world!"* I wanted to reach every soul possible, give them hope and let them know, "You can make it! You can heal, forgive, love, be free and be whole!"

I struggled with sharing my personal experiences and releasing my story for open criticism and unfavorable remarks. I was still not confident in my own transformation. I fought negative and self-corrupting thoughts. *"No one wants to hear your story. Everyone has a story. Why do you think anyone wants to hear yours?"*

I felt as if my mind and heart were against each other. My heart refused to give up, but my thoughts caused me to feel defeated. Yet, as I grew inside, strengthened my spirit and reminded myself daily who I truly was, I began to believe it and walk in it. I looked myself in the mirror every day and told myself, "I love myself. I am the best. I can do it. God is always with me. I am a winner. Today is my day." I believed that as I repeated these affirmations, I would eventual internalize them, believe them and become them.

I felt uncomfortable the first time I tried to talk to myself in the mirror. I had already come to grips with the fact that I would be speaking to a broken soul. However, when I looked into my own eyes and said "I love you," I did not believe it. I walked away from the mirror, feeling defeated. I was frustrated. "This is stupid! This doesn't even work! I don't feel different at all!" I did not give up though. One morning, as I got ready for my day, I decided to try again. I stood in front of the mirror, pushed my shoulders back and stood with my posture erect. I was ready to face myself. I looked into my eyes again and said the same words I said the first time I tried this exercise. "I love you." Tears flowed down my face as I realized I did not love myself. I desperately wanted to love myself. I decided to repeat this act as many times as it took for me to finally start loving myself.

There were several other positive affirmations, quotes and scriptures that I spoke to myself to fight the negative thinking and self-hatred that constantly attempted to penetrate my mind, thoughts, and actions. They gave me hope. They enabled me to believe in myself and strengthened me to reach out to others and share what worked. I made a habit to speak life into my own life, so in turn, I could speak life into others.

I began to think and speak more positively each time I recited Biblical scriptures and positive affirmations. I learned to quote scriptures over my life from spiritual leaders whom all had a profound impact on my life; specifically, my pastor from Carbondale. She told me how she adopted me as her "spiritual daughter" and often spoke so many positive things to me. She told me how I had a "great calling" over my life and how much God loved me. Her words somehow stuck with me.

I learned about the positive affirmations from Lucas's Aunt Michelle. She opened her home to me when I went to visit in Florida for vacation and to bring Amari home from spending time with his dad. She covered each room of her home with loving, enlightening and positive words and quotes; sometimes even writing them in lipstick on her mirrors. She inspired me to do the same.

Each time I glanced at my vision board, the positive affirmations written in lipstick on the dresser drawer mirror in my bedroom, scanned over the printed positive quotes and scriptures taped on the walls, and glared at my own reflection in the mirror, I saw a new person. Someone who had rediscovered herself, fought to heal and now resembled change. I could have been crying, depressed or in distress. Instead, I was grateful for each experience I encountered and counted them all as a life lesson. No more "woe is me." I was a different human being - a changed person.

Knowing what I put into practice worked, I had to figure out a way to share it with my clients. There was a client who battled with severe depression. She arrived to appointments unkempt. Her hair was not combed, she wore pajamas and often appeared destitute. Rather than judging her, I understood. I had an honest talk with her and suggested she begin to speak positive affirmations over herself to lift her spirits. I warned her that at first, she may feel funny talking to herself in the mirror, or that it is not working, but to trust the process and to "fake it until she makes it."

I also had an honest talk with her about her appearance and how the way she carried herself could be contributing to the way she felt inside. I wrote down the positive affirmations, asked her to tape it to her mirror, recite them daily and come to her next appointment with her hair combed and dressed.

I wanted to cry when I saw her sitting out in the lobby! She was dressed and her hair was combed for her next appointment! I knew that what I put into practice for myself worked for others as well. She mentioned how the positive affirmations were working and she was beginning to feel better about herself. I never shared with her how I personally knew this method worked. I desperately wanted to share my experiences and how I understood everything she was feeling, but I couldn't. I took pride in having a certain level of professionalism in the work place, specifically in working with my clients. I also valued the importance of ethical standards and abiding by the rules set forth by the employer. Therefore, I was limited in how transparent I could be with my clients. I remained completely neutral when conversing with them.

I had other situations with clients where I shared methods, thoughts or encouraging words to help them through their situations. Although they were on probation for a criminal offense they were convicted of, they had deeper issues which needed to be addressed and resolved. I realized that I had experienced a lot of their deeper issues just the same, but addressed them and either resolved them or was in the process of doing so.

There were many times I wanted to say, "I know, I went through that too!" Or, "You can forgive, you don't have to hate them forever, take your power back!" I wanted to share I knew what it felt like to face trial and tribulations, to get knocked down and feel like the world is standing on top of you. I experienced the aches and pains of broken hearts, one right after the other. I experienced the misery of suffering from depression and recurrent suicidal thoughts. I had disappointments and was betrayed from those closest to me. I had turned to alcohol and partying to suppress the pain, or have sex to feel loved and wanted.

I felt if I could personally share my empathy toward them and their pain, then maybe they would be more susceptible to change and believe that they too could change. Seeing them in the state they were in motivated me to continue moving forward with my journey in forgiveness, healing, self-love and being whole. I wanted to be an example for them, that they too could experience the freedom I was experiencing.

CHAPTER SEVENTEEN

Stranger

One morning I received a random message from someone I knew from high school, Rachel. We didn't go to the same high school, but knew of each other from being opponents during track and field season. She contacted me because her friend, Rob, mentioned how he saw me at a Greek event a few months back, but never got a chance to introduce himself. After he discovered Rachel knew who I was, he asked her to contact me. She told me about their conversation and that I could inbox him on Facebook if I did not feel comfortable giving him my phone number.

Being my friendly self, I thanked her and told her I would look him up whenever I got a chance. I didn't really give it much thought, nor think it was worth entertaining. As soon as I sent that message to Rachel, Rob had already reached out to me.

"Good morning Casandra. I know you don't know me, but I remember seeing you at a Greek mixer this summer that the ladies of AKA sponsored. I wanted to introduce myself then but I noticed that you were conversing with friends and I didn't want to intrude. Nevertheless, I still remembered you and asked my friend (Rachel) about you and that I still remembered you from the event. I'm not sure what your situation is (single or involved) but I just wanted to reach out and see if you'd entertain my invitation to get to know one another. Maybe an exchange of numbers and then dinner sometime. Hope to hear from you."

I was flattered, yet unmoved. I had just begun a new position and was experiencing transformation in my life. I was not interested in being with anyone and was simply just enjoying general 'me time.' I did not want to be rude nor come off as a snob. I responded tactfully. I told him I was open to meeting new people and developing new friendships for the purposes of networking only, but I did appreciate his kind approach. When I discovered he was a young, black educated professional, I merely saw another person I could network with.

However, something unexpected happened. We began to have candid conversations about ourselves and life in general once we got past the initial back and forth correspondences of introducing ourselves. We ate the same foods, enjoyed the same activities, both had eclectic tastes and were intrigued by our intellectual responses to one another's inquisitiveness.

He taught an African American Studies course at the community college as another stream of income. I minored in African American Studies as an undergrad. The similarities and commonalities were becoming limitless between us. Several weeks passed as we shared glimpses of each other's world over the phone, text and email. He never pressured me to see him in person, but would be persistent at the same time in suggesting public places we could meet.

I had not experienced a connection with a man in nearly 10 years. It was refreshing and scary at the same time. I did not want to experience anymore hurt or disappointment, but did not want to pass up on a potential opportunity due to fear. The catch for me was our conversations about God and our faith for a promising future. He sent prerecorded prayers to me via text and we prayed over the phone as well. He was even looking for a church home when he first began pursuing me. The same friend that facilitated our 'meeting' recommended he visit a church in Springfield. Rob worked and lived in Decatur. He was the Assistant Dean of Student Inclusion at Milliken University. I was shocked to hear he was looking for a place in Springfield to meet his spiritual needs since Decatur and Springfield were about 35 miles apart. He had tried various churches in Decatur, but had not found what he was looking for or needed. I was also on the same search and had yet to find what I was looking for.

I asked him to keep me abreast on his experiences. He went to Bible study and prayer first and then to a Sunday service. He felt to get a good understanding of how a church taught the Bible, he needed to attend all services offered to gauge if it may be worth revisiting. He had raving reviews and suggested I visit with him. I was still hesitant about seeing him in person. I felt he would actively pursue me afterward and I was still scared. I had not felt the comfort level needed to ensure us meeting in person would not result in an epic failure.

After speaking on the phone, for sometimes hours a day and for several weeks, I finally gave in to seeing him in person. We decided to meet at the public library. I went a little early to see if I could see him before he saw me. I made sure to go in my gym clothes. I wanted to appear as unattractive as possible. I was testing him. The library we met at had large size windows which overlooked several blocks. I could see him as he walked up to the door. He told me he would have on a purple sweater, my favorite color, in which he did. He walked into the library with a plum sweater on, black slacks, and black dress shoes. He appeared to be in decent shape, which was a plus because I believed being healthy was paramount.

I grew nervous as I knew he had already begun coming up the stairs to the floor where we had agreed upon to meet. *"He's not lazy."* I thought to myself. He could have very well taken the elevator, but he walked up the stairs. I was impressed. I carefully observed everything about him that I could; the way he walked and carried himself, how articulate and eloquently he spoke. I wanted to be sure I was not meeting with the same type of person I had ever dealt with in the past. I was mindful and wanted to use discernment when I finally interacted with him in person.

I had all intentions on going to the gym after meeting with Rob. I did not anticipate we would spend the next few hours at the library talking about many topics. He had a hard time looking me in my eyes that day and I kept pointing that out to him. He told me he was shy and how beautiful I was in person. He already had complimented me on my outward beauty after seeing photographs. I figured I looked the same in person as I did in photographs, until I realized he was seeing all of me in person.

We talked until it was time for the library to close. I was careful in how I handled myself in getting to know him. I made sure to not divulge too much information about myself, particularly experiences I had during my childhood. I did not want to scare him or run him off by projecting myself as some scorned woman. I had already addressed many of the issues I had, was actively engaged in counseling and was very in tune with myself and my own healing. I wanted him to know me for who I was at that present moment.

We walked out of the library together. He walked me to my car, opened my door and gave me a hug before I went inside to drive back home. He embraced me tightly as I got a whiff of the cologne that was still emanating from his presence. A part of me wanted to go for a walk with him and continue conversing about the interesting topics we had briefly touched upon. Yet I did not want to rush or get too attached as I had done in my past. I left content, knowing I did not share too much of myself, but just enough to expose a small piece of who I was.

Rob and I could not stop talking about how much we enjoyed seeing each other and the conversations we had. We couldn't wait to meet up again and see where else our minds could lead us in discussions with one another. I felt him speaking to my soul. The way he encouraged me, spoke life into me and allowed me to see myself the way God sees me was truly a remarkable experience. I had already moved toward loving myself more, spending time with myself and improving upon myself. He just showed me I was on the right path.

I agreed to meet with him on my lunch one afternoon to see if our first meeting was just a fluke. We only had roughly thirty minutes to chat, but like before we had a good conversation. He picked me up from my office and had a flower arrangement for me. He told me he initially was going to have them delivered, but felt compelled to deliver them to me himself.

Our conversations were never dry, nor boring. We seemed to be able to converse about anything. We talked to each other during various parts of the day. Good morning texts or phone calls, followed by phone calls to check on how our respective days were going, evening conversations and our nightly prayers before bed. I was beginning to pray and ask God was this the man he sent to me?

Rob was very consistent. We spoke frequently. There was never a dull moment and we didn't miss prayers. I agreed to visit a Wednesday night Bible study with him to see how I liked the church. I still had not found a "church home" and figured it wouldn't hurt to visit with him. I enjoyed the service and felt the teacher did a great job breaking the content of the Bible down for even the simple minded to understand.

I finally agreed to go on a date with Rob. I didn't want to go on a traditional dinner date, so I told him to pick something fun to do. I was not ready to share with him where I lived, so I met him at a destination we both agreed upon and got into the car with him. We went on a haunted hayrack ride. It was a chili October night, and I could not believe I had agreed to this. He seemed more relaxed than before. After our first few meetings I thought he was a poindexter type of guy, who talked and walked a certain way. Yet this night, I saw a different side of him. He seemed more relaxed and comfortable around me. I enjoyed this side more. We laughed all night and had a great time. We even went to a few lounges afterwards for cocktails and conversation. We were beginning to tell each other more personal, and intimate details about one another. I was becoming more and more attracted to him and viewed him from a different perspective.

Though we both did not want the night to end, we knew it had to. He took me back to my car, but before I got out we sat and listened to some slow jams. I asked him to sing a song, since he had told me previously that his family told him he had a nice voice. I thought it was sweet as he attempted to sound like the artist on the track as he closed his eyes in shyness. I didn't laugh. I just listened and appreciated the effort. He then looked at me and asked could he kiss me. The mere fact he asked first was appealing. Folks these days just go straight in for the kill, with no regard for the other person's wants or feelings! I also felt he had read my mind.

We had already shared horror kissing stories up into this point. So, the expectations and bar was raised high for him to kiss me the right way. I even told him, "If I don't feel any butterflies then this will be the first and the last kiss. So, I better feel some butterflies!" I was serious! As he leaned in to kiss me, his hand softly grazed the side of my check as he used slight pressure to reel me in closer to him. When his lips pressed against mine, I felt my heart beat faster and my stomach flutter. I couldn't believe what was happening! What started off for me as just a mere acquaintance was beginning to turn into a love story. He told me how soft my lips were, and how he appreciated the fact I could kiss. We both smiled and I got out of his vehicle. He got out, opened the door to my car, hugged me as if he never wanted to let me go, and then I drove home.

Our next date, Rob invited me to his place so he could cook dinner. When I arrived, he had on a blue apron, which was one of the colors of the fraternity he was in. He also had a single pink rose and card waiting for me. *"How sweet,"* I thought.

I admired the books he had on his book shelf and noticed we even had some of the same reading materials. I went from wondering if he was being forthright with me about who he was, to believing the words he told me. He handed me picture albums of himself for me to look through as he finished preparing our meal. I browsed through the photos and saw graduation pictures, pictures of his children and family and more. *"He's real,"* I thought. He wasn't making anything up just to impress me, this was really him.

We both enjoyed and wrote poetry. Rob did more spoken word and I wrote my work. As he was cooking, he shared a spoken word piece for me about us meeting. I was beyond impressed, I was mesmerized. His talent in choosing just the right words to spell out a story in rhyme was amazing. He spoke effortlessly and with passion. Almost as if he was speaking directly to my heart.

Rob plated our meal like a chef would at a five-star restaurant. He broiled the salmon to perfection. The asparagus was just how I liked it and the brown rice pilaf was very flavorful. *"He can cook too!"* I thought to myself. I was impressed with his cooking and at the fact he could cook the type of foods I enjoyed. I was a stickler on what I ate and had the most difficult time conveying that to others. Most people wanted to go out to eat, or eat unhealthy foods. Rob however, enjoyed eating the same type of foods as I did and enjoyed preparing them. I wondered was this too good to be true? After we finished our meal, we watched a documentary on Netflix and he held me in his arms. It was the most natural, and comforting feeling I had in a long time. My body melted in his arms as he held me firmly, yet with care. I never wanted that moment to end.

From that moment on, Rob made it clear he was dating me with a purpose and marriage was the goal. I heard the church folks talk about this. I thought, *"this has to be it, no one has ever pursued me or courted me in this manner before."* He told me how he had prayed about me and God revealed to him I was "the one," but that we had to take our time and he had to be patient with me. I believed him and allowed him to take the reins with us in putting God first, trusting he would lead this relationship with a purpose. *"Finally, my prayers are being answered,"* I thought.

We both began to brag to friends and family about each other. We were so excited about what we were about to experience with one another, we could hardly keep our mouths shut. Neither one of us were ashamed of each other, nor wanted to hide each other. We held hands in private and in public places. We were affectionate with each other. We showed each other the appreciation we had and the growing infatuation we had for each other through both words and actions. I had never experienced anything like this before and was in total bliss.

As I began to like him more and more, and could see a future with him, my friends and family began to bring up Amari meeting him. "You need to know now if Rob and Amari can get along or not, before the two of you get serious. You don't want to fall in love with that man and your son doesn't like him." My best friend Christy was always wise beyond her years, and did a lot of thinking for me when my mind was elsewhere. She was right. I did not want to move forward and have a full-fledged relationship with someone who may not have been fitting for my family. Rob had two children of his own. His son, the oldest, from what he claimed was a one-night stand in college; and his daughter from his previous marriage.

I was leery in the beginning about developing an interest for a man who one, had been married and divorced, and two, had two children by two different women. That was not on my "future husband" list I had sitting inside of my Bible. I preferred someone who had not been married and had only one child, or at least his children were by the same woman. Yet, as I got to know Rob, I put my high demands to the side and accepted him for being human.

April suggested I have Rob and Amari interact with each other in a public place so that it did not seem as if I was introducing Amari to a potential boyfriend; but could still gage if they would be able to get along or not. I asked Rob to meet us at the park. I brought my nieces along with us so it did not seem obvious something else was going on. I knew if Amari was anything like me, he would be suspicious regardless, so I wanted to be as discreet as possible.

When we all arrived at the park, I introduced Rob as my friend to my nieces and Amari. I could see the puzzlement on Amari's face. I had not brought a man around him in this manner before. The curiosity plaguing his mind was apparent in his facial expressions. I also used this as an opportunity to test how Rob interacted with children in general. He always spoke of loving children and someday wanting more, but I wanted to see the action behind it.

We played tag with the kids, walked through the trails, and Rob pushed my nieces on the swing. Rob engaged in conversation with the kids, asking them questions about their interests and what they like to do for fun. I began to see him in a new light. I saw the potential of Rob moving from the friend zone to the mate zone. I was attracted to him even more when I saw the father in him. My feelings for him deepened. I was frightened that I was beginning to feel like this about a man. I had not experienced these types of feelings since Lucas and I were together. I did not want to experience the same hurt either, so I remained cautious.

Due to our hectic work schedules and the small distance which separated us, we were unable to see each other as often as people beginning to date someone new prefer. Weekends were usually what we had to look forward to, with occasional once a week visits for Bible study on Wednesday nights, or just to have dinner. We used Skype, talked on the phone, texted, e-mailed and used just about every sort of technology out there to keep our conversations fresh and our interest peeked.

What drew me even closer to Rob was how he mentioned he always wanted to practice celibacy in a relationship and he felt he never could because women were always so aggressive in sleeping with him. I had already promised myself to not become intimate with someone too quickly as I had done in the past. I was ecstatic when he wanted to practice celibacy. He did not pressure me into having sex, yet was so emotionally in tune with me. He gave me gifts, opened doors for me, wrote love letters and poems, sent flowers to my job and gave me flowers in person. He treated me like a queen, without getting sex from me. I had never experienced this and was enjoying every single minute of it.

Rob always expressed how he felt about me and did not hold back. He told me he couldn't see his life without me, how I was the woman of his dreams and how beautiful I was inside and out. At this point, I did not doubt a single word he said and believed he meant every word. I began to envision a future with him, and picture a life with him. Yet, I was still guarded emotionally trying to hold on to every ounce of control I could to not fall in love with this man. I knew once I fell in love, there was no coming back. Being in love would put me at risk for heartbreak, which scared me more than anything else. I was tired of being in dead-end relationships and getting my heart broken. I wanted a love that would last and endure the test of time. I wanted to be with my soul-mate.

The night Rob told me he loved me, we had just gone to Decatur after going to a Canvas and Cocktails event in Springfield. I enjoyed the painting and went often with girlfriends of mine, although my painting skills were very novice. We sat on his couch, he looked me in my eyes with his palms braced against my cheeks, and told me he loved me. I began to cry. He did not ask me why I was crying, he just embraced me as my tears dampened his shirt. I looked at him and told him, "no one ever told me they loved me before I had sex with them." I knew he meant it. I could see it in his eyes. "You don't have to tell me back. I just want you to know how I feel about you." Rob assured me. He never pressured me to do anything I did not want to do or felt uncomfortable doing. I felt safe with him.

Rob began inquiring about Amari and having more interactions with him. He felt if he was going to be a part of my life in the capacity he spoke of, he needed to develop a relationship with Amari. This frightened me more than me falling in love with him. Amari was already dealing with his dad living across the country. He only saw him maybe once a year, sometimes, only every other year. I did not want to introduce a man to him that was not going to be around for the long haul. I not only wanted to protect my heart, but I felt a charge to protect my son's heart as well. I knew what type of man Rob was and that Amari would love him once he got to know him.

I decided to start slow, like I did in my process in getting to know Rob. I decided to bring Amari to church with me and told him we were visiting a new church and my friend from the park went there as well. Amari would go to church with April and her husband at times, especially when I was working shift work at the detention center. I wanted to show Amari I had been "church shopping" and found a potential candidate.

Rob was there and complimented Amari on how nice he looked. We enjoyed the service and Amari enjoyed it as well. As we began to head toward the door to exit the building, Rob asked me to wait in the lobby as he walked Amari over to his car. He had bought him a batman belt with gadgets to accompany it. He told Amari he loved to reward positive behavior and heard how good of a kid he was and how well he did in school. A part of me questioned his motive. I wondered if he was doing this to get on me and Amari's good side. Yet, I also knew how passionate Rob was about education and being a positive role model for young black males. Regardless, I was happy Amari could interact with a positive black male.

It did not take long for Amari to see the qualities in Rob that caught my eye. As time progressed, we continued to spend more time with each other as Amari interacted with Rob more often. He eventually grew very fond of Rob. "Mom, I have something to tell you, but you can't say a word." Amari whispered in my ear after service one Sunday. "Go ahead Amari," I responded with curiosity. "I want Rob to be my step-dad!" Amari said with so much excitement in his voice. I paused, and got quiet for a moment. I asked Amari why he said that. He began to ramble off the admirable qualities Rob possessed, felt he was nice to his mom, and would make a good candidate for a potential step-dad. I still could not believe what I had heard. It only had been a couple of months and already Amari was talking about something so serious. I was taken aback.

It took me a while to feel comfortable before allowing Rob to come into our home. We sat on the porch together, and enjoyed the beautiful weather. I had not yet invited him inside. I did not want to give Amari the wrong impression, especially after he made such a bold statement regarding Rob. I did eventually give in, and asked Amari was it ok if Rob came over so we could watch a movie together and he cook us dinner? Of course, Amari was all for it! It was me who was hesitant and withdrawn about taking steps forward.

The first time Rob came over to cook in my home, he bought Amari and I aprons of our own. I thought it was kind of him to make Amari feel included. It was just one more addition to the list of the many qualities I liked about him. He also helped Amari with his homework that night! A man who goes to church with me, is educated, has a career, dresses nice, can cook and is helping my son with his homework, I felt like I had hit the jackpot! Not to mention, we were practicing celibacy together. The bond we were creating was unlike any other I had ever experienced. It felt genuine and real.

As time progressed and we continued to grow both as individuals and together, Rob asked if Amari and I would join him in riding down to Arkansas to attend his family reunion. Again, I was hesitant and guarded. I felt I was taking my time, but this seemed sudden. *"He wants me to meet his family? All of them? He must really be serious about me!"* These thoughts and questions ran rampant through my mind as I asked him to give me a chance to think about it. After spending about a week pondering, I eventually accepted the invitation.

This was a first. A man who literally comes out of nowhere, sweeps both myself and my son off our feet, and wants me to meet his entire family without having my body first?! I admired him even more. I had never met, nor been in a relationship with, anyone who asked me to meet their family before having sex with me first. Usually it was the other way around, especially when I was with Lucas. Although I met his dad and brother before I was pregnant with Amari, we still had sex prior to me meeting them. I did not meet the rest of Lucas's family until after I gave birth to Amari. Rob was giving me an experience I never had, and I was enjoying every bit of it.

The ride down to Arkansas was long, but fun. We stopped in Kansas City, Kansas to pick up his daughter. He was such a family man and a devoted father, yet another quality I appreciated. With Lucas being so inconsistent with Amari, and then only seeing him during the summers for the most part, watching Rob taking this drive without hesitation spoke volumes. In an indirect way, he assured me he would do whatever he had to do for his children. What woman wouldn't love that about a man?!

We stayed with his mom after she insisted. His family was very loving and accepting. They reminded me of the way Lucas's family accepted me as their own when I first met them. I've always loved southern hospitality and how hospitable folks down south are. They're kind, polite and overall good people. Amari even enjoyed playing with Rob's son, who was around his age. We had a great time.

At this moment, I realized I was falling in love with this man. I was scared to death to express this to him. The last man I expressed my heart to and fell madly in love with abandoned me with a baby and moved on with his now wife. I could not risk that hurt again. Yet, I reminded myself, in life I must take risks to get something I've never had. I did not tell him I loved him while in Arkansas, I allowed myself time to meditate on it before I opened my mouth.

On the way back to Illinois, we stopped in Kansas City again to meet his ex-wife to drop his daughter off. I introduced myself as I extended my hand out to her, "Hi, I'm Casandra." Amari was so eager to introduce himself, he did not allow her time to introduce herself to me and extended his hand out as well, "Hi, I'm Amari." The excitement on Amari's face was evident. "Hi, I'm Cammie." She responded to both of us.

Now by this point, I had already addressed a lot of my self-esteem issues. It was liberating to be able to meet this man's ex-wife and not feel insecure. I was proud of myself for the growth and progress I had made. I was more aware of my inward self. I did, however, make sure I kept an eye on their interaction to see if there were any sparks between the two of them. I was using common sense. After my experiences with Lucas, I knew firsthand that a man, or woman, could be with someone else, but still have something there for their former love. Rob being married and divorced concerned me. I knew I was only hearing his side of the story, I wondered what her side was.

Nonetheless, I was happy Rob felt comfortable enough to have Amari and I meet his entire family - ex-wife and children included. He demonstrated his seriousness in courting me and leading our relationship with a purpose. I was more than willing to follow at this point.

Things between Rob and I began to pick up. We began to see each other more often, with more frequent weekday trips to see one another. This led to us spending the night at each other's respective homes.

The first time he held me in his arms my body melted into him like butter. I had never slept so comfortably with another person in the bed with me. *"I can get used to this,"* I thought to myself. He held me with such care, yet made me feel protected. His arms wrapped around me in such a way I would have to pry them off to get up from underneath him. I liked it that way. My man, holding me tight and close to him, whispering sweet nothings in my ear as we went to sleep, this is what I had been waiting for.

Although we were practicing celibacy, we did have conversations about sex. We began to talk about sex more, and went to church less. We went from going to Wednesday night bible study and Sunday morning service, to watching TD Jakes online sermons. We did continue to pray daily together though.

The first time we had sex I was devastated. I knew we were playing with fire by spending the night at each other's homes and sleeping in the same bed together. He would caress me and kiss on me, and I enjoyed it. I knew if we continued in that manner, our kissing and touching would turn into more, in which it did.

Despite being disappointed and me expressing that, we continued to have sex. He called it "making love to the woman he loved." I called it "sex." I could not get to the point of calling it "making love." For some reason, I still did not feel secure in our relationship. I knew we should not have been engaging in that act, yet my flesh wanted to be pleased.

Rather than listening to my heart and intuition, I ignored it and listened to my loins. He looked me in my eyes, expressed his love for me, recited poetry to me all while he was "making love" to me. I was mesmerized. I fell into his trance and decided, *"I'm going to be with him anyway, we might as well learn each other's bodies."* He reassured me he was not going anywhere, and that I was the woman of his dreams.

We often watched HGTV together and discussed our dream homes. We had similar tastes and both agreed on several designs and color schemes. One Sunday afternoon, after we watched TD Jakes sermon, Rob went online and began looking at homes in Springfield. He asked me to think of a price range that was modest and reasonable. We went on to spend the next couple of hours looking at some of the finest homes in Springfield and the surrounding areas. I was imagining our life together, getting his kids and having family gatherings, hosting dinner parties and cooking together in our "state of the art" kitchen. I could see myself as this man's wife.

Rob even asked me about my ring size and my preference in the cut, band and metal. *"He's serious."* I thought to myself. *"He's really dating me with a purpose!"* We e-mailed rings from different sites to each other back and forth, trying to find the perfect ring I would love for him to propose to me with someday. The process made me fall more madly in love with him. He continued to pour into me, telling me how I could do and be anybody I wanted to. He supported my dreams and visions. He listened to me, even when I would ramble on and on about the same things over and over - he listened. He always showered me with surprise gifts and bouquets of flowers, to show me I was his queen.

Then things shifted. He began to drink a little more than our occasional glass of wine. He wasn't as attentive or encouraging. He slowed down on expressing himself and being affectionate. We were spending less time with each other. We stopped going to church together at all. I felt an overall change in his demeanor and the direction our relationship was heading in. I wasn't sure if it was because I had sex with him or if he was losing interest.

When I approached him with my concerns, he told me to "back off." This did not sound like him and I had never heard him speak that way. *"Who is he?"* I wondered. He was such a kind and gentle man, I did not know he had this side to him. I was beginning to wonder if I met his "representative" and now I was beginning to see the real him.

Things progressively got worse between us. He began to share his uncertainty about having a future with me and felt he needed time to figure that out. My gut told me our demise was forthcoming. I was worried. I was not sure what was happening or why. I thought we were heading in a good direction. We communicated well when we did have a disagreement or a discussion. I knew something was not right.

He started getting his daughter and going to Arkansas by himself, without asking if I wanted to tag along. He used the excuse he did not know if I wanted to go or not so did not bother to ask. "Of course, I would want to go!" I told him. I reached out to friends and family and shared what was happening. I knew I was going to need the support of my loved ones for what was yet to come. "He's getting back with his ex-wife. I can feel it!" I shared with my sisters. Everyone encouraged me to remain optimistic and to not give up, but my heart and gut told me otherwise.

I began to be honest with myself, and ask if I had missed any red flags with him. The obvious being how desperate he was in the beginning, but I misread it for interest. I also didn't pay attention to him sharing how he ran from his problems, beginning with his failed marriage. Something inside of me had questioned was he truly over his ex-wife? He shared how he cheated on her, regretted it and made every effort to try to restore their relationship after he confessed his infidelity. Despite his efforts, she still divorced him. It seemed he never wanted their marriage to end and realized he made a huge mistake. Yet, because she was a couple of states away, I did not give it any further thought.

I began processing our interaction from day one, realizing my hesitations in the beginning may have been for a reason. When I initially began getting to know Rob, I did not feel an instant connection. I forced one. I looked at his status and prestige and thought, *"no one of this stature has approached me before. I'll just give him a try."* Despite my intuitive urge to resist him in the beginning, I pushed those instincts to the side and decided I was going to go full force ahead. I felt if he was so interested in me and was consistently expressing such, I could learn to love him. After all, love is what I desired from a man all along.

Rob eventually began sharing what had been going on with him. He was being investigated at work for accusations he had inappropriate interactions with a student, another red flag. He shared he left the previous institution he worked for, due to the same reason. However, he was allowed to resign to save his reputation. *"A second time? He must have done something!"* I began to feel there was something about him I did not know, that maybe he was living a double life.

He then said with the stress of the investigation, he felt it was "a sign" that he needed to return to Kansas City, the same city his ex-wife lived in, and finish his dissertation for his PhD. I tried so hard to be an encouraging and supportive girlfriend. I told him we could both work on our goals while he was away and maintain a long-distance relationship. He did not wish for the same. He told me that he would not have time for a long-distance relationship, or any relationship for that matter, and that he needed to focus all his energy toward completing his dissertation. I tried to believe him, but I couldn't. My gut was still telling me there was something else to this story.

He told me conflicting statements from what he did when he was actively pursuing me. "People are sometimes only in your life for a season. It's not you, it's me." I knew he was giving me one of those cliché "I'm about to be with someone else" breakup statements, without directly telling me. I decided to just come right out and ask if he was getting back with his ex-wife. He denied it. I knew he was lying.

Rob eventually made the final decision to return to Kansas City. I was devastated. *"This cannot be happening to me, again!"* I could not believe that another man I thought I would spend my life with, was leaving me and moving states away. I thought I was being pranked. I felt bamboozled. The empty promises he made to me, promising me a future, they were all lies. He even had the nerve to tell me he was not doing the same thing Amari's dad did because he "poured into my life in a positive manner." He completely and totally disregarded my feelings. I cried out in agony, feeling betrayed once again.

I tried everything to keep us together. We even went to my counselor for a session. What a waste of time! When it was his turn to speak, he folded under pressure and turned into a mean, arrogant imbecile who did not need to explain himself. I did not know who this man was. He was not the man who pretended to be prince charming and swept me off my feet in the beginning. He turned on me, and he turned on me quick.

I finally had to come to terms and accept he was leaving. I had reached out to my old pastor in Carbondale and her daughter for support and encouragement. I felt as if I was falling apart. Rob was not the man I thought he was and it pained me that I gave my heart to someone who did not cherish it.

The night before Rob was expected to depart for Kansas, I got an eerie feeling in the pit of my stomach, urging me to drive to Decatur at 10:00pm at night. I was dressed for bed, and this feeling would not let me have peace until I got into my car and began driving. I called ROB once I arrived. He was out with his friends watching a ball game, but came to his apartment to let me in and left again.

There were packed boxes everywhere. He was clearly leaving the following day. This was real. I needed to see it. At first, I just sat on the couch and was going to wait for him to return. Yet, I got the urge that came over me nearly a decade ago when I used to invade Lucas's privacy to unveil his dishonesty. Yes, I did it! I did what most women do when they're looking for answers and are suspicious they've been lied to. I began going through his shit!

His tablet was out in the open and unlocked. I looked through there first. I discovered he sent his ex-wife flowers while he and I were still in a relationship. It was also prior to him even telling me of his confirmative plans of moving. Then the trash… A used condom and black panties, which did not belong to me, sat right on top in plain view. I was utterly disgusted and in total disbelief. "You've got to be kidding me!" I told myself. Using a pencil, I tossed the evidence toward the middle of the floor, so that he could see it as soon as he walked into his bedroom.

I called him immediately. "You need to come back. I need to talk to you now!" I couldn't hold it in, I wanted to show him he was exposed and walk out of his life! "The game is still on. There's 2 minutes left and I'll be over there." In the meantime, I calmed myself down and promised myself to not go off on him. He did not deserve that sort of reaction out of me. I prayed, cried and got out whatever needed out of my system before he returned.

The moment he walked through the door, my heart dropped to the pit of my stomach. Although I planned every detail in my mind as to how this conversation would go, I was unsure of how it would play out once he saw I went through his belongings. I didn't care. I stood in the middle of his bedroom, with my hand on my hip and watched his reaction as he saw his own evidence on the floor. He sat on his bed, placed both of his hands on his head, leaned back and let out a sigh of guilt. He was speechless and had nothing to say for himself. I then revealed to him that I saw the email in his tablet, confirming his order of the flower delivery he had for his ex-wife.

"You went through my stuff?!" He had the nerve to question me, after being caught red handed. "You're damn right I did! I knew you were lying to me! This was the only way I could see the truth!" He continued to sit in silence. I became emotional after a few moments. I couldn't hold it in.

"Who are you?! Who the hell are you?! I don't even know you!" He tried to grab me by my arms to console me, but I resisted. "Don't touch me! Don't put your nasty, filthy hands on me! I don't know who you've been touching!" He tried to explain himself. I was not hearing it. There was nothing he could say to rectify the situation. The damage was done. I had both the proof and closure I had been seeking. The next step was for me to accept it, walk out of the door and begin my healing process so I could move on.

"You be blessed and take care..." I walked out of the door and did not turn around. I decided I would walk out of his life with class and my dignity. I did not yell at him; hit him, or do anything that would demean myself as a woman. I remained as calm as anyone possibly could in a situation such as this. I felt like I took my power back by walking out of his life. It was not him leaving me. It was me leaving him. It felt good, even though I hurt at the same time. I was changing the way the story ended. It ended on my terms, not on his. This was the peace and closure I needed to put him in my past.

Once again, I felt the adverse effects of another failed relationship. I knew that I did not want to go back to Eva as I had done before. I also did not want to continue repeating the same cycle of jumping in the bed or in a relationship with someone else to mask the pain. I realized I needed to love myself. I knew I had to take the same advice for myself, in which I often gave to my clients at work. I had to go through the pain, allow myself to feel it so I could move on and be healed from this person.

I began to experience panic attacks. I had never experienced these before. I called my counselor in a panic while at work one afternoon. "My heart is racing; my breathing is weird and I feel anxious! What's wrong with me?" My counselor suggested I imagine a bell curve, take a deep breath, picture my breath reaching the top of the curve and slowly release the air (or negative energy as I liked to think of it as) back out. I had never truly allowed myself to do this - feel the pain of heartbreak without partying, jumping into another relationship, or having sex to cope. I felt every ounce of the agonizing daggers that tore at my heart like a sword piercing its enemy. Once again, I lost myself to another relationship.

CHAPTER EIGHTEEN
Self-love

As a little girl, I often went into the front room of our house, put the window curtain on my head and pretended it was a veil. I could hear the wedding processional playing as I walked down the aisle to meet my groom. As the curtain fell down my back from walking too far away from the window, I turned around and repeated this act over and over again. I dreamt of being a bride - marrying the one who would stick by me through thick and thin. I imagined having a happy marriage and being with someone who truly loved and adored me. I didn't want what Mom and Dad had. I wanted something better.

As I reflected upon the poor decisions I had made in regards to relationships, I recalled this childhood dream and decided to make some changes to make my dream a reality. First, I needed to be in complete solitude and work on myself to ensure I would be ready for whoever was meant to be my life partner. I needed to love myself more.

I was tired of giving my body away and having nothing to show for it. I didn't want to just say I had obtained monetary possessions out of an unhealthy or failed relationship. I wanted to say I had someone who was going to stick with me regardless of the fight. Someone who sees who I am through God's eyes and desires no other woman to be in their life, but me.

I wanted to be a wife. I wanted to be someone's queen. I wanted to be a Mrs. and share a last name with the one who loves God more than they love me and even loves me a little more than I love them. I decided to practice celibacy while I worked on myself.

I made attempts in the past to not have pre-marital sex, but failed each time. Presumably because I was still struggling with unresolved hurts and pain. Each time I had a sexual encounter with someone, I felt guilty afterward. I knew it was wrong and should not have been giving my body away, regardless if I was in a relationship with that person or not. I was taught in the church to wait until marriage to have sex. However, I was exposed to sex at such an early age. A seed was already planted to have premarital sex.

I used sex to suppress the pain and feel a connection with another human being. Yet, after having a transformational experience where healing, revelations and self-empowerment occurred, I felt I had a chance at redemption to truly abstain from sex until the right one came along. I realized I was having irresponsible, pre-marital sex and was not engaging in this sacred act for the right reasons. I even put myself at risk for attracting an illness I could not get rid of. Thank God, the testing I had completed revealed otherwise and that I was fine! I used sex to cope, to suppress and to feel a false sense of security, while giving pieces of myself away to the wrong people.

Friends and family mocked me for this; they told me it wasn't possible to wait for the right one and that I would never be able to do it because everyone wants to 'test the water before they swim.' They reminded me of how "everyone has needs," and that it was "okay to have at least a friend with benefits." I, however, was thinking deeper into this. I knew the only way they could possibly understand my rationale was to show them.

What I desired and was determined to seek out was more than a euphoric thrill. I wanted to have the epitome of a friendship, companionship, spiritual partner, business partner, confidante and lover wrapped into one person; my life partner. And if this was the fleshly sacrifice I needed to make for it to come into fruition, then I was more than willing to go through with it.

Practicing celibacy and remaining abstinent from sex caused me to experience loneliness. I was so used to having someone there, albeit if it were a significant other or just a sexual partner. I was not accustomed to spending time alone with myself. I knew time alone was needed to enhance my growth and healing. I needed to hear those thoughts which surfaced when no one was around - the good and the bad - the insecurities, doubts, fears, and any old resentment that may have been lingering on. I had to address these thoughts on an individual basis, to their root and why they continued to perpetuate and remain in my conscious mind.

I didn't like being alone though. Granted, there were those moments I enjoyed alone time, mainly because I found something to preoccupy my thoughts. Whether it were running and/or exercising, reading or writing. I found busy work to do while alone. It was those moments, when everything got quiet, and no one else was around that I was avoiding, but needed to face. It was just me, my thoughts, my heart and God. I was avoiding this alone time of hearing what they had to say. I did not want to face it, but knew it was time that I did.

While Amari was away with his dad and his other family in Florida for the summer, it turned into a critical time for me. It was after Rob and I had split up and I was still struggling with coming to terms with what happened, why and moving forward. With Amari gone, I was in the house alone. I began spending more time with family and friends, doing anything possible to get out of the house to ignore the thoughts I had. I even caught up with old friends and hung out with them at a lounge or night club. But it was different this time. I didn't want to cope with alcohol to suppress my pain, or meet someone new just to have someone around, nor did I enjoy myself at these establishments. I was transforming, while realizing I was not that same person and I had the strength and courage to be alone, stop running from my problems and address them for the betterment of self.

This walk of celibacy wasn't just about not having sex to show my power as a woman by standing up for myself and what I believed in while valuing my worth, or a vow to God to wait until he sent me the one he made especially for me. It was about learning why I continued to have sex, address every thought and feeling associated with the act so I did not continue to repeat the same mistakes twice. It was both a learning and growing phase.

Once I changed my perspective on being celibate, I no longer looked at it as just me sacrificing fleshly desires for an ultimate purpose and goal. I searched for a deeper resolve. It was about recognizing that I did not need another person to validate my existence, or have sex to feel loved, wanted or feel secure. God validated my existence. I was working toward loving myself more and I valued my body so much so I only wanted my future life partner to have me in that manner.

Each person I had sexual encounters with, either made withdrawals or deposits, neither of the two being beneficial toward my well-being. Those who made withdrawals took pieces of me along with them when they left or I left because it wasn't a good situation for me. Ultimately, pieces of my heart were scattered about with various people. Those who made deposits left me with their past hurts, a mess which they released inside of me - new burden for me to carry. This caused me to not only have to deal with my own issues, but now have someone else's negative energy attached to mine.

I no longer wanted anyone else's withdrawals or deposits in my life. I decided to wait on the one who needed me in their life and they were willing to wait to have my body and get to know me first, from the inside-out.

Knowing this made it easier to not become desperate for a mate. Rather, I exercised patience. Desperation always ended badly. I ended up with someone whom I probably would have never been with if I weren't desperate. Seeking love in all the wrong places or looking for someone else to validate me caused me to give my body away to undeserving takers who did not value the soul which resides inside of the vessel. Because I earnestly sought after their love and approval, desperation caused me to not value or love myself first before being with someone else.

I felt like a dope fiend who was having constant withdrawals. I had a poor attitude. I could not stop thinking about having sex, or being intimate with someone. I questioned why I had decided to make such a drastic change. It was time to address the origin of my engagement with sex. I had a general idea of what it was, but I did not want to face the reality of it. I did not want to admit how I was originally introduced to sex.

I talked about others who had multiple children out of wedlock, especially if fathered by multiple men. I struggled with coming to grips that I was no different than them I just did not have the evidence, or the same number of children, to show for it. I too, spent most my life looking for love in all the wrong places. I did not want to be alone. The quiet time frightened me. I wanted to mask everything and pretend I was fine – just as I had been doing all along. I wanted to believe I had myself all together and did not need to work on my inner self. That was a lie. I still had another layer to unfold and another area of my past to address. An area which contributed to my sexual behaviors as an adult...

"He wasn't supposed to be out of prison yet!"

I was furious. Brian was out of sight, so I kept him out of my mind. I knew something happened to me as a little girl, but I did not have to face or deal with it. Brian was a drug dealer who had been incarcerated most my adulthood. I had not seen nor heard from him since I was a youth.

"I don't even want to see his face! I don't want to hear his voice! He makes my skin crawl!"

Crystal and I had been discussing the shocking news of Brian being released from prison earlier than expected. Family members, who were unaware of this burden I had been carrying, were excited about him being back home. I grieved him being out. I dodged phone calls and avoided being home just in case a family member stopped by unannounced and brought Brian with them. I did not want to face my demons. You know, "get the monkey off my back."

I met with my editor on a Sunday afternoon. She was returning my first three chapters she carefully reviewed and critiqued. As we got to the chapter regarding Brian, she mentioned how I did not express myself in the same manner as I did with the former chapters. I wrote from an objective point of view and basically skimmed over the facts without providing detail to the events which occurred concerning Brian. A profound epiphany came over me, as if a light switch were flipped on in a dark room. As I was writing my testimony to be an inspiration for others, I myself still had something to face, and had yet to do so.

"You're going to have to confront him, Casandra." Crystal had been encouraging me that Brian being out of prison may not be as awful as I portrayed it to be. I had an opportunity to face him, just as I had done with Dad and Mom. I could be completely set free from everything hurtful in my past. My breakthrough was at my fingertips.

"I'm scared!"

"What if he tries to minimize my feelings? Or make light of what he did to me years ago?" I thought I was never going to have to face him, and was okay with that. It was easier to not face him. I did not have to relive the moments. I did not want to remember the intricate details I blew away on those white seeds.

I spent weeks wrestling about how this conversation would occur – when, where, how, etc. I was nervous that I would sob uncontrollably, rather than articulate what I had been holding inside of a cage for so many years. Unexpectedly, on a Wednesday evening as I was driving to church for Bible study, I heard someone call my name and honk their horn. I turned my head to the left, and there he was.

"What's up cuz!" Brian was sitting on the passenger side of the car as Hank drove. I instinctively felt that this moment was approaching, but did not anticipate it to occur as soon as it did. "I need to talk you!" I boldly responded. The light was red and I obviously was not going to engage in small talk while in the middle of traffic. I wanted to get straight to the point. "You can get my number from Hank, he has it." Then I drove off and continued driving to church.

As I sat in Bible Study, I tried to concentrate and focus on the teachings, but it was difficult straying away from the multiple scenarios running through my mind of how this conversation between Brian and I would go.

"I wonder if he already knows what I want to talk to him about." "Does he remember what he did? Of course, he does! How could he forget that?!" The thoughts continued to get louder, as the Bible lesson was turning into background noise.

My phone was on silent, but I had it facing upward. Brian was calling. I mean at least I figured that was him. I did not recognize the number and assumed he had just gotten my number from Hank and was calling me to see what I wanted to talk to him about. A voice message icon popped up on my screen next. I couldn't listen to it because I was still sitting in Bible study. Eager to see what he had to say, I eventually excused myself from the service and left. It was nearly pointless for me to be there anyway because I was not attentive and my wandering mind would not allow me to focus on the message. My impatience got the best of me.

As soon as I walked out of the building, I listened to the voice message. "Casandra, this is your cousin Brian. This is my number, call me back." My heart began to race. Hearing his voice made my heart feel as if it were dropping down to the pit of my stomach. Anxiousness consumed me as I wondered how this conversation between us would go. I did not return his call. Instead, I called Crystal to let her know what happened.

I continued to avoid him. I had not seen him in years and was not prepared to face him. Yet, I knew it was necessary for me to heal and move forward. He continued to text me and call me days following our encounter. I ignored him. *"I'll call him when I'm ready."* I told myself.

I began thinking about the conversation Crystal and I had regarding me telling everyone else the importance of healing, and yet I was avoiding my own healing. What was I scared of? Why was it easier for me to face Dad, but I struggled with facing Brian? I decided to call Eva and ask her if she would come with me to go talk to Brian. She came with me when I went to talk to Dad, and for some reason I felt compelled to ask her to come with me again. We had not been on the best of speaking terms. She was still mad at me for going back to men. Yet, out of the kindness of her heart, she obliged. She knew what I had been through and felt this was very important.

"You need to do this." Eva always encouraged me to face my past, so that I could heal. It was admirable of her to put her personal feelings to the side and encourage me through a major moment in my life. Brian called me while I was at work. I knew I could no longer avoid him, so I answered.

"Hey, I'm at work. I'll text you when I get off." I whispered as I quickly hurried Brian off the line. I texted him and asked could we meet in a mutual place when I got off work so I could talk to him. He said we could. I called Eva and made sure that time was conducive with her work schedule. Thankfully, it was. Once I got off, I called Eva first to let her know I was going to pick her up. I text Brian informing him I was off work and asked where we could meet. "Come to my mom's." He replied. I wondered again if he was aware of what I was going to talk to him about.

"There's no way he knows. He wants me to meet him at Aunt Carol's! She doesn't even know about this!" I didn't care. I needed to get this off my chest and release the heavy burden which had been weighing down on me for far too long.

"I feel sick to my stomach." I didn't even give Eva a chance to close the door once she got inside of my car before I began rambling off about my nervousness. "Why? What's wrong?" She asked of me. "I just feel scared. Like I feel like that little girl in the bathroom again. What am I going to say to him?" I was beginning to feel so nauseous that I thought I was going to have to pull over to the side of the road to vomit. My pulse began to increase as my heartrate rose. My palms were sweaty and my thoughts were racing. Fear slowly took over my body.

"Maybe I should just turn around. I mean, he knows what happened. What's the point of talking about it, right?" I was trying to convince myself that this conversation was unnecessary and that I could heal without confronting him. "No, you need to do this, just like you did with your dad. Just talk to him." Eva was not going to allow me to back out of this. She knew how much I needed to talk to Brian and get this burden off my chest.

I called Brian to see where he was. He was in the car with Hank, and had just left his mom's house and asked me to just meet him on the street she lived on. As I drove on the street Aunt Carol lived on, I saw Hank's car parked on the side of the road and parked in front of him. It was a warm summer day and the sun was shining, like the days when Brian caught me in the bathroom. I had just left work and was still in my uniform. When I got out of the car, Brian was already standing behind my car. Eva and Hank remained in the respective cars they arrived in. It was just Brian and I, like before. This time it was *my* decision to be alone with him.

"He's shorter than I am." I thought to myself. He did not appear as the giant he did when I was a kid. "Are you going to take me to jail?" Brian asked of me in a jokingly manner, but seemed somewhat serious at the same time. "No, I'm a probation officer, not a cop and I just got off work." I began to see how the power had shifted. It was no longer I who was inferior to him. Here I stood, taller than he and in an authoritative position with my uniform on. Confidence began to calm me.

"Do you know why I need to talk to you?" I asked of Brian.

"No." He stated as he casually leaned against the car.

"I want to talk to you about something that happened years ago. When I was a little girl." I felt my voice gaining strength. I was about to release the words I wished I had said nearly 20 years ago. He continued to lean against the car and stared at me with confusion.

"Something you did to me. At Madea and Paw-Paw's house. In their bathroom." I paused. I was waiting for him to interject and say something. But he remained silent.

"You touched me inappropriately. You did things in that bathroom that affected my life!" I felt myself feeling empowered. I wanted to take my power back from him.

He continued to look at me with confusion. "I don't remember."

"What in the hell does he mean he doesn't remember?" I thought to myself.

"I had to go to counseling for that! You were wrong for that! I did not realize it then, but I know now that you were wrong! What you did was wrong!" Wow! It felt awesome saying those words! The little girl with the little yellow shorts had a voice and she spoke - firmly, confidently and with courage. She spoke!

"I don't know if you did it because something happened to you too or what, but I came to tell you that I forgive you. Not for you though, for me. I need to put this behind me, so that I can heal and move on with my life." It was short, sweet and to the point. I did not feel the need to go into grotesque detail. I wanted to acknowledge that I knew what he had done, that it was wrong and how it affected my life, but that I forgave him and was putting it behind me.

A moment of silence sat between us. He appeared shocked. Here I stood taller than him, with my blue polo uniformed shirt, which said "Adult Probation Officer" above the county shield and my hand on my hip. I spoke up for myself, for the first time ever to him and he was speechless.

"I'm sorry. Thank you for forgiving me."

"Ah, an admission of guilt!" I thought to myself. He spoke the words so softly when he said them, as if he didn't want anyone else to hear them.

We both continued to stand in silence. I had nothing else to say to him. I felt as if a huge weight had been lifted off me and was free from the secret which I carried for nearly two decades.

As soon as we left, I dropped Eva off to her car and went to April's house. I needed to decompress. I pulled my cell phone out, and began to journal the encounter I had. I told myself that as the words left my fingertips into my cell phone, so did the painful and burdensome feelings attached with them. I was freeing myself from another experience that had too much power, for too many years over my life.

I confronted my past, forgave those who offended me and took major leaps and bounds toward healing and restoration. Yet, there was another piece to the puzzle missing. I needed to forgive myself. I needed to love myself – truly and wholeheartedly love me. I did not love myself as much as I thought, and I could not fix this alone. I needed something only God could give me. To obtain self-love, I had to go into solitude and seek Him- the Creator alone. Not a man, or a woman, not a friend, or a foe, or another hobby or endeavor could resolve the lack I had and the void which needed filled. I needed a touch from God. I knew if I could connect with God on a deeper level, my life would never be the same.

I needed to do this without anyone being there to validate me or a date to make me feel special. I needed to do this without someone holding me at night, giving me a false sense of security. I needed to do this without having sex, just to feel wanted. I needed to learn how to love Casandra, flaws and all, by myself. I needed to do this without the help of others, but with the help of God. I knew it was not going to be easy, but I had to do it. My breakthrough – my life - depended upon it.

I felt like I had to teach myself how to be a strong, classy, and fearless woman. With Mom, not being home much the older I got, I learned a lot from Dad and my environment. I only remember a couple of lessons about being a woman from Mom.

One late night, or even possibly early into the next day, I went into the bathroom to urinate. Mom was taking a bath. She began telling me how it was time for me to start shaving. I could hardly keep my eyes open from being in a deep slumber. It was rare to have these sorts of talks with Mom since she wasn't hardly home. Hell, I had to learn about proper hygiene and what to do when my period came from Ebony. Go figure. She taught me more than I wanted to know at one point, and on the other hand she taught me all that I needed to know.

I learned how to be a woman from whomever I felt could teach me: teachers, Aunts, family, friends and their mothers, co-workers, colleagues, celebrities, etc. I watched and observed their mannerisms and demeanor. I picked intricate details from certain women that I admired and applied them to my life.

I even learned a lot from Lucas's Aunt Michelle. She taught me more than she will ever realize. "I wish I could jump into your body, gorgeous. You don't know what you have." When I first met her, she constantly complemented me on my outward appearance. "Darling, you are so beautiful!" She called me complimentary names in lieu of Casandra most times. Her compliments were the catalyst for me building up my self-esteem. She also taught me about the power we have in our words.

Her home was covered with positive affirmations and declarations in various forms. She had them everywhere; her kitchen, bathroom, living room, bedroom and even in the hallway. I had never seen such a thing before. It was intriguing. Even after Lucas and I split up, Aunt Michelle welcomed her home to me for vacationing. She and the rest of her family told me I would always be family to them and was always welcome in their homes. The energy and the environment in general was peaceful and calming. I looked forward to not only having a good time in Florida, but rejuvenating my mind, body and soul.

Over time, I began to borrow her ideas for home décor. I wrote out positive affirmations, found décor with positive statements, and cut out clippings from magazines and placed them everywhere in my home. I knew I needed to surround myself with my own positive energy and affirmations if I was going to embark upon a journey toward self-love.

I went on a hiatus. I did not accept dates from men, nor their contact information. I stopped going to the bars, clubs and special organized events, stayed to myself and did even more work on myself. I did things that made me happy and feel loved. I began buying myself flowers and placing them in a vase at home. I took candle lit baths, listened to music or read, and enjoyed a glass of wine. I ran while listening to audible devotions or motivational speeches. I even went out to eat to my favorite restaurants and dined alone. I began to feel comfortable being in my own company.

I fought through loneliness and the fears I had of being alone by praying more and asking God for guidance. I looked myself in the mirror, directly into my own eyes, in attempts to connect with my inner being. I talked to her. I told the little girl who blew the white seeds that everything was going to be okay. I reassured her that the love she builds for herself will enable her to love others greatly. I built confidence inside of her, pointing out her strengths and the obstacles she overcame. I told that little girl inside of me, to rise and be the mighty woman of God she was created to be.

CHAPTER NINETEEN

"Because You're Human"

I used to think that if I was perfect, Mom and Dad would love me. I felt if I could be presumed as perfect, maybe Dad would be nicer to me and Mom would be home more often. I tried to be the best at everything. I thought if I got first chair when I played the Clarinet, they would start showing up to my musicals.

I thought by getting good grades, they would want to spend more time with me or do something fun as a reward. If I won track meets and they saw my name in the newspaper, they would come to cheer me on. I assumed being the best would capture their attention. If only I could catch their attention, they would praise me for the good things I had accomplished and want to be a part of it. They would celebrate *me*, in an essence.

Unfortunately, this mindset spilled over into my adulthood. I used it as a means for acceptance and praise from others, an ego booster if you will. Perfection is what I thought was needed to be accepted and loved by others. I wanted my outward appearance to be perfect. I wanted to wear the perfect outfit, have the perfect hair style and decorate my home perfectly. I wanted to be the perfect mom, have the perfect son, be the perfect employee and overall, be the perfect woman. I generally wanted to be and do everything perfectly.

Mistakes and flaws made me feel as if I was the scum of the earth. Any fallible thing I did I immediately condemned myself for, feeling as if God Himself wouldn't dare forgive this old retch. My heart burned with grief and my stomach felt soiled with poison as shame and sorrow consumed my inner being. All of this was because I wanted to portray perfection - something that does not exist.

Over some time, I had come to the realization that perfection was only a façade. The image in the mirror did not resemble perfection. Unbeknownst to me, I was poisoning myself rather than helping myself. This mindset robbed me of being my true and authentic self. Perfection does not exist. This is the reality I finally had to face. Perfection does not exist and it is completely normal and human of me to be imperfect.

I had yet one more person to face – myself. I had become disgusted with the poor decisions I made from the hurt and pain of my past. I was very self-critical of my own self and often beat myself up for the choices I had made and the outcomes of those choices in my life. I was embarrassed about being a single mother. I felt that it made me look incompetent, like I was unable to be woman enough to keep a man, or hold a family together. I felt the lack of financial, physical and emotional support I had not consistently received from Lucas for Amari was a direct reflection of who I was as a mother. I felt like I had failed Amari because his dad was living clear across the country, only seeing him once a year and had minimal to no involvement in his life. I felt pathetic each time I called Lucas, pleading with him to help with Amari and to at least be more involved in his life.

I felt less than a woman because I was in my 30's and had not even been married yet. I felt that each man who had left me, regardless if they were good for me or not, meant something was wrong with *me*. I continued to blame my past for the reasoning behind being a single mother, in her 30's, who was on this mission in life to find herself. *"I mean, who waits until this point in their life to find out who they really are?"* I thought something was wrong with that.

I was tired of using my past as a crutch to not do or be more. If I was going to use my past as a crutch for anything, I wanted to use it to enable me to forgive more, love deeply, be kind, and generous. I knew how it felt to not have these components which are crucial to healthy self-development.

I didn't even know how much I hated myself. I thought perfection produced love, but I did everything out of hate for my own self. Once I got past the point of running to heal, I worked out for other reasons. I hated my body. I read more and studied because I thought I was stupid and not adequate to associate with intellectuals. I went on spurts of eating healthier because I thought it would make me appear slimmer – I despised the aftermath of having a child. I tanned in the summer time because I hated when my complexion looked more Caucasian than black. My actions were out of self-hatred, not love. I was failing at producing desired results.

I thought if I loved someone else, then they would love me in return and fill the empty void that was still taking up space in my soul. I put all my energy into loving others, in hopes they would love me the same way, if not more. *"If I could just love them perfectly, then they would love me perfectly in return."* This method was not effective, to say the least.

The desire to be perfect to produce love was not working out as I had anticipated. I read through old journal entries, some dated from even a few years ago, and realized I was going around in circles. Each year, around the same time, I went around the same mountain. There were vicious and unhealthy cycles which needed to be broken. By doing things out of hatred against myself with the need to be perfect, depression easily settled in. It prevented me from being grateful and seeing the good in all things. This mentality only allowed me to see flaws and negativity.

As the depression took root, the emotional eating began. I used food to comfort the uneasy feelings and discomfort I felt from focusing on the wrong things. Then the weight gain came in from stuffing my face to suppress the monster inside of me. From there, I began hating myself all over again. Then the cycles repeated themselves. I began working out again, because I hated my body. I then masked the ugliness dwelling inside of myself, by wearing a smile and making sure my appearance did not reflect such.

I beat myself up inside until the point of crippling myself on the outside. It prohibited me from functioning in a productive manner. I was unable being able to be consistent when working toward goals I set for myself. I also did not allow myself the freedom to make mistakes and learn along the way. If I was not perfect, then I was not enough.

I often gave up on myself. I stopped caring about my health and began eating poorly and exercised less. I stopped caring about maintaining healthy relationships with others. I allowed my career to consume me to the point I hated it and wanted to give up. I lost all motivation to simply continue to strive to become a better and happier person. I felt that if people, places, and/ or things could not make me happy, then I would never achieve happiness and just wanted to give up on life.

"I want to live! I want to live!" I kept thinking about death. I wondered if anyone would notice if I was gone, but somewhere inside I wanted to fight. Tears streamed down my face as I chanted, *"I want to live!"* to myself. I knew I had to fight this thing. I had to do the opposite of what I normally had done in past times when this ugly thing tried to consume my life! I had to turn the lights on at home and stop sitting in the dark. I had to surround myself around family, friends and loved ones and stop isolating myself. I had to eat a healthy and well balanced diet and stop emotionally binge eating on carbs and sugars to cope with my emotions. I had to get up and exercise and stop sleeping my life away. I had to smile and stop frowning. I had to fight! Fight for my life! But most importantly, I had to learn to love my life.

As I drove home on a cold December night, I began to cry. I tried to not let a sound part from between my lips and just let the tears stream down my cheeks. Amari was in the passenger side and I did not want him to worry about his mom. I didn't cry because I felt sad, or sorry for myself. I cried because I desperately wanted to beat depression once and for all and was feeling defeated. I cried because my son had to wake me up some mornings because I could not bring myself to get up. I cried because my son recognized a pattern with this ugly monster that would creep in and take over my life and he just wanted his mom "to be happy." I cried because I wanted to fight like I had never fought before and I was scared I would fail or the depression would win.

As I drove home, I started thinking about Christmas lights. I thought about the time Grandpa Frank drove us around as kids to look at the Christmas lights while we were in Huntington, Indiana for Thanksgiving. I drove Amari around different neighborhoods and shared with him this very story. We pointed out our favorite light decorations and admired how pretty and bright the neighborhoods were. I immediately felt relief. I kept driving. Eventually my smile returned, and we went home. I knew each moment I had to fight. But I'd rather fight, than give into the ugly monster and allow it to win. *"I am stronger than depression. Depression has no power over my life. I will live and be victorious! I am an overcomer!"* I began to feel empowered all over again as I repeated these phrases to myself.

In overcoming depression, I had to remind myself that *"this moment does not define my day and this day does not define my life."* A bad day, or not feeling "happy" now, did not mean I had a bad life. I tried to catch the negative thoughts as they surfaced to the forefront of my mind and cancel them out with a positive affirmation. I even spoke the affirmations aloud to audibly hear the positivity penetrating my mind.

I lacked consistency in working toward my goals and aspirations, because I was fueled by hatred. I started goals with all the motivation in the world, but once that motivational high came down, I was back at square one. I was consistent in being hard on myself, giving up on myself and starting over. I was consistent at being inconsistent. I wanted to be consistent in following through on goals, completing tasks I set out before myself and most of all doing them all out of love. I wanted to turn this into a life style, not just a temporary fix. I needed to love myself first, before I could produce an action out of love.

I thought that by healing from the emotional wounds and scars of my past, I had overcome the aforementioned. I was always in a constant battle with myself and my thoughts. *"I mean, didn't I already work hard enough to overcome all of that? Why do I still need to do "self-help" type of work to feel better?"*

I finally had come to the realization that the work never ends. If I wanted to maintain healing and continue to grow in life, I had to continuously water the seeds I planted inside of myself. I needed to continue to do the things which initially brought me to a better place: listening to devotionals, reading positive and motivating material, exercise and eat healthy, be compassionate, kind and loving toward myself, being aware of myself, affirming my worth, etc. I could not stop doing these things just because I felt good or better for a moment and thought I had "arrived." I could not only maintain the healing I had achieved, but could no longer continue to grow as an individual if I ceased in using these helpful tools. The work never ends.

As I got adjusted by my chiropractor on a Tuesday evening after work, I began complaining about my inconsistencies in achieving my fitness goals and eating clean on a consistent basis. I wanted to know *"how did everyone else do it?"* How did those who had the well envied six-pack abs, achieve the body of their dreams? Why couldn't I remain consistent to reach those goals?

My chiropractor said something so simple, yet so profound, "because you're human." He reminded me of how a lot of those people I was referring to were either professionals or had hired personal nutritionist and a trainer who guided them each step along the way. I had an "aha" moment. *"Yes! I am human!"* I needed to accept that. I needed to accept that it was okay to be imperfect. I decided to let go of my need to be perfect and to be more loving and compassionate toward my own self.

I had to accept that perfection does not exist amongst humans. It is only a figment of our imagination. I needed to learn how to be okay with being imperfectly perfect. I needed to learn how to love my imperfect self. I had to learn to accept my own self, flaws and all. I had to accept the pudge left on my belly as a reminder I could bring another life into this world, the gap between my teeth, the large sized hands and feet my ancestors passed down to me that they once needed to survive, my coarse, red hair that had become my trademark to most, in addition to many other flaws I harped on about myself. I had to accept all of me, once and for all.

If I wanted to live a life full of abundance, happiness, peace, love and joy, I needed to consciously decide each day that I was going to live just that way. I realized the life I desired would not live itself or magically appear. I had to make a choice and put in work to see the fruition of the life I desired to live.

It can be a bit overwhelming when you try to look at the bigger picture and see how far you have yet to go. In the grand scheme of things, I had a general idea of the woman I wanted to become, the life I wanted to live and the amount of people I desired to reach through my transparency. Because I had not achieved nor become those things yet, I did not think I was enough. I needed to love myself at the place I was at in my now.

I began by looking at how far I had come. I thought back to the days where I washed clothes for five people in a bathtub, with my feet. Now, I have operable washer and dryer machines in my home. I recalled the days where I had to boil hot water to take a bath. I now had heat in my home. I remembered the days when we had to walk, take the bus, or catch a cab to wherever we had to go. I became filled with gratitude that I had transportation of my own. I recounted the countless times I searched for love in all the wrong places and gave my body to undeserving takers. I now valued my own self-worth and knew what I deserved and refused to settle for less. I learned how to get to know someone without feeling I had to give away my body to hold their interest in me! Relief consumed me as I began to know the new me.

This journey that I am on is a lifelong journey. Happiness comes from within. It comes from an intentional choice I make each day to want more, to be more and to apply what I've learned to my life to achieve that. I had to let go of my fears, doubts, and insecurities and accept the woman I have turned into, while growing into the woman I aspired to be. I was tired of falling in and out of depression, failed diets, giving up on myself and not loving myself more. I decided I was going to be the change that I wanted to see.

CHAPTER TWENTY

Let Go, Let God

The need to have complete control in my adult life was a direct result of the lack of control I had in my childhood. I felt to prevent hurt, pain and any other form of unfortunate happenings from reoccurring in my life, I needed to have control over everything and everyone. I felt powerless if I did not have control. I felt my destiny was in someone else's hands if they had all the power and control. The need to have and be in control was the root of fear and worry. These fears were developed during my childhood; mainly the fear of never being loved or being worthy of love.

By living in constant fear and worry, I developed anxiety. I experienced my first panic attack after Rob broke my heart. I was petrified of being hurt again. I wanted to be able to control and create optimal outcomes from my encounters with others. After being left in similar ways by two men in my life whom I cared deeply for, I began to think it was due to a lack of control on my end. *"Had I just controlled my emotions more and not loved them so much, maybe they would have stayed."* I was convinced if I had controlled the situation better, the outcomes may have been different.

When I tried to seduce Lucas in attempts to make him stay with me, I was trying to control the outcome of our relationship. I didn't want to be alone, nor a single mother. When I began seeing women, I was trying to control not getting hurt again. I feared being hurt again; specifically, by a man. Fear and worry made me want to have control over everything. Eventually I had come to the realization that I could not control other people or certain outcomes. After reflecting and viewing those situations from a different perspective, I realized their rejection was God's protection! Lucas turned out to be an inconsistent dad at some point. Dating women did not save me from getting hurt, and Rob turned out to be a womanizer and a liar.

After some time had passed, Rob reached out to me. Initially, I had received phone calls on my office phone at work, with someone on the other end saying "I'm coming back for you" and then hanging up. This happened several times and I figured it was Rob reaching out to me. He began texting me from an unknown phone number, telling me about his "woe is me" life. I ultimately decided to accept a phone call from him to hear him out and let him say whatever it was he felt he needed to say.

Rob was going through a lot of unexpected turmoil and desired my sympathy and forgiveness to give him another chance. At this moment, I questioned, *"was it him, and not me?!"* After Rob left, I felt like something was wrong with *me*, as a woman. I questioned if I had not done enough of something or too much of something else. Yet, when he called to beg for another chance, I suddenly felt like maybe it wasn't *me* after all.

Rob admitted to returning to his ex-wife, believing they could rekindle what they once had for the sake of their daughter. He expressed how he later realized she jealously wanted to pull him away from me. He continued to share the unfortunate happenings he was experiencing since leaving Illinois. I was relieved that he was receiving his karma for hurting me and shared it with me. I didn't know if it was true or not, but the mere fact that he was begging for my forgiveness and asking for another chance to make things right with me showed me there was nothing wrong with *me*. He continued to beg and plead for another chance for the next few months. He appeared convinced if he continued to profess his love for me, that I would eventually give in and give him another chance.

Deep down, I had hoped he would come back for me because Lucas never did. I always wanted a man to become aware of what he had with me, and return begging. I wanted this from Lucas years ago. After Rob pleaded for another chance, I became aware of my worth. If he truly loved me, he would not have left me for another woman and cast me off. I deserved so much more than that. I told him I was not interested in rekindling anything with him. I suggested he move on with his life, as I had done the same with mine.

I not only gained my power back from the heartbreak *he* caused, but the heartbreak Lucas caused as well. The old Casandra would have taken him back, thinking this was love because he came back for me, not remembering the pain he caused and inflicted. I took my power back from any man who had ever left me by not getting back together with Rob. I took my power back by valuing my own worth and trusting that God had someone for me who would not leave me and would value me in their life. I stood on that. I stood up for myself. I decided to protect my heart this time and learn from my past experiences. I decided to love *me* more.

My first feelings of rejection came from Dad. I never felt like his little princess or "daddy's little girl." I thought something was wrong with me and that is why he was abusive towards me. Going forward, I was mistreated by men in relationships. They cheated on me, abused me, used me for sex, abandoned me with a baby, left me for other women, etc. I never had a man treat me right and stick around. I wanted love so badly that I was willing to sacrifice myself for it.

Not this time! If anyone deserved my love more, it was me. I decided to love me more than I had loved anyone else. I decided to let go of the need to be loved by another to feel love for myself. I let go of the need to be validated by others.

I let go of my fears and worries that another man would not love me again. The old Casandra would have taken Rob back for many reasons, including the fear that this was my only opportunity to have love from a man. I gave up fearing the unknown. I had peace in knowing there was a Higher Power other than myself. One who was in control, watching over me and protecting me to ensure that I would be just fine if I listened to the inner voice placed inside of my being. It was the voice of God whispering to me - guiding and directing my path.

When I was with Eva, I isolated myself completely because of her possessive, abusive, and jealous nature. I failed at maintaining healthy and positive relationships with those important to me. I knew if I loved myself, my family and friends, it would fill the voids of needing a romantic partner to make me feel loved.

In letting go of the need to be in control, I also needed to let go of my expectations of how I thought others should be and do things. I felt if people weren't reaching out to me, then they did not care about me. My mind was so conditioned and brainwashed from years of abuse and neglect that I did not know what a healthy relationship was. I realized I could only control myself, and no one else. I could not control any of those men leaving my life, but I could control not allowing them back into my life.

I learned to meet people where they are. I stopped trying to fit people into a mold of who I thought they should be. I often created personalities and characteristics in my mind of how others should be; specifically, to benefit my own needs. I had to accept that no one is perfect. I could either accept people for who they were, or if I did not care for them enough, I simply did not have to deal with them at all.

I had gotten into a pattern of expecting others to motivate and encourage me out of a longing desire for my parents to do it. When I allowed negative thoughts to fester until the point I fell into a depression, I wanted someone else to pick me up and tell me things would get better – that I "could do it" – that I was loved and someone was proud of me. I reminded myself of the moments I motivated and encouraged myself. I encouraged myself to begin to face the hurts of my past. I decided to let go of my need for approval from others and find approval within myself. I did not need others to motivate and encourage me all the time. I had learned to do that for myself.

This process began by letting go of the expectations that my parents should reach out to me for a relationship. I was very upset because they both promised to be more involved in me and Amari's life when I confronted them about my childhood. However, nothing had changed. They were there when I seldom asked them to help me with Amari (because I had no other options), but they were not reaching out to me for a relationship.

I decided if I wanted a relationship with them, that I needed to be proactive and reach out. I needed to meet them where they were. It began with simple things, such as acknowledging my parents on holidays, like Mother's Day, Father's Day and birthdays. I randomly sent them text messages, telling them I loved them. I had not yet come to a place where I could call and tell them verbally. There was still an awkwardness of not having an actual relationship with them that lingered inside of me. I started where I felt most comfortable.

For Mother's Day one year, I arranged for all of us to get together and meet for breakfast at a restaurant. I even paid for Mom and Dad's meals. I wanted to show them I did not hate them. For Father's Day, I rallied April and Crystal to assist me in cooking Dad a home cooked meal. I delivered it to Dad by myself and sat in the very house where the horrific memories of my childhood resided, and sparked up conversation with him. I also invited Mom and Dad to Amari's school activities and athletic events.

I thought if I could show them that I was inviting them into my world, it would tear down the walls of fear, guilt and any other barriers which hindered the fruition of our relationship. I decided to let go of the negative memories I had of my parents. I decided to embrace the lessons I learned from them, which molded me into the woman I was today.

Not only did I decide to let go of the negative memories I had of Mom and Dad, but I wanted to let go of all the negative memories I had of my childhood. I wanted to learn as much as one possibly could from those adverse experiences and use them as tools to help me be a better person. I decided to stop blaming Mom and Dad, and anyone else for the matter, for my own unhappiness.

I frequently blamed them, or whoever I was in a relationship with for my own happiness, or the lack thereof. I decided to point the finger back at myself and dig for the truth. I realized that I controlled my own happiness. That it was a decision I had to make daily. No one could give or take away my joy. Nor was it anyone else's fault if I was happy or not. I had to take responsibility for myself, the choices I made and the outcomes that were a direct result of those choices.

I no longer wanted to be a broken, miserable and bitter woman. I wanted to be happy, free, and love as much as one possibly could. I got tired of building a life based upon hurts from my past. No, I could not change my past, nor the events that occurred, but I could change myself with hard work, dedication, and persistence. Life is too short to hold onto anger, resentment and pain. It felt better to forgive, allow myself to feel the pain, let it pass and heal from it. It was as if an enormous amount of weight had been lifted from my entire being.

Once I stopped blaming Mom and Dad, and everyone else from my past for my outcomes or shortcomings in life and decided to make different choices, my life began to transform right before my eyes. Through prayer and strengthening my spiritual life by having a closer relationship with God and consistently going to counseling sessions allowed for the manifestations of a new me to occur.

I drove past Madea and Paw-Paw's house every day on the way to work. On the way home, I drove past Mom and Dad's house, the house I mainly grew up in and they still lived in. At first, this was unintentional. My position as a probation officer required me to work downtown in the county courthouse. Each time I drove by a house, I remembered a thought, a feeling, a smell or an experience. I began to make this scenic route intentional. Sure, I could have chosen other routes, but there was something about driving past those houses that reminded me of the strength I had. They held so many of my secrets, memories, nightmares, laughs and cries. If the walls could talk, I wondered what they would reveal? Images replayed in my mind as if recollecting scenes from a film.

I could still see so vividly those yellow shorts I wore the first time my older cousin caught me in the bathroom; smell the booze on Dad's breath and feel my other older cousin touch me in the same place her brother had. I could hear Mom's cries for Dad to stop, see the bruises on her face and feel the anger that grew within me over the years.

Yet, I also saw this little girl who pleaded to God for a miracle, ran with tranquility and freedom, and laughed until tears fell upon her cheeks with her younger sisters. Of course, I remembered the bad, but as I drove past these houses I desperately wanted to remember the good. I wanted to replace those haunted memories, with pleasant experiences, to remind myself to see the good in all things. I wanted to let go of my painful past and embrace a promising future. I no longer wanted to remember them for the negative experiences I had, I wanted to thank them for the strength it all gave me. Driving past these houses, daily, was a transformative experience for me. I changed the way I viewed them, the world, and myself, one drive at a time.

I used to despise Mom and Dad. I even took after some of their unfavorable behaviors by coping with life through substances and alcohol, food, or staying in unhealthy relationships that I knew were not good for me. As I learned to let go of the negativity and release the harmful memories that caused me no good, I embraced whatever good I could find in Mom and Dad. Throughout the growth and transformative experience, I didn't mind recognizing the favorable traits which were passed down to me.

I took after Mom's professional work ethic, yet added my own niche by learning how to balance being more involved in Amari's personal interests. I also took Amari to the same library I went to with Mom on the weekends. We checked out various books in the genre of our liking. I wanted to pass down this tradition to Amari. Mom usually stayed on the first floor as she explored the science fiction section. I used to wonder if she used the books to escape her reality. I, however, chose to roam about on the second floor where most of the non-fiction, self-development books were. I desired to improve and work on my inner self, not just to be a better person, but to be a better mother.

I learned how to be stern and assertive from Dad, yet, tried to have respect and tact when addressing issues or standing up for myself in various situations. I also ate healthier and still exercised in my adult years. I valued the background I had on natural home remedies. I attributed this to Dad. I thought about how Dad could have buckled with the pressure of raising three girls and left. Yet, he stayed. I started to appreciate the good in them.

Because of my experiences, I became a strong, independent and bold leader. I no longer despise Mom and Dad. Now, I thank them. I am grateful for it all, because each experience taught me something, built my character, and developed my strength.

Life is too short to hold onto to anger, bitterness, resentment and pain. It was like poisoning my own soul and often hurt me more than the people I was holding grudges against. It felt so much better, more liberating and more rewarding to forgive, heal and let it all go. It felt as if an enormous amount of weight had been lifted from my entire being. I felt free to finally be the fearless woman I was created to be.

Forgiving those who wronged or disappointed me was not about letting them off the hook or making light of the offense. It was about releasing the power and the strongholds they held over my life. The strongholds which caused me to be so bound and restricted internally that I was unable to be free to love, even my own self. I learned to see life through the lenses of the ones I had been harboring ill will against. It enabled me to have more compassion for them, making room for forgiveness to occur. Hurt people, hurt other people. This mindset helped me to forgive my dad. When I realized he was drowning his sorrows in a bottle, and that at one point I too had done the same, it allowed me to forgive him.

Forgiveness is for you too! It's for your peace at night, your sanity, your health, and your freedom. If you will take steps toward healing, and lay your burdens at God's feet, your life will never be the same; YOU will never be the same! Internal transformation is not different than external transformation. You can't eat healthy and work out for one day and expect to jump in front of the mirror and voila! A six pack of abs has magically appeared! That's not realistic. Internal transformation is the same in terms of going through a process which requires hard work, dedication and consistency. But the fruit of your labor will be worth it and you will reap many rewards if you do not give up.

I also went back to the root of when my change initially started. During the summer while Amari was away with his dad's family, Grandma Cassie called me. She asked if I wanted to accompany her in going to Aunt Katie and Aunt Molly's house in Indiana. She was taking a couple of my nieces, and welcomed help. I thought this was my perfect opportunity to thank all of them for being a part of the reason I had become the woman I was today. I accepted her invitation with much excitement.

Aunt Katie and Aunt Molly were so excited that I was visiting them. I had not seen them since April's wedding, but had not been in Indiana since I was 19 years old. Our first night there, Aunt Katie and I went to the store together. I began to share with her why I came to live with them 13 years ago. I shared with her the abuse I endured, the domestic violence I witnessed, and the times I was molested at Madea and Paw-Paw's house. As she drove to the store, she silently listened. 13 years ago, while we drove to Indiana for me to start my new life, they asked me why I was coming to live with them. I had finally mustered up the courage to tell her.

She did not appear to be shocked about the abuse and domestic violence. She was, however, disturbed and quite upset to hear I had been molested as well. She shared with me that she had asked Mom to leave Dad. "Your mom said 'Oh, I could never do that. He told me I could go, but I was not taking his kids with.'" Aunt Katie went on to tell me how she tried to convince Mom to leave and take us with her, but that Mom refused. "Your mom said, 'I couldn't. He would hunt me down.'"

I just listened. The little girl inside of me, who fought, begged and pleaded for Mom to leave, got angered all over again. I thought, *"She had a way out and she did not take it?!"* At that moment, I felt she never truly wanted us, she just wanted Dad. Knowing that Mom had a way out, an option to bring us up in a different way, in love and serenity and she didn't take it pained me.

I imagined what life would have been like, had she left Dad and we lived in Indiana. I imagined the three of us girls running around, in the country, chasing each other. We were laughing and having fun. We were happy. I pictured myself going to sleep and waking up in complete serenity, with no fighting, yelling or crying waking me up out of my sleep. Then I snapped back into reality. It was ironic that I still ended up in Indiana. I knew then that my destiny was to eventually arrive to that safe place I had come to know.

I thanked Aunt Katie and told her that by them accepting me into their home, and loving me the way they did had such a profound and positive influence on my life. I was certain that was the reason my life went in a different direction. She encouraged me and told me that I am who I am today despite of my upbringing because of the choices I made. She told me that those choices led me to where I am today.

I learned that everything in my life was a direct result of the relationship I had with God and the choices I had made. The consequences or rewards resulted from those choices. I preferred to reap as many rewards as possible. While embracing the consequences of the lessons learned from my mistakes, I decided to let go of the vicious lies I told myself over the years.

I let go of the lies that I was not good enough. I was not smart enough. I was not worthy of love. I let go of the lies that I can't do this or that. It was time for me to let go of those crippling and debilitating lies which had more power than they deserved for far too long over my life. I had to embrace who I truly was - an ambitious, loving, caring, giving, intelligent, bright, witty, fearless, God-fearing woman and mother, who was beautiful from the inside-out. I no longer allowed others to define who I was.

I questioned my ability and the power of God that resides on the inside of me. I feared failure and doubted if I had the capabilities to touch that one soul whose life could change for the better. Confiding in God for reassurance, I was given a new perspective which caused me to have an epiphany.

"This isn't about you. This is for that little girl or boy who's waking up to abuse by their mother, father, or whomever and can turn to your words, your story and find a way out. If you only touch that one person, your mission would have been accomplished."

Then it came to me, at one point in time that was me. The little girl who searched for a way out and thirst for inspiration from someone, somewhere to overcome my adversities, was me. Then I decided I would share my story for the little girl I once was.

I let go of my fears, insecurities, doubts, the need to be perfect, in control and the need to be accepted by others. I let go of the broken woman I once was and all the pain that she carried. I had to forgive myself for poor choices I made throughout my life. I spoke to the little girl inside of me, who still desired to be loved and supported by her parents. I told her that she had love and support from so many others. I had to tell the little girl inside of me that she grew up to be a strong and bold woman. She was enough and had enough. I spoke to the woman the little girl had become.

I told myself, *"I am enough. I am worthy of love and have love for myself and others. I have to be who I am today, not who I used to be."*

I continue to go to counseling for maintenance. I believe this journey I am on will last a lifetime. There will always be an area to overcome, and an area that needs to be addressed. During a session with my counselor I shared how I wanted to help others with my story. I shared my doubts and insecurities, and my hopes and dreams. At the end of the session, my counselor gave me a hug and reassured me of the changes and continuous progress I have made over the years.

I felt empowered and encouraged by her feedback, especially coming from someone who's initial encounter with me was shortly after a suicide attempt. As I walked back to my car, I told the little girl inside of me, that those seeds she once blew off the dandelions into the sky, which held her wishes and dreams, were coming true.

I let go of my old negative and stinking way of thinking, and began to learn new positive and healthier ways to think. I let God heal me, mold me and shape me into the awesome woman I was created to be. I decided to live a life of purpose. I shifted my focus toward running after my destiny.

I stopped running away from people, my fears and problems. I decided to run with God. I felt I owed the Creator my life. I gave it back to the One who placed me on this earth, to use me in the capacity in which God saw fit. I let go of what I thought my life should have been, and was allowing God to use me to help other people in a way I had never imagined. I am letting go, and letting God have Thine own way in me…

Tears were streaming down my face as I was writing and talking to God about how scared I was to tell my story and to lay myself bare for others to see. I thought Amari was asleep at the time. However, as the tears continued to run down my cheeks, I felt two arms come up from behind me, squeeze my neck and ask me if I was okay. Amari kissed me on my cheek and told me he loved me. I smiled and told him I loved him back. I explained to him I was praying and was just fine. As this happened, Kirk Franklin's 'Imagine Me' was playing in the background. At that moment, I realized everything I had ever been through and felt was gone. I am healed. And I pray for the soul reading this to be healed as well.

Acknowledgments

First and foremost, I MUST give all the praise, glory and honor to the Most High, my Creator. God has never left me, nor forsook me. I am eternally grateful for Thee…

Mom and Dad, thank you for listening to me when I had the courage to speak. Grandma Sandy, thank you for being the family "grammar Nazi!" Your wisdom, knowledge and love helped to shape and mold me into the woman I am today. Thank you. Aunt Patty and Lisa, thank you for always loving me and supporting me. You two are truly my earthly angels. Hope and Tasha, thank you for your friendship and sisterly love. Liz, thank you for reminding me of the progress I made. Thank you for listening to my innermost thoughts, without judgement.

Coach McBride, thank you for telling me I can do anything I put my mind to. Aunt Clemma, thank you for telling me "it gets greater later." Pastor Holder, thank you for showing me how to stay connected to the Most High, and for all of your continuous prayers. You are a God-send. Alyssa, thank you for being my spiritual sister. You are the epitome of a Proverbs 31 woman. Jamie, thank you for being my spiritual brother. Your intellect and humor inspires me.

Ashley, thank you for being a true friend indeed. I don't know what I would do without you. Pastor Jessie, thank you for praying with me at work, and praying for me. Rohan, thank you for being you- understanding, supportive, and loving. Kedeka, JoAnne, and LaDonna, thank you for your friendship, both then and now. Nicole and Ashlynn, thank you for the memories and years of friendship. Melissa, thank you for suggesting I record myself speaking when I had "writer's block." Chesa, thank you for your prayers, support, encouragement and friendship. Falon, thank you for the unexpected spurts of encouragement. Your timing was impeccable. Tyra, thank you for checking on me to make sure I was writing. Tiffany and Neesa, thank you for your sisterly support. Sai, thank you for reminding me that my feelings are important too. Ms. Jacqueline, thank you for reading chapters while I twisted your hair. Gabby, my editor, thank you, thank you, thank you! Thank you for your suggestions, patience and kindness. Thank you for encouraging me to continue writing!

To all my mentors and life coaches, thank you for pushing me, challenging me, and believing in me. To all who have ever said a prayer for and/or with me, gave me a word of encouragement, inspired me, believed in me, helped me, forgave me, blessed me and loved me – thank you. It all brought me to this moment.

About the Author

   Casandra M. Austin is a transformation consultant who is dedicated to helping others transform their lives from the inside-out through inner healing and self-love. She founded the transformation movement, *Be Pretty Inside* in 2014. Casandra is a bold and dynamic speaker who shares her story fearlessly. She earned her Bachelor's Degree from Southern Illinois University in Carbondale, with a major in Administration of Justice and a minor in African American Studies. Casandra has worked with both juvenile and adult offenders in the criminal justice system for nearly a decade using evidence based practices and motivational interviewing techniques. Casandra attributes her strength in overcoming adversities to her close and intimate relationship with God.

website: www.casandraaustin.com

61496806R00186

Made in the USA
Lexington, KY
11 March 2017